Cattle Trails and Animal Lives

ANIMAL VOICES
ANIMAL WORLDS

Robert W. Mitchell, series editor

Cattle Trails and Animal Lives

THE FOUNDING OF AN AMERICAN
CARCERAL ARCHIPELAGO

Karen M. Morin

The University of Georgia Press
ATHENS

Printed digitally

EU Authorized Representative
Easy Access System Europe—Mustamäe tee 50, 10621
Tallinn, Estonia, gpsr.requests@easproject.com

Library of Congress Cataloging-in-Publication Data

Names: Morin, Karen M. author
Title: Cattle trails and animal lives :
the founding of an American carceral archipelago / Karen M. Morin.
Description: Athens : The University of Georgia Press, [2025] |
Series: Animal voices / animal worlds | Includes bibliographical references and index.
Identifiers: LCCN 2025003804 | ISBN 9780820374451 hardback |
ISBN 9780820374468 paperback | ISBN 9780820374475 epub | ISBN 9780820374482 pdf
Subjects: LCSH: Animal rights—United States | Beef industry—Social aspects—
United States | Cattle trade—Social aspects—United States
Classification: LCC HV4764 .M67 2025 | DDC 179/.30973—dc23/eng/20250616
LC record available at https://lccn.loc.gov/2025003804

CONTENTS

FIGURES

ACKNOWLEDGMENTS

I offer my first and most sincere thanks to Lori Gruen and Justin Marceau for inviting me to the Against Cages and Carceral Logics Workshop at the University of Denver Sturm School of Law in 2019. There I was able to first float some of the ideas for this book among a group of talented legal scholars, attorneys, and activists. Lori's and Justin's feedback on my less-than-thought-out original contribution to their edited book that emerged from that workshop (Gruen and Marceau 2022—it's open access; check it out) formed the cornerstone to this book, and it simply would not have happened without their generous and insightful feedback.

From there this became my 'pandemic book'. Like scholars across the world, many types of research were suspended for a number of years while covid-19 took its toll on scholarly production. Conducting research and writing a first draft of the book during covid times were both pleasantly and sometimes not so pleasantly affected by the freedom of working from home amid the endless Zoom calls, household commotion, daily crushing routine, and limited movement. Combined, this made me greatly appreciate the support of the many museum docents, curators, archivists, and librarians in Kansas, Oklahoma, Texas, and California who helped me navigate and access primary resources for this study amid uneven and unpredictable closures and delays. Many of them allowed me to access their sites in person while also introducing me to numerous online library resources and archives. In particular, I want to offer thanks to Warren Stricker at the Panhandle-Plains Museum in Canyon, Texas, as well as to the museum's Jennifer Modzel and Jenni Opalinski; to Michael Grauer at the National Cowboy and Western History Museum in Oklahoma City and Samantha Schafer and Lulu Zilinskas at the museum's Donald C. & Elizabeth M. Dickinson Research Center; to Michael Hook at Old Abilene Town in Abilene, Kansas; to Lea Ann Lust at the National Ranching Heritage Center at Texas Tech University in Lubbock, Texas; to Kathie Bell, at the Boot Hill Museum in Dodge City, Kansas; to Lisa Keys and Lauren Grey of the Kansas Historical Society in Topeka, Kansas; and to Shannon Gering at the University of Oklahoma Press.

Archivists and film librarians in California, whose archives were closed or restricted to outside researchers during the pandemic, also managed to so kindly guide me through online film resources for my chapter on Hollywood cattle drive films. I am indebted to Maya Montañez Smukler at the Film and Television Research and Study Center at UCLA; to Genevieve Maxwell and Edda Manriquez at the Academy of Motion Picture Archives Film Archive in Los Angeles; and to Liza Posas and Maxine Hanson at the Gene Autry Museum of the American West in LA, along with Bob Fisher from Gene Autry Entertainment. The Autry staff placed me in touch with Clay Lilley of Movin on Livestock, a company that arranges animal actors and other stage materials for film, who put me in touch with his father, the western stuntman Jack Lilley, for a fascinating interview. A number of other scholars greatly aided my entrée into the world of animals in film, including filmmaker Ilisa Barbash and Bucknell University's treasured film afficionado Rebecca Myers. Finally, Courtney Penley and her team at PETA's division of Animals in Film and Television instructed me on the overall legal and ethical standards in place for use of animals in film, historically and today.

So many other scholars and professionals helped me chart my way through this research and offered feedback, scholars I know, as well as those who graciously responded to my many cold calls working in areas outside my specialization. These include Katie Gillespie, Zeb Tortorici, Kelly Struthers Montford, Alexandra Isfahani-Hammond, Carol Wayne White, Erica Fudge, and Lance Esplund (who gave me a hilarious insider's view of Dodge City, Kansas); as well as the York University Animal Research Roundtable in Toronto led by the intrepid Alice Hovorka. A generous year's sabbatical provided by Bucknell University helped me finish a draft of the book. I especially thank the provost's office for the time away; Wes Bernstein, for providing truly invaluable technical help with the book's images and know-how with their production; and Dan Heuer, for his assistance with procuring so many interlibrary loan resources.

I also thank the staff at UGA press, particularly Beth Snead, and the Animal Lives series editor Robert Mitchell, for sticking with the project through delays and setbacks. This material was maddeningly difficult for me to organize, and I took it apart and put it back together three times. I appreciate Beth's and Robert's graciousness and patience in dealing with a disgruntled author. Unlikely as it may sound, I owe the most for the ultimate shape of this book to someone I don't know. Looking back, I have to appreciate the incredible time and personal effort put forward by one particularly devoted (anonymous) reader of the manuscript, and to that person's many constructive suggestions, especially for a more coherent organization of the material. I hope this individual will contact me one day so that I can offer my thanks personally. Also at UGA Press, I acknowledge the extraordinary responsiveness and professionalism of Jon Davies and the pleasure it has been working with him and his production team.

This book represents, in many ways, my research program coming full circle geographically, as a case study in aspects of animal agriculture that I introduced in *Carceral Space, Prisoners and Animals* (Morin 2018), and tying back to some of my early scholarly research on Great Plains travel writing. The work also connects to my own personal origin story. I was born in Omaha, Nebraska, that merciful blue dot on the map (if you follow U.S. politics), home to the Oracle of Omaha and the NCAA College World Series, as well as, unfortunately, at least three large meatpacking plants (one of which Timothy Pachirat so gruesomely covered in his *Every Twelve Seconds*, 2011)—and, naturally, Omaha Steaks. This project definitely sent my memories of home and western animal (beef) culture on an unjoyous collision course. Now, it's all for the animals.

As we headed into the postpandemic period, the last couple of years things got a bit challenging at home while I was still plugging away on this book, and I tremendously benefited from the support of an army of Morins, Olivettis, Matterns, our big, beautiful extended family, our dear Lewisburg friends and those farther out, all of whom helped in ways that still pull at my heartstrings. An eternal thank-you to my life partner, Dan Olivetti, who among many other things drove with me all over the country to visit western museums and so expertly handled all the photography in Abilene and Dodge City, Kansas, and in Canyon, Lubbock, and Fort Worth, Texas. Finally, I dedicate this work to the kids: to my millennial children Nina and Nick, with their blessed understanding of animal suffering and the need to share the earth and its resources with the animals; and to our beloved toddler Elliott, who gave me so much joy, and believe it or not, inspiration, these past few years. Sitting with me at my desk, Elliott talked often with me about the tragic death of the celebrity owl Flaco, who died in 2024 by slamming into a Manhattan apartment window. To this day Elliott believes my book is about Flaco. Why not—here's to Flaco too.

Cattle Trails and Animal Lives

Bovine Lives and the Carceral West

The observable everyday lives of cows on the American agricultural land-scape today present one of two main images: either a picturesque scene of a few animals peacefully grazing on grassy hillsides or thousands of them intensely concentrated, shoulder to shoulder, eating grain out of troughs within one of many vast industrialized factory farms. In the first, the 'carceral' apparatuses—structures, tools, and practices that enclose and hold animals captive, such as barbed wire fences—oftentimes are hidden from view, while in the latter, they are completely obvious. We know all too well where animals are headed within a scene of industrial beef production—what all the pens, ramps, drainage systems, grain elevators, transport vehicles, and power plants are about. Both images very differently send messages about where bovine animals 'belong' on the landscape, as well as the terms of that belonging (after Gillespie forthcoming). In the first, they belong on the rural farm setting that seems an echo of a quaint and venerated American past made up of yeomen farmers who, along with their animals, built the nation through inventiveness and hard work; and in the latter, they represent successful capitalist industrialization of the cattle beef business.

While it might not be obvious that animals in the first landscape typically end up in the second before slaughter, recognition of these carceral framings is important in that they both tend to create an impression of almost inert, unconscious animal life. Cows are the most 'universal' of animals due to their close relationship with humans and long-standing domestication; no animal has been written about and studied more (Alio 2021). And yet, what does the casual observer really know about them? What does the casual observer know about their sentient lived experiences and inner lives, or whether they in fact have them? In both scenes, the animals have been so thoroughly objectified and commodified that to think of them as having *lives* at all, to think of them as anything other than "beef" is a challenge for many (Royle 2018; also see Philo and Wilbert 2000: 6–14). Yet if we consider bovine animals as shapers of histories and geographies, with thoroughly active inner lives, as Anderson (2004), Crosby (2003), Pachirat (2011), Gustafsson and Haapoja (2015), Fudge (2017), Gillespie (2018a), Specht (2019), and many other scholars have argued, we must entertain the notion of them as actors with lives, kinship relations, emotions, preferences, interests, and agency along with those of their human captors.

Cattle Trails and Animal Lives can best be described as 'early western Americana meets critical animal studies', with my conceptual intervention occurring specifically at the interface of carceral geography, critical animal histories, and material culture.[1] In this book I attempt to understand the lived experiences of bovine animals within historical carceral landscapes as well as interpret how these experiences and landscapes are culturally 're-narrated' to contemporary audiences. Popular as well as more scholarly literature on the history of western cattle ranching is well-trod territory. Thousands of scholarly books and articles, memoirs, biographies, illustrated weeklies, films and documentaries, museum artifacts and exhibits, and paintings and other artistic works have depicted the history and geography of the western 'open range', the early ranching empires, the nineteenth-century cattle trails and cattle drives, and the small rural towns that sprung up at their termini. (Among classic scholarly examples see Dykstra 1968 and Skaggs 1973.) This outsized body of American West literature and culture has collectively depicted bovine animals as an instrument, albeit an integral one, of cowboys, ranchers, cattle barons, and a multitude of other enterprising entrepreneurs who heroically 'conquered' the West and who economically, politically, and culturally maneuvered control over the emerging U.S. cattle beef industry.

My assessment of this body of work is that real animal lives and stories are nearly totally absent from it and remain to be studied and documented. Western history and western Americana museum culture about the early cattle trade are built on or around the bodies of these animals, yet the animals' lived experiences are nearly completely absent from them. In many important ways, they are 'absent presences' within American colonial history, yet such animals played an integral role in the U.S. settler colonial project. A central fact of that colonial project, basic to settler colonialism itself, was the changing of human diets toward meat consumption (Few and Tortorici 2013: 12; Specht 2017). Specht (2017; 2016: 345) shows how bovine animals were vital to the food revolution in America; between 1870 and 1890 fresh beef was transformed from "delicacy to daily fare." The 'healthy beef' movement would come with the late nineteenth-century slaughterhouses, but quite significantly the origins of the cattle beef trade date much earlier, to Spanish colonialism in the West.

In this work I offer what might be called a lived origin story for bovine animals within what was an emergent carceral system of captivity and control in the American West; the origins, as it were, of where bovine animals 'belonged' from their arrival with the Spanish conquistadors to the emergence of industrial beef production in the mid-nineteenth century. In so doing I attempt to access historical bovine animal experiences and subjectivity to try to understand the worlds—albeit colonial carceral worlds—that they cocreated with humans and for themselves. These were beings under intense external human carceral control, captured and moved along a 'carceral archipelago' that was created to commodify them, accompanied nonetheless by their everyday experiences of walking or running across pastures and streams, eating, resting, playing, fighting, caring for one another, procreating, and so on, with all the emotions associated with such activities. As many have argued, animals, including farm and ranch 'livestock', experience wide-ranging emotions such as joy, contentment, pride, love, grief, anxiety, embarrassment, fear, and empathy (e.g., Gillespie 2018a; Gruen 2015). Yet as we also know, animal cultures, identities, experiences, and so on are not simply a function of species habits and characteristics: different environments or communities produce different kinds of animals and animal experiences and behaviors (as would also be true of the human animal), on an individual as well as group level (Fudge 2017; Nance 2013: 10–13). Decentering our human, anthropocentric interpretations of animal perspectives and experiences, of carceral or any other spaces, remains our collective challenge (Probyn-Rapsey 2018).

So, unlike the scores of works that have focused on the early cattle trade from other cultural, economic, political, agricultural, or social lenses (many of which are referenced throughout this book), I want to think about how historical bovine animals lived within colonial-carceral structures, operations, and practices, all informed fundamentally by 'carceral logics' underlying the emergent beef industry (Gruen 2014; Moran, Turner, and Schliehe 2018; Marceau 2019). Thus, it is the framing of the carceral as a lived experience for bovine animals that structures what follows in subsequent chapters.

Accordingly, my first aim in this work is to center animal experiences, identifying some of the material, social, emotional, and psychological experiences and trauma of becoming an 'animalized' commodity—an exploitable, disposable, killable being—within settler colonial structures and infrastructures. Studying the lives of cattle fundamentally involves understanding their gradual commodification—these formerly free-roaming beings were literally turned into money: 'free for the taking', with virtually no official regulatory apparatus in the nineteenth century (or prior) guiding their capture, enclosure, movement, exploitation, and, of course, eventual death. I propose understanding the West as a 'carceral West', meaning understanding it as a place where the captivity, enclosure, bodily modification, suffering, and death of these formerly feral or semiferal animals were normalized and, indeed, celebrated and honored in countless ways.

Writing a critical historical geography of bovine animals offers an opportunity to examine a range of questions about their lives—their *stories*. What are their stories? My project is one that, as Gibbs (2020: 771–773) articulates it, attempts to understand "animals creating their own life worlds . . . to hear the cry" of the nonhuman. And if trying to write a 'story' of cows is too anthropocentric a term for the likes of Yong (2022) as it implies a (human) narrative structure to that lived experience—'animals don't have stories'—I can live with calling my work a study of animals seeing, hearing, smelling, and feeling the carceral (after Gustafsson and Haapoja 2015). The new vantage point offered here helps us understand the material, physical, social, and psychological experiences of 'cattle' gradually becoming animalized commodities.[2] In this book I investigate the ways in which a collective of people, practices, and places helped create the conditions for this commodification to occur: the animals' forced movement over sea and land and the various environmental conditions they encountered; the multiple human players who were involved in their coerced movement; the legal apparatuses (or lack thereof) that were implicated in animal capture, transport, and consumption; and the tools and technological 'advances' of the emerging cattle beef industry in the nineteenth-century Great Plains and West, such as railroad cattle cars, barbed wire fencing, stock pens, and numerous instruments of bodily control such as branding irons, dehorning tools, and devices designed to prevent calves from suckling their mothers' milk. These material artifacts offer insights into animal experiences, as do a variety of textual archival sources such as agricultural advice manuals, veterinary medicine documents, patents, journalistic accounts in newspapers and illustrated weeklies, photographs, and memoirs, biographies, and autobiographies.

The symbolic importance of bovine animals to the American past and in American culture, particularly the Texas longhorn with their majestic horns, is an important part of their story as well. In this work I tie together the mythology surrounding the romanticized cowboy, cattle baron, and cattle town entrepreneurs to the cattle themselves, a collective of actors who are cast in numerous cultural and historical sites as mutually taming the wild frontier.

Thus the second aim of this work is to engage with the 're-presentations' or 're-narrations' of the nineteenth-century cattle trade: in museums, such as in study of exhibits explaining the purported advances in barbed wire and breeding technologies; at living history sites, such as those of the Kansas towns Old Abilene and Dodge City; other touristic re-creations of historic cattle trails, such as the twice-daily Fort Worth 'cattle drive'; specific artistic artifacts such as taxidermied animals presented in museum dioramas, as well as heroic statuary and paintings of bovine animals; and, last but not least, through Hollywood westerns. Mid-twentieth-century films about nineteenth-century western cattle drives and cattle towns (and there are many) are important cultural resources in helping to understand how specific kinds of depictions of animals helped promote and entice a post–World War II public toward beef eating. I question how the carceral spaces of the cattle trails were portrayed in film, including analysis of the mutual 'work' that cowboys and cows engaged in together, arguing that the normalization and neutralization of carceral practices and logics were important in prompting audiences to not only accept but even enjoy images of the carceral.

Museums and other sites that renarrate the early American cattle trade and cattle empires tend to represent these to contemporary audiences as sites of adventure, work, endurance, heartiness, and romance, for both humans and nonhumans. Bovine animals, along with the beloved cowboy with whom they 'partnered', are presented to contemporary audiences as symbols of the success of the industrial cattle business via these ostensible American traits, and in so doing, come to stand for American national identity itself. The story that emerges from these historical sites, implicitly, is a story about the carceral landscape itself. Thus, digging a little deeper I propose that carceral landscapes, structures, tools, and practices—the success of the carceral archipelago itself, if you will, which is by definition the exploitation and death of animals—is what is actually celebrated and honored as an important piece of the American past.

In the remainder of this introduction I discuss in more detail how I understand and apply the concepts of carceral logic and carceral space in this work; and how these intersected in the creation of a set of spatial 'nodes' to form the rural western carceral archipelago I am identifying. 'The carceral' intersects with numerous themes of the book that I introduce in the following pages—for example, how the carceral helps produce, and not just reflect, the boundaries between humanness and animality, as well as the terms of agency and resistance that both humans and animals expressed in their encounters in the carceral archipelago. I then delve into the methodological challenges scholars face in attempting to access historical animal lives, and my principal interventions in recovering them from historical archives and material artifacts. Finally, I overview the themes and contents of the book.

Carceral Logic and Carceral Space

Animals had not heretofore figured in the field of carceral geography until my attempt to conceptualize a 'trans-species carceral geography' in *Carceral Space, Prisoners and Animals* (Morin 2018), in which I considered factory farms, slaughterhouses, research labs, and zoos as prisons or prison-like spaces, with those incarcerated within them as animalized prisoners. In the book I placed into parallel conversation the connected and entangled spatial, structural, operational, and embodied carceral practices and processes of a number of industrial sites and institutions in the present-day United States. I aimed to uncover the epistemic violence that pervades spaces of both human and nonhuman animal captivity, confinement, exploitation, and death and yet is normalized and neutralized in countless ways in everyday life. Naming spaces of animal captivity and confinement as prison-like allows insights into the way that 'carceral logics' extend throughout the prison-, agricultural-, medical-, and entertainment-industrial complexes in similar ways, and impact both human and nonhuman animals in consistent and detrimental ways via processes of animalization, racialization (particularly via anti-Blackness), and criminalization (after, among others, Moran, Turner, and Schliehe 2018; Gruen and Marceau 2022).

To the extent that the present work is a *historical* animal geography (see Howell 2021 for a useful overview), my spatial history or historical geography of animal lives rests on identifying an emergent rural carceral archipelago designed and developed to capture, enclose, transport, and eventually kill bovine animals for food and other commodities. When writing about a colonial 'carceral archipelago', I am borrowing from Michel Foucault's *Discipline and Punish: The Birth of the Prison* (1977), wherein he argued that this island concept can be appropriately applied to a set of institutions, surveillance systems, and technologies that 'discipline' and exert power and control over populations and indeed whole societies in a spatially ordered and universalizing way (discussed in Morin 2018: 21–25). It is not my purpose to engage in an overall critique of Foucault's conceptual framework, but I do highlight the fact that carceral sites and institutions share a particular spatiality encompassing animalized bodies. Recent work in carceral geography contends that 'the carceral' extends well beyond the prison and jail—though these are quintessential carceral spaces—illustrating that the defining characteristics of the prison extend well beyond it (after Moran 2015). Thus, the carceral is understood as far exceeding imprisonment for criminal activity and embracing the myriad spaces and ways in which people (and animals) are disciplined and confined by the state, for example in extensive surveillance systems, electronic monitoring devices, and through migrant detention, to name a few (Moran, Gill, and Conlon 2013; Mountz 2010; Loyd, Mitchelson, and Burridge 2012; Routley 2017; Morin and Moran 2015). In the present case I am applying the island concept of archipelago to refer to a set of spatial nodes that included the open range, cattle ranches, cattle trails, and cattle towns that diffused northward from Mexico and Texas to Kansas, creating a specific production chain on the American landscape in which bovine animals were captured, moved, and transformed into marketable industrial commodities.

Spatial confinement and incapacitation are key to the carceral, but again, these go beyond the narrowly geographical to include a variety of practices, meanings, and social relations of surveillance, discipline, control, and domination. The carceral thus exceeds categories of criminality and penality, involving systems of confinement that differ from those that a sociology of punishment or criminality would address. Moreover, the carceral is achieved through spatiality; it is always related to some kind of space—that is, where the carceral is conducted. Carceral spatiality is thus characterized by a technology of confinement: (intentionally) keeping in, (detrimentally) containing those within (after Moran, Turner, and Schliehe 2018: 679). This can be especially applied to institutional spaces, but carceral spatiality can emerge in many ways: through actual walls, through restricting mobility, and in the ways that intention and detriment have influenced those incarcerated after their confinement.

Underlying my work is the concept of 'carceral logic'—the meanings, ideologies, philosophies, and thinking—that are contrary to and challenge the rationalizations that give taken-for-granted credence to spaces such as fenced pastures, ranches, and stockyards in popular discourse and practice. Gruen and Marceau (2022: 4–5) discuss two interrelated meanings of carceral logic that I employ throughout the book: the first emphasizes the 'logic' of carceral systems—"the laws, rules, design, and practices of courts, police, and prisons." The second emphasizes "how the 'carceral' and its practices inform, surveil, limit, and constrain our thinking in contexts that go beyond prisons." Philosophers such as Gruen (2016) focus on carceral logic as the logic of domination itself, shaping our social and political relations in order to naturalize domination and fix inclusions, exclusions, and disposability of certain bodies in the process.

Thus, in a broader sense my interests lie in defining carcerality in its many facets: its functional/physical form, its mode of operation and practice, its technologies and techniques, and especially in its experiential aspects. In carceral spaces, social ties of inside and outside are broken, and a type of disciplinary power spatially restricts bodies and manages them within highly orchestrated visible or 'invisible' structures, technologies, and practices. In addition, and quite foundationally, the bodies of the incarcerated are subjected as well to routine processes of animalization while their status as property and commodity is continually created and reinforced. Ultimately in this work I attempt to recover the 'absent presences' of bovine animals in historical carceral settings, focusing more on their social life than their social death—or, perhaps more accurately, recognizing the inseparability of their social life from their social death upon captivity within the carceral archipelago.

It is important to examine the specific context of captivity with respect to animal experiences and behaviors, as behavioral norms and outcomes are not simply 'givens' by species, communities, or breeds of animals, but are rather *produced through* encounters with carceral structures, operations, technologies, and practices. What this means is that structures and practices of captivity, control, restraint, restriction, and so on themselves create the conditions within which certain bodies (both human and nonhuman) can be 'animalized', which in turn reinforces or validates the carceral structures and practices they are captive within, as well as validates the exploitation and disposability of their bodies. To the extent possible I stay attuned to the fact that while captivity itself produces many similar carceral effects that are physical, behavioral, emotional, and psychological (Gruen 2014; Gillespie 2018a; Morin 2018), individuals may also experience captivity differently, and those differences are acknowledged and taken into account. Foundational questions locate around how the carceral spaces and practices were experienced. Did they involve suffering? Enjoyment? Grief? Were these carceral conditions resisted? In fact, numerous eyewitnesses to the early cattle trade (e.g., Cox 1895; Rollins 1922; Dobie 1941) described a range of animal responses to their incarceration, which can be attributed to factors such as kinship relations, environmental conditions, and the relative brutality of specific carceral spaces, structures, and practices.

A Rural Carceral Archipelago

In this work I re-map the historical and empirical geography of the open range, the ranch, the cattle drive, and the cattle town as comprising a 'rural carceral archipelago'—an archipelago of nodes and sites characterized by a specific rural spatiality. Foundationally this archipelago was enabled by the forced removal and land dispossession of Indigenous peoples, along with the massacre of the previous bovines in North America, the buffalo. Southern Texas emerging as the epicenter of western cattle ranching and origin point of the cattle trails dates to the Spanish colonial period of the fifteenth and sixteenth centuries, representing a significant Spanish legacy to the development of U.S. carceral geographies. Studying the forced migration of bovine animals from Europe to the Caribbean and North America via sailing or other ships is one important conceptual intervention I propose in this book. I usefully draw on Hodgetts and Lorimer's (2020) argument about the "ordering practices" of sovereign, disciplinary, and biopower that govern such animal mobility in carceral spaces. Once on North American soil, the carceral archipelago advanced along the nodes of the open range from Mexico to Texas and development of the cattle ranching empires, the cattle trails that led from Texas to Kansas, and on to the Kansas cow towns where the trails met the railroad. A typical nineteenth-century American frontier 'cow town' was a small settlement that lay at the junction of the cattle trail and the developing railroad lines that were emerging to transport animals to points north and east for slaughter.

What was it like for these animals to be transported across the Atlantic, 'rounded up' from their free-range lifestyle, enclosed in rudimentary cow pens on the range and ranches, then driven as quickly but also as efficiently as possible by workers (cowboys) who were themselves laboring under difficult circumstances? How did the cows experience the new technologies such as barbed wire fencing? What forms of bodily modification and appropriation were they subjected to along the way, for example, the brutality of branding, earmarking, castration, and dehorning that marked them as property and commodity? How did they experience being loaded onto railroad cattle cars for the two-week trip to Chicago? What were the physical, emotional, and psychological implications of existing as beings with no legal standing or protections, outside of the informal claims made by cattle barons and others? No ostensible protections for farmed or ranched animals would appear in the United States until well into the twentieth century, and these to an extremely restricted degree. Even today, the only law that governs treatment of farmed animals is the Humane Methods Slaughter Act of 1958 (amended in 1978).

To preview some of what follows subsequently: in 1830, 100,000 cattle roamed Texas, and just three decades later, on the eve of the Civil War, that number had increased to an estimated 3.5–5 million (Rifkin 1992: 68–70; White 1991: 220–225; Starrs 1998). During those years, these longhorn cattle wandered on their own, finding themselves shelter, foraging, grazing, and caring for their young. By the end of the Civil War, 6 million Texan longhorns wandered wild and untendered. These animals were informally (and later far more formally and systematically) captured from the wild, enclosed, and immediately turned into individualized human property as they were sep-

arated, branded, and prepared for the cattle drive. The most well known of
the western cattle trails ran from Texas northward to the state of Kansas, as
herders drove millions of cattle from the mid-1860s through the 1880s (Sherow 2018; Ludwig 2018; Welch 2017). As the railroads began to extend and
connect to rural outposts in the Great Plains and West, entrepreneurs in the
new cattle towns such as Abilene and Dodge City, Kansas, sought out Texas
livestock trails to reach them, benefiting greatly from the new trade. Sites
such as Abilene were still relatively unpeopled, well-watered, and offered
plentiful grass for the incoming herds (although environmental hazards such
as winter blizzards ultimately derailed the entrepreneurial aspirations of
many cattlemen). The geography of Abilene and other such cow towns would
reflect their central nodal function in the developing meat industry and today have become notable tourist attractions.

It is important to recognize that the carceral archipelago I describe was
enabled via some characteristic spatial and geographical features of rural
places. Rural places themselves have been traditionally defined as areas
dominated by extensive land use in agriculture or forestry, or by large open
spaces of undeveloped land containing small settlements. Recent studies
have challenged, modified, or enhanced those definitions (Argent 2017, 2019;
Woods 2009; Cloke, Marsden, and Mooney 2006).[3] Generally speaking, rural
places have been defined by: (1) function—by land use, by geographical location, and/or as sites rich in primary resources and commodity chains; (2) as
places with unique political economies subject to and the product of broader
uneven social, economic, and political parameters incentivized by or subjected to particular governmental regulations and state processes; and (3) by
the social meanings that people ascribe to them and their inhabitants, often
as mythologized or romanticized places that have particular moral values
that are nature- or eco-friendly. All of these features are germane to my study,
both through analysis of the lived experiences of animals as they passed
through the nodes on the carceral archipelago and through re-narrations of
the American past via museum artifacts and living history sites such as the
cow towns. As Woods observes, the spatial settings within which rural and
urban identities are most entangled and where distinctions are most elusive
are in "small towns in rural regions" (Woods 2009: 851–852).

One aspect of rurality that I develop relates to the 'Wild West' land grab
that directly impacted animal lives. Nineteenth-century rural land laws ostensibly governing the private takeover of public land offered opportunities
for considerable abuse and the creation of the carceral landscape I describe
and, within that framework, localized structural, infrastructural, and technological developments such as stockyards and fencing of grazing lands. Scott's
(1998) analysis of land, agriculture, and rurality adds depth to understand-

ing the 'invisibility' and hiddenness of the infrastructural and technological apparatuses of the carceral in rural spaces. Scott usefully outlines the state-sponsored simplification and abstraction of modernist scientific agriculture in rural locations, meaning the 'general shift toward monoculture agriculture and production and the profit motive as the only motivator'. This had (and has) the effect of failing to represent real spaces and local biotic communities (1998: 262). Scott shows how this "radical simplification" under the guise of science reduces places to a single outcome such as a crop (or may I suggest, cattle raising), and has the effect of rendering everything else invisible—externalities only receive attention when they begin to affect production, or are resisted (1998: 263). Immerwahr (2023: 28) argues that "rural America" is actually a highly artificial concept and place, particularly as rural places are as much a "creature of state power and industrial capitalism as their city-dwelling counterparts." The state was obviously heavily involved in settler co-lonialism—displacing Native peoples and massacring the buffalo, implanting newcomers, providing land ownership to these newcomers, and facilitating corporate dominance of industrial operations. Yet such influences are invisible within the overarching myth of rural places as inhabited by (white) people who lead a supposedly more authentic, independent, traditional way of life.

The entire apparatus of the carceral archipelago is one that fundamentally involves the gradual commodification of bovine animals in rural spaces—the process by which they became both 'live' or living property as well as 'dead' property through the act of consumption—being sold, traded, and eventually killed (see Wadiwel 2015: 147–157). That said, industrial violence is obviously not unique to or restricted to rural places; plenty of violence toward animals occurs in slaughterhouses and other sites located in urban areas—and no place is essentially dangerous and violent. And yet such an observation does not preclude a timely and worthwhile analysis of the oftentimes invisible violence foundational to development of the rural carceral archipelago and emergent U.S. cattle trade.

Carceral Animality and Resistance

A key aspect to the carceral logic behind the capture and enclosure of bovine animals along the carceral archipelago was in their objectification as animal-ized beings; as exploitable, disposable, and killable beings. Basic to creating and upholding carceral systems is this animalization of the 'prisoner'. Both humans and nonhumans may be assigned putatively 'human' or 'animal' characteristics. More than two decades ago Wolfe and Elmer (1995) offered a useful typology of how the human and the animal as ideological constructs intersect within various social spheres in hierarchical and value-laden ways.

Their four types were: (1) "animalized animals" (animals we eat, wear, and test our products on); (2) "humanized animals" (pets and other animals endowed with presumably positive anthropomorphic/human features; (3) "animalized humans" (human beings subjected to all manner of brutalizations carried out by cultural prescription, as well as those who serve as reminders of human beings' bodily, organic existence); and (4) "humanized humans" (the category of pure human, 'sovereign and untroubled').

'Animalization' and 'humanization' then are processes that place humans and nonhumans into hierarchies of worthiness and value. These attributions are applied to various bodies via a number of different mechanisms and processes that either amplify the status of certain humans and nonhumans—humanizing them—or reduce the status of others and animalize them. Processes of animalization are common throughout any number of social sites and institutions, yet they have particular salience within carceral spaces—human and animal distinctions are made *through* carceral spaces and carceral processes (Morin 2018). That is, the distress caused by carceral structures and practices can produce behaviors understood as animalistic, which are then used to justify the carceral captivity in the first place.

The social construction of 'the animal' or the subhuman other—that is, the derogatory social meanings attached to various beings—has been invoked to perpetuate hierarchical human-human and as well human-nonhuman relationships, in countless historical as well as contemporary sites and spaces (Kim 2011, 2015: 24–60; Deckha 2010, 2013a; Cacho 2012; Jackson 2013; Glick 2013). In the process both certain human and certain nonhuman bodies become valued and protected, while others become vilified, reduced to the status of beastly animal. The carceral logics underlying domination of numerous vulnerable populations intersect and are deeply intertwined (Deckha 2013a: 515). Manifestly, what may be done to or with nonhuman animals that represent various social categories—pets, performers, wildlife, livestock, vermin, beasts of burden, seeing-eye dogs, and so on (Morgan and Cole 2011)—mirrors the ways in which different human groups are endowed with humanness or animality and are subsequently protected or deprived of protections. The most vulnerable are animalized lives such as vermin, pests, and livestock.

Moreover, what becomes constituted as human and what becomes constituted as animal, as numerous authors have shown in other contexts (e.g., Ritvo 2010; Deckha 2010; Kim 2015), is profoundly and fundamentally shaped by human-animal interactions and relationships. Human-animal interactions and relationships occurred at sites throughout the carceral archipelago I study here, were implicit within it, and directly impacted an array of legal, political, and cultural outcomes for bovine animals. I specifically examine human cowboy and bovine animal interactions in their mutual 'work' on the cattle trails, in re-narrations of cow towns, and in cinematic portrayals of cattle drives, arguing, among other things, that these had the effect of blurring the boundaries between human and animal, with both cast as partners in their masculine, triumphant mastery over the West—a highly incongruous message when considering animal death at the end of the trail. While my work is not intended as a multispecies ethnography as such, it does contain the elements of one, including those that Gillespie (2018b: 163) and McLauchlan (2021: 393) describe. These authors argue that multispecies ethnographies are useful in thinking through human-animal experiences, relations, and boundaries by, among other practices, 'witnessing' interactions, recognizing the relationality of all existence, and decentering the human in our histories and studies. To McLauchlan (2021: 396–402) the best we can do, since we cannot speak for others, is to develop partial affinities with them, focusing beyond behavior (ethology) to lived experience—for example, knowing the world through the sense of touch (cf. Gustafsson and Haapoja 2015), which is the centerpiece to my focus on material artifacts.

Scott's (1998: 263) observation that externalities to the order of rural places only receive attention when they begin to affect production or are resisted is worth further consideration as well. Relative animal agency or resistance expressed within the conditions of their captivity is an underlying theme throughout this book. Clearly there are many types of agency/resistance and definitions of it—philosophical, ethical, psychological, behavioral, and so on—and these have evolved with understandings of various 'agenic' forces across time and place (Fudge 2017: 264–270). The concept of agency, of both humans and nonhumans, has been studied from countless perspectives, although it is colonial and postcolonial scholars who have best helped us interpret how the agency of the historically colonized or otherwise voiceless subjects from the past could be grasped from the historical record or archive (Spivak 1988 influentially problematized the task). In this sense agency is often framed within resistance to colonial and imperial encounters. Scholars have addressed the broader impacts of historical animal agency in mythology and anthropology, as well as ecology—a standpoint animals have rarely been accorded (Few and Tortorici 2013: 7). Many scholars, such as Fudge (2017: 258–260), encourage us to think of animals as always affecting spaces and changing environments and cultures they inhabit: "they are world-producing beings"—and in that way animals have been a powerful force in history. If we accept that animals are actors in the making of histories and geographies, then a very different version of the past will ensue (Few and Tortorici 2013: 3).

Commonly, agency might be thought of as having and exercising higher-order purpose or cognitive intentionality, but a more expansive definition than this anthropocentric one is obviously needed to account for the agency of creatures with other forms and types of capabilities, decision-making processes, and impacts on their life-worlds. Much of the scholarship on animals within settler colonial contexts has tended to emphasize animals' agency as primarily ecological 'impact' on the land, and in the case of the United States, thus indirectly on the conquest of Indigenous peoples and their land dispossession (Crosby 2003, 2004; Anderson 2004). Anderson usefully describes animal domestication and cattle-grazing herds in the eastern colonies as a principal goal of colonization and "an emblem of civilization" itself (2004: 6, 76–77). The animals took care of themselves in this free-range style of animal husbandry that required "far more space than [the colonists] anticipated," and thus they could "see no alternative but to appropriate Indian land" for the animals (10). The fact that animals took care of themselves—were left to their own devices for survival and self-regulation within early American colonial agriculture—offers an insight into their labor as well as their reputations for hardiness and independence in this labor (Anderson 2004; Ogle 2013; Specht 2016). Ogle (2013: 4–5) makes similar points, that cattle required low human labor demands but also that a single animal required an astonishing 5–20 acres for grazing. They overgrazed areas, and then would move on to new spaces. Bovine animals' participation in the settler colonial project in the American West mirrored these patterns, if on a remarkably larger scale than the small-scale farming enterprises in the East.

Throughout this book I identify the many ways in which cattle resisted their captivity. This ranged from trying to resist capture and enclosure in the first instance, to mother cows protecting and hiding their offspring from carceral structures and practices, trying to throw their captors off their scents, voicing their opposition to carceral practices through sounds and bellows, and even attempting suicide to escape the carceral (Wilkeson 1885). The western cow towns and the railroad infrastructure that developed in them, including the practices of forcing cows through pens, ramps, chutes, and other devices, offers innumerable clues about the meaning of the encounter to animals: they oftentimes attempted to escape from and resist these spaces, and would have been more successful at doing so were it not for the prods and whips and other pain-inducing equipment and tools that prevented them. In the following sections I develop this methodology further, including paying attention to what was likely experienced as ordinary daily life for the animals within carceral spaces as well, and the potential for not just pain and suffering within them but also caring, playfulness, fighting, and the pleasures of grazing and rest. It may often be the case that subjects might not be aware of their own confinement; they may understand their conditions as 'normal' and thus not resist them (Morin 2018).

Methodological Challenges and Interventions

The preceding discussion outlines how animal experiences can be productively framed through the carceral. But it is also important to lay groundwork around some basic methodological issues involved with trying to bring forward animals' 'point of view', particularly historical animals, in the first instance. I recognize the challenging epistemological, conceptual, ethical, and methodological questions and issues that this project poses. Recent scholarship in critical animal studies offers helpful understandings of the lived experiences of captive animals on farms, in zoos, in research labs, and in other carceral spaces within which they undergo harmful processes and practices, and beyond what ethology and other animal behavior studies have contributed to date (e.g., what frightens them, what makes them anxious, and so on). Gillespie's *The Cow with Ear Tag #1389* (2018a) offers an empathetic example of witnessing bovine social, emotional, and psychological responses to a number of settings such as auction yards and dairy farms, as well as sites of refuge. Critical animal studies work such as this and others focus on contemporary experiences of animals unfolding in real time.

But how might one engage such affective, visceral knowing in a historical context? A different or more expansive approach is needed to understand the experiences of historical animals, those long dead and no longer able to be directly 'witnessed'. Thus, an important question revolves around how to access animal experiences to try to understand the worlds—albeit colonial carceral worlds—that they cocreated with their human captors and for themselves. Many scholars of animal histories and historical geographies have demonstrated that this can be done and have modeled useful approaches (Few and Tortorici 2013; Fudge 2002, 2017; Nance 2015; Wilcox and Rutherford 2018).

Colonial and postcolonial scholars have taught us that the experiences of those heretofore silenced in the human historical record or archive can be made accessible—indeed must be made accessible—and in much the same way that we understand the historical experience of any 'other other' whose lives and stories were represented in archival, textual, and photographic sources by someone else. Erica Fudge reminds us that past subjectivities, human and nonhuman, have always been difficult to access—that the archive is always already fraught as a representational tool. Both humans and nonhumans have been shaped by an archive not of their own making. As Fudge observes, humans can write anything about animals, whether 'true' or 'false', but this applies to *all history* and any being written about: "these are problems of history in general and not specifically about the history of animals" (2002, 2017: 261). One can access animal experiences in much the same way that one accesses anyone else's experience or history—any 'other other' subaltern whose experience has been produced and represented and mediated by someone else.

Obviously, animals express themselves. But as Buller maintains, though we may not "share language with non-humans we do share embodied life and movement and, in doing so, different—yet both biologically and socially related—ways of inhabiting the world" (Buller 2015: 378). The Finnish authors and editors of *History According to Cattle* (Gustafsson and Haapoja 2015) offer a most provocative attempt to try to capture this embodied way of inhabiting the world for bovine animals, via an exhibit called the Museum of the History of Cattle. The exhibition and published book evoke a dark, subliminal, shadowy experience and existence. To these authors, for example, the "cattle tongue is not a written language. In cattle culture, the tongue is a means of touching others." Installations feature partial, blurry images of light, objects, and landscape as well as intensely vibrant magnified images of other objects within close range such as companion species' dress patterns and the veins on a leaf, all imaginings of bovine perspective.

If we are to construct a meaningful and 'reliable' methodology to study and apprehend historical animal experiences from the written, documented, and material archive, what would it look like? How would we know animal experiences of suffering and pain—or enjoyment and contentment for that matter—and how could we understand any agenic attempts, if such existed, to resist or respond to their conditions of confinement and captivity in historical carceral spaces (Gillespie 2015; Wadiwel 2015; Buller 2015; Colling 2020)? Can we ever know what animals thought and felt? How do we not silence beings who speak other than human languages? Can we ever really 'know' the suffering, pain, or experiences of another being? Are such experiences (only) culturally or subjectively specific, or can we establish some objectively harmful detrimental parameters produced in carceral settings (after Moran, Turner, and Schliehe 2018)?

Much empirical evidence points to the potential suffering and pain of animals in the carceral settings I discuss, yet it is important to be able to establish, from the point of view of the subjects, that they indeed suffered through violent practices and processes and not just assume it to be so—and moreover, to consider the possibility that even within these spaces, care and contentment might have been possible. While it might seem that how humans treated cows is more easily extracted from the historical record than how cows felt or experienced life, Tortorici (2015: 94–96) usefully argues that textual images of animals in the archive nevertheless have the potential to shape our affective engagement with them, in both the past and the present, and that we do not necessarily need to be present with them to understand their experiences.

Since humans produce the archive, in what ways could animals speak from it? If we acknowledge that there is always a 'politics of the archive'—a politics about who creates, controls, and disseminates information contained in the archive and who is silenced and left behind (Morin 2010), such would only seem to be more so the case when considering animal voices whose languages humans are not particularly adept at understanding, limited as we are by our own notions about what language is, and how communication takes place. Humans have a limited capacity for understanding nonhuman linguistic systems. Yet there are other forms of language than the human spoken and written word—bodily language, for example—that we do share with other animals and that helps us understand them (Buller 2015). There are ways of communicating we can study with the aim of understanding across species lines. And if we can accept that all historical accounts are potentially problematical as representations written from particular points of view, if we 'read against the grain', human perspectives will still be of value: "Histories of animals that rely on human representations can still broaden our understanding of the past to include animals as animals, rather than only as human tools or ideas, and so can give us glimpses of life that would otherwise remain invisible." As Fudge asserts, "an imperfect history is better than no history at all" (2017: 261, 268).

Scholars have developed many methods for understanding animal experiences. Buller describes the observational, mechanistic methods of animal study within the natural and behavioral sciences that rely on human representations of animal experiences, arguing that we must find alternative ways to allow animals to speak and represent themselves. Hodgetts and Lorimer (2015), for example, discuss developing tools and methods that (at least arguably) 'leave out [interpretations of] the gatekeeper', such as monitoring and tracking devices. Griffin (1992), in discussing his cognitive ethological (vs. behavioral ethological) method, asserts that we must start with the proposition that animals are (and were) sentient and conscious, albeit with fundamentally different types of experiences and consciousness than humans. As Gibbs (2020: 774) suggests, as animal geographies and more-than-human scholarship come together, researchers have adopted a more-than-human—that is, material and relational—conceptual frame. In the present case, the 'sensory' is read through the textual as well as material artifacts, at least partly through what would be the sense of touch (after Gustafsson and Haapoja 2015). Historical eyewitness human accounts of animal behaviors, alongside study of carceral structures and instruments, helps concretize what animals' lived experience might have been like. Supporting documentation of such devices from institutional sources such as the U.S. Department of Agriculture, veterinary history, illustrated weeklies, and advice manuals of various sorts support an understanding of the 'intentionality' behind the uses of numerous carceral structures and instruments.

Moreover, one might question whether there is any real difference between trying to access the experience of animals, to represent the experiences of animals in history, versus one from a (contemporaneous) distant geographical location. Both could be equally 'distant', inaccessible, or hidden, and involve bodies with whom one has no direct contact. Thus, seeking out proxy animal sites and experiences for those of the past are useful for my purposes, such as study of today's longhorn animals trudging through the paved streets of Fort Worth's twice-daily 'cattle drives'. It is also useful to think them through and alongside the behaviors and experiences of other domesticated livestock animals as well as those more free-roaming. One recent study in Australia (Hanson 2020) found, not surprisingly, that cows express a range of vocalizations related to different feelings, such as when experiencing hunger or isolation. Farmed animals in particular, as Buller observes, offer distinctively visceral, performative, and affective opportunities for exploring co-presence and mutual becoming within the context of animal welfare (2015: 379–380), particularly in ethological studies of animal confinement. Intra- and interspecies communication has been a focus of such ethological research: "This communication tends to be aural, consisting of calls, barks, whoops, growls and the like; and researchers are able to develop a degree of understanding through investigating the consistency of aural communications between individuals in relation to external events" (Hodgetts and Lorimer 2015: 288–289)—as one alternative to the visual bias of most observational methods. Documentary traces of such aural communications in the historical record are valuable and add an important dimension to the more readily available visual evidence such as that provided by photographs.

Dalke and Hunt (2017) undertook a study under the U.S. Geological Survey of 317 free-roaming adult mustangs (horses) compared with their domesticated counterparts. They discovered thirteen distinct behaviors that are helpful for comparing the lives of other free-roaming versus domesticated species. These behaviors included resting, feeding, locomotion, and grooming, with the researchers studying how these animals used their time in each activity and behavior, and questioned the extent to which domestication, and the length of domestication, altered behavior. Their results: feeding occurred 84 percent of the time across all animals, with resting the second most frequent activity, occurring 10 percent of time. Locomotion was third, at 1.1 percent, followed by grooming, at 0.7 percent of their time. For more nuanced results comparing domesticated versus free-roaming animals, see Dalke and Hunt (2017)—such as that wild mustangs rested less, and domesticated animals spent less time grooming themselves than their wild counterparts since they could retreat to shelters to avoid insects.

These basic traits and behaviors are worth noting simply to provide a context for interpreting the behaviors of bovine animals within the conditions of captivity I study; that the carceral logics, practices, and spaces tremendously impacted and curtailed behaviors that may otherwise have been meaningful and important especially to formerly free-roaming animals. Derby (2011: 605) notes that the successful survival of animals prior to captivity depended on their habitat, such as thickets that provided protection from the weather and ample foraging potential. The emergence of carceral conditions and the cattle trail and cow town in the nineteenth century replaced a life of animals left on their own, foraging in the thickets, developing strategies for finding shelter, food, and ability to care for their young. Once captured within carceral spaces and unable to move about freely, bovine life experiences changed dramatically—from being caught against barbed wire fencing and freezing or starving to death, to becoming a branded piece of property for the cattlemen, to the crowding in the cattle car onward toward death in the slaughterhouse.

Recovering Past Animal Lives: Artifacts and Archives

In this work I follow two main tracks in attempting to reconstruct lived animal experiences of carceral spaces: the textual and the material artifactual. Historians have typically relied on narrative mechanisms to understand animal pasts. Archival documentary sources and narratives produced by humans provide one access point to these lives—memoirs, biographies, journalistic accounts, photographs, instruction manuals, patents, films, paintings—even if they offer only traces of historical animals' lived experiences. When examining such representations we must think seriously about the extent to which human ideas about bovine animals were invented by certain actors whose purpose was to produce certain kinds of bodies and behaviors upon which to profit. A poignant example we might turn to is a seemingly innocuous but unforgettable scene in the 1948 western film *Red River*, whose depiction of branding restrained animals—searing hot irons onto sizzling animal flesh—is gruesome in its realistic detail. And yet, the overall effect of this film is wholly artificial and sanitized for a post–World War II meat-eating American audience; the real, live animals undergoing an undoubtedly painful procedure lie still and are portrayed as eliciting no reaction at all. When examining such representations, we must think seriously about the extent to which human ideas about bovine animals were created by certain actors who produced certain kinds of bodies and behaviors, oftentimes backed by a profit motive.

The second access point to past animal lives are historical-material artifacts that can speak to the kinds of bodily management practices and tools
that cowboys and ranchers employed to capture, enclose, move, and commodify animals—the carceral apparatuses named previously, such as barbed
wire and stock pens, and numerous bodily modification tools such as branding irons and dehorning tools. The tortuous dehorning tools and associated
chemicals, instruction manuals, and practices together destroyed the bodily
integrity of bovine animals while causing untold pain and disorientation.
Such should be considered crucial and relevant archival evidence to the development of carceral landscapes and spaces, to both human-animal interaction as well as animal experiences. They allow us (or force us) to consider
more nonrepresentational, emotional, affective approaches to the study of
animal suffering; 'visceral knowing'.

Examining samples of instruments and artifacts at western museums
alongside eyewitness accounts of animal carcerality and visual or photographic evidence of carceral structures and practices can help us begin to
triangulate important understandings of animals' lived experiences. As
Fudge writes, the "material and rhetorical are linked in their context, and the
history that recognizes this can, in turn, force a reassessment of the material
through its analysis of the rhetorical strategies of the written record" (2002:
11). Artifacts derived from sources as diverse as western popular culture museums and natural history museums, and archival sources such as veterinary
medicine and government agricultural manuals, together offer important
clues to the experiences of historical animals, some carrying more weight
of 'science' (and thus authority) than others. My work is thus situated at the
intersection of such authoritative science and popular western culture.

Tolia-Kelly (2011: 435) helpfully overviews how geography has been impacted by such material culture studies, particularly subsequent to Jane Bennett's influential *Vibrant Matter* (2010). Bennett in this work theorizes a 'vital
materiality' that takes seriously active participation and agency, the web of
forces including those of the nonhuman, which affect and co-constitute sit-
uations and events (such as those of stem cells, fish oils, electricity, metal,
and trash). Tolia-Kelly's is a cautionary piece about "new" materialisms and
orientations that followed, suggesting that many studies only offer a shallow
engagement with things and material. To her, these lack reflection, critique,
engagement, or evaluation; leaving a surface recording, a superficial description, a mapping or illustration of materialities (2011: 153–154) but without
an engagement that is seemingly purposeful or political, and that does not
take into consideration hierarchical power relations (my words). Her broader
view of materialism in any case "accords ontological priority to the material

conditions of existence" and rejects nonmaterial (e.g., spiritual, metaphysical, and other transcendent) prime causes. "Materials are live, active, agenic and powerful," imbued with hierarchies, patterns, and significations; and which have a performative role and effect in shaping place (after Hetherington and Munro 1997). Tolia-Kelly's observations are useful to keep in mind for the present study, as my principal contribution to a historical-carceral geography is to engage deeply with the material physical and spatial conditions of the nonhumans (and humans) under study—to consider their uneven social hierarchies and power relations, and to weigh their respective agency to impact and be impacted by their material circumstances.

Heintzman (2021: 357–358) helps frame my study too by categorizing material culture or material cultural artifacts as tangible objects, as distinct from textual, visual, and aural ones. The textual includes things like written letters; the visual includes paintings, posters, and film; and the audio includes things like music and speeches. As Heintzman observes, these all are constituted and made from materials, of course, but as archival sources they are used to textually study the *ideas* contained within them, not the thing itself. Material sources, in contrast, are those items that lie outside of the written record, including sensory data, that are the 'thing itself' and can help build an experiential aspect to the study of history. Bennett (1998), for context, provides detail on the materials and composition of tools and instruments used to control animals (primarily horses but also cows) in the New World, as well as specifics on how they were used, thus providing a useful model for engaging with material cultural artifacts found in American cowboy and cattle museums from centuries later and, as noted, indicating an important Spanish carceral template for the study of such artifacts. As Bennett (1998: 317) posits, the vaqueros of Mexico invented most modern 'cowboy' tools and techniques.

Wilcox and Rutherford (2018: 2) observe that histories and memories are passed down through generations of animals in ways that humans cannot fathom. For scholars attempting to materially reconstruct past animal lives, though, little remains that testifies to these prior existences. Individual lives are erased by chemical, biological, and physical processes acting on the landscape that wipe away identifiable traces, tracks, and remains. Nance (2013: 10), though, argues in her work on circus elephants that animals left a material record:

> Although elephants never kept diaries or wrote newspaper columns, they marked the historical record with footprints and dung, the accounts of injured or amazed bystanders, broken bridges and barns, images and photographs, the shape of harnesses and fetters, and other "traces" that we will

find if we look for them. At the same time, we can be frank that the sources depicting historical elephants consist in large part of evidence collected by people immersed in cultures of seeing and interpreting animals that are very different from our own.

Cox (2015: 101–105, 110) illustrates how such material objects in the archive—in her case, veterinary archives—are useful in writing the history of animals. Cox interestingly found that such objects and instruments contained traces of fur, skin, and blood of real deceased animals that can help formulate theories about emotional and psychological stress. While I do not engage this sort of biological analysis at the cellular level, such insights nevertheless prompt me to recategorize objects such as fences, branding irons, ropes, whips, and a myriad of restraining devices as important and relevant archival evidence, to human-animal interaction as well as to interactions among animals. These insights also help us appreciate the value and importance of shifting from (only) written discourses on or about animals to the material histories or historical geographies of those animals, when and where possible (after Tortorici and Few 2013: 18).

Gardiner (2021: 497) develops the veterinary angle further, asking whether we could write a veterinary history that is *for* animals. To take one piece of his argument, Gardiner outlines how treatments for animal ailments were only possible to the extent that animals consented or yielded to them (501–503): "Animal 'consent' becomes a practical, everyday matter, based on what animals can or cannot tolerate." Gardiner offers an example of dentures for dogs—which did not catch on—compared with limb prostheses. Thus, he considers animals as active participants in their own treatments. Gardiner continues: "However just because an animal tolerates or allows a certain treatment does not make it right. . . . Animals are severely limited in their ability to express 'compliance' in the sense in which we usually think of it" (503). These observations seem expressly relevant within carceral spaces as 'consent' or resistance within the restrictions and practices imposed most assuredly influenced human narrative accounts of them.

I examine a broad range of tools and practices and their embodied effects in carceral spaces, some whose use was under the auspices of veterinary medicine and/or the U.S. Department of Agriculture. Such tools and instruments are available in an array of visual and written media as well as directly available at museums and other sites. Artifacts such as those held at museums in Texas, Oklahoma, and Kansas are the basic building blocks of this study; indeed, foundational to it. The Barbed Wire Study Collection located at the National Cowboy Hall of Fame and Western Heritage Museum in Oklahoma City, Oklahoma; branding irons at the National Ranching Heritage Center in Lubbock, Texas; and the tool collections in the natural history hall of the Panhandle-Plains Museum in Canyon, Texas, and the Boot Hill Museum in Dodge City, Kansas, among many others, offer essential entreés into the technologies, instruments, and practices of animal control and dominance as well as how such artifacts have been represented to today's audiences as producing a particular story about the emergent beef industry and national meaning-making for ranching dynasties, cowboys, and longhorn cattle.

Themes and Contents of the Volume

Chapter 1, "First Encounters with the Carceral: Forced Migration and Animal Mobility," begins with the observation that the transport or movement of bovine animals to and within America must be framed as a 'forced migration', basically in three phases—first via Atlantic Ocean (and other) sailing vessels, then through land via cattle drives to the cow towns such as Abilene and Dodge City, Kansas, and finally via railroad to awaiting slaughterhouses. The colonial epicenter for the forced migration of bovine animals in the United States was in what we today call southern Texas, the origin point of cattle ranching dating to the Spanish colonial period and subsequent origin point of the cattle trails east (before the Civil War) and north thereafter. An important aspect to the U.S. carceral archipelago is the legacy of many tools and practices brought with the Spanish colonizers. The chapter traces bovine mobility from the Caribbean to Mexico to southern Texas, and the importance of the Texas cattle ranching frontier to the emergence of the cattle carceral archipelago. In this chapter I also link to the larger-scale colonial-carceral processes taking place just prior to the emergent cattle industry, that of land dispossession, forced migration, and removal of Indigenous peoples, which coincided with the mass extermination of their food source and basis of their livelihoods, that of the previous bovines in North America, the buffalo.

Chapter 2, "Enclosing the Range: Carceral Tools, Practices, Structures," opens with the cattle 'roundup' on the open range. These wild or semiferal animals living independently in dense thickets were captured and then moved into stock pens where they were held, separated, branded, and prepared for the cattle drive north. In this chapter I examine various insidious carceral tools, technologies, and practices used to capture, enclose, and restrain animals, and animal responses to them. These include hot iron branding, earmarking, and castration tools, collectively representing a carceral experience amplified. This chapter frames such experiences within the enclosure of the open range by the emergent cattle baron class in the nineteenth century, enabled with new technologies such as barbed wire and an infrastructure behind them such as land laws that quickly and quite dramatically impacted the lives of animals. Acquiring physical control over the herds and land was more efficacious for the cattlemen than seeking legal control over them. Those who were most successful at turning these animal lives into personal property simply rounded them up, claimed them, branded them, and enclosed them on mostly illegally acquired public land (itself appropriated Indigenous territory). In particular, I highlight the impacts of the new barbed wire technology on animal experiences, including study of the 'fence cutting wars' among cattle kings, other ranchers, and farmers, and the emergence of 'drift fences' in Texas to prevent animals' movement to preferred habitats and feeding grounds to the south. Celebration of so-called advancements in barbed wire technology as well as other carceral instruments form an important celebratory component of the re-narrations of the cattle trade in western museum culture.

Chapter 3, "The Cattle Drive: Cowboys and Cattle at Work," centrally examines the experiences of animals during what I consider a "carceral death march" on the cattle drive from Texas to Kansas. In addition to the human-imposed carceral practices involved in moving, resting, grazing, and disciplining animals along the cattle trail, as well as the resultant occasional stampede, I highlight the numerous environmental factors that they encountered during their journeys—dangerous river crossings, blizzards, and droughts—and the tortuous impacts on animal lives and survival. The experiences of mother cows and their calves during the cattle drive, and various eyewitness accounts of the ways in which mother cows attempted to mediate the carceral experiences for their offspring, and care for them, helps concretize the emotional and psychological experience of the cattle drive for many animals—even if the common practice was to simply kill the calves. This chapter also takes up the important question of how study of the carceral spaces of human-nonhuman interactions and relations on the cattle drive can illuminate human-nonhuman boundary construction—humanness and animality—within the U.S. historical context. Such analysis forces a reexamination of how cows and cowboys' mutual 'work' on the cattle drive shapes much of the mythmaking surrounding the conquest of the West by heroic cowboys and those animals with whom they were closely, even intimately, connected in the settler colonial project. While 'work' performed by animals during the early American colonial period as well as on the western ranches and cattle drives was in simply feeding themselves on pasture grasses and transporting themselves to awaiting railroad cars, here I contribute an analysis of this work within its carceral context.

Chapter 4, "Cow Towns and (Lost) Animal Lives: A National Celebration," outlines the development and emergence of the Kansas cow towns whose specific rural spatiality was fundamental to the carceral archipelago of which they were a part. Numerous structural, infrastructural, and technological developments of these towns aided in the unprecedented growth of the cattle trade during the mid-nineteenth century; most significantly, they were nodal points where the cattle trails met the awaiting railroad cars that would transport animals to the slaughterhouses beyond. The actions of multiple economic and political entrepreneurs enabled them to make enormous profits on the lives of animals during the heyday of the cattle trail and town, ca. 1865–1885. How the towns of Abilene and Dodge City, Kansas, have become popular tourist destinations is a key piece of cattle trade history, and I unpack how important artifacts such as taxidermied animals in museum dioramas represent a distinct carceral condition for animals, and they, along with town monuments, convey mythologized stories of an imagined past where the longhorn animals were important players in the heroic winning of the West. This ostensibly hearty, rugged, independent breed became an important signifier of American national identity itself. I juxtapose the symbolism of these animals and their majestic horns against the reality of the business problems that the horns posed to town builders and the cruel, painful practice of horn removal—a contradictory practice in that while the horns were (and are) celebrated, they are at the same time subject to erasure.

Chapter 5, "Cattle-Drive Westerns: Carceral Space and Bovine Actors," focuses on classic Hollywood post–World War II American western films that feature cattle drives and cattle towns as central plot lines. I argue that bovine animals have not been heretofore discussed in the literature on animals in film, including in the literature on western films; they feature prominently in such films yet only as backdrops to human dramas taking place. These films typically portray animals as either peacefully grazing in beautiful pastoral landscapes or wholly out of control and wildly stampeding in clouds of dust. Reconstructing the cattle drive from fictionalized films offers an important entrée into a nostalgic mythic past within which both humans and animals prevailed in their masculine conquest of the West. The films harkened to a nineteenth-century American past and helped justify and neutralize the carceral conditions bovine animals experienced. These portrayals of the nineteenth-century West in films produced in the mid-twentieth century dramatized a type of postwar mentality that infused American culture with meat eating itself as a patriotic act. This chapter thus considers the extent to which human representation of cows in these films invented ideas about them that were subsequently used to produce certain kinds of bodies and foodways, as well as encourage audiences to enjoy and celebrate the carceral. This chapter also includes discussion of experiences of animals who 'acted' in these films, most of whom were rented from the carceral spaces of then-operating ranches.

The afterword, "Bovine Lives and an Ethical West," first recaps and summarizes the main arguments of the book, reiterating that real animals with real lives have been heretofore absent from our understandings of the emergent cattle trade, and that the present intervention into western history, historical geography, and historiography necessarily changes how we think about and study the past. History will be on the side of taking animal lives seriously, particularly the bovine animals discussed in this work who are among the most objectified and animalized of animals. This 'origin story' offers tremendous potential to rethink the treatment of animals who have been ensnared in the cattle beef industry, and to challenge the unprecedented levels of violence inherent in it, historically and today. Although this work is primarily focused on the lived experiences of bovine animals in the past, the chapter also includes some reflections on the subsequent threats to contemporary animal lives as well.

CHAPTER 1

First Encounters with the Carceral

FORCED MIGRATION AND ANIMAL MOBILITY

Bovine animal experiences that began with their forced migration to North America in slings on Spanish sailing ships in the fifteenth and sixteenth centuries and ended with their boarding railroad cars bound for Chicago abattoirs in the nineteenth century represents a singularly poignant historical example of how violence toward nonhuman animals with attendant pain and suffering is a basic ingredient—and outcome—of industries whose design is based on carceral logics. My discussion in this chapter charts the early migration and subsequent mobility of bovine animals to the point where Texas became the primary epicenter of the American cattle industry. The chapter begins with a conceptual intervention into the appearance of bovine animals in the Americas in the first instance. I consider transport or movement of these animals as a colonial 'forced migration', a migration that would ultimately unfold in three phases—first via Atlantic Ocean (and other) sailing vessels, then over land via cattle drives to the cow towns such as Abilene and Dodge City, Kansas, and finally via railroad to awaiting slaughterhouses.

Animals have not typically been considered 'migrants' in migration studies, although more-than-human advances to human migration studies are taking shape (e.g., Alkan 2022). This chapter outlines bovine animals' migrations (forced and otherwise) from Spain to the Caribbean, to Mexico, and to Texas, and the parallel draw of human immigrants West from the eastern colonies to the cattle trade along the Atlantic coast and Gulf of Mexico prior to the Civil War (e.g., Davant and Herskowitz 2016; Sherow 2018). I detail some of the processes and practices involved in cattle migration, with the earliest forebears' first encounters with the carceral by sea, followed by increasingly intensive carceral encounters over and on land. It is important to document the early experiences of these animals, or to at least acknowledge the challenge of doing so. Their seafaring experiences often get left out of their stories; as Tortorici (2021) explains, scholarly focus has been not on their journeys, but on very bureaucratic accounting of their numbers only on arrival.

Specht (2019: 4) writes of the early industrial "cattle beef complex" as a system reliant on movement—from the cows essentially walking themselves to market, to the physical labor of the cattlemen driving them, to the development of the railroad. The history of the American beef industry and the development of national markets was fundamentally about such mobility—the moving of live or dead bodies long distances—which was enabled via government regulation combined with a standardization of the spaces through which cows and people moved (Specht 2019: 15, 122). To this useful theorizing I propose beginning discussion of bovine movement with their transatlantic crossings, and their subsequent migrations north from Mexico and Texas prior to the expansive ranching and cattle trailing periods.

When considering cattle movement within these carceral infrastructures it is useful to frame it around what Hodgetts and Lorimer call the "ordering practices" that govern animal mobility (2020; also see Lorimer 2006). These authors make the distinction between "movement" of animals, as simply a shift in their spatial coordinates in Euclidean space, and animal "mobility," which refers to the politics and ethics associated with that animal movement (or stillness; Hodgetts and Lorimer 2020: 5–6). This distinction helps us understand forced migration as a type of mobility—and not just a passive transport of commodified bodies—and to recognize that animal movements are always produced within (and are productive of) relations of power between many actors.

Various sorts of power dynamics and practices govern or 'order' animal mobilities, including *sovereign power*, associated with the totalizing control over the movement of life, such as human sovereign power over the ability to take animal lives (or let them live); capture and transport of them over long distances; and control of them via technologies of spatial confinement such as fences, cages, nets, tanks, and so forth. *Disciplinary power* and *biopower* refer to ways in which animal governmentality operates; the ways in which the mobilities of individual subjects are enabled and constrained, with the former concerned with human shaping and training of individual animal mobilities—such as through whistles, bits and bridles, whips, and electric prods—and the latter focused on the modification and modulation of aggregations of animal bodies and their collective properties such as in selective breeding programs

(Hodgetts and Lorimer 2020: 15). Disciplinary training has been central to intensive animal agriculture, in which animals are subjected to a range of technologies and controls designed to rationalize bodies and behaviors in the interests of maximizing production. Much of the animal mobility I discuss in this chapter falls under the aegis and oversight of numerous sovereign, disciplinary, and biopowers but is also combined with a type of independent movement on the part of the animals as they migrated north from Mexico to what became Texas in search of abundant grasses. Thus, at a broader historical and spatial scale, the forced migrations I discuss should be considered alongside some self-directed movement on the part of the animals.

Focusing on animal mobilities offers an opportunity to take account of animal lived experiences as part of their spatial movement within carceral spaces—multisensory, affective, embodied experiences of moving about in different ways, and concomitant bodily capacities, emotional experiences, and social relations (Specht 2019: 8). Research on captive animals has demonstrated that the emotions of pain, pleasure, boredom, joy, grief, anger, and surprise can be elicited by controlling animals' movement. As scores of animal researchers have confirmed (Gruen 2014; Urbanik 2012; DeMello 2014; Gillespie 2018a), restrictions on movement—such as captivity via structural mechanisms such as a boat, fence, or cage—can cause an animal distress, even when the movement no longer serves a functional purpose. Movement is associated with rhythms for eating, sleeping, and socializing; and different experiences are elicited in the absence or presence of known predators, with those confined too close to predators experiencing anxiety (with humans the 'apex' predator; Hodgetts and Lorimer 2020: 10). Such observations help contextualize the life experiences of animals during ocean voyages as well as their further movements along the carceral archipelago on land.

I follow discussion of bovine animals' early seafaring experiences from Spain to North America with examination of their subsequent migrations from the Caribbean to Mexico and to the emergence of the Texas cattle ranching frontier as it eventually took shape in the mid-nineteenth century amid the contours of the American Civil War. Their numbers greatly increased as they migrated north. This empirical grounding helps set the stage for what would become 'industrial' beef production in the United States beginning in the mid-nineteenth century.

This chapter also adds another important dimension to the story of this colonial-carceral archipelago: the simultaneous eradication of the former bovine lives on the continent, the buffalo, parallel to the nineteenth-century human colonial-carceral system writ large. Here I outline the direct relationships between settler colonialism, Indigenous carcerality, and the vast destruction of the buffalo herds, and how this destruction was foundational to the cattle beef industry that emerged to replace the buffalo. So while my focus is on animals, the carceral enclosure of Indigenous peoples and stories of cattle drives through the ever-shrinking geography of so-called Indian Territory provides enhanced understandings of the early historical geography of the emergent cattle beef industry.

Forced Animal Migration in Colonial-Carceral Context

Bovine animals' appearance in the Americas was an integral piece of a specifically colonial-carceral enterprise. One possible, and provocative, strategy for attempting to understand and frame the carceral experiences of these animals is to consider them as beings subjected to forced migration within the context of North American (and other) settler colonial interventions. Thinking of them as forced migrants—as opposed to simply transported cargo—within what could be thought of as perhaps one of the first transoceanic carceral migrations adds an important dimension to carceral studies as well as studies of migration and mobility more generally (see Moran, Gill, and Conlon 2013; Loyd, Mitchelson, and Burridge 2012). This framing challenges taken-for-granted empirical understandings of bovine animals' appearance on the continent as the result of simple transport or movement within early settler colonial encounters. It also intersects with the carceral logics and violence of the forced migration of Indigenous communities as part of the emergent cattle industry and well beyond it across the North American continent (e.g., the Trail of Tears), as well as, of course, the transatlantic human slave trade.

The forced animal migrants at subject here primarily originated as part of the Spanish colonial enterprise in the fifteenth and sixteenth centuries via sailing vessels, later mixing with other animals shipped as part of the British colonial enterprise to the eastern seaboard. Very different exigencies surrounded these settler colonial (and imperial) migrations, and these origins are an important part of animals' stories, as is their role in the colonial project itself. Thus, I interrogate what we might consider another type of 'New World chattel' aboard the ships and early land encounters of European colonizers in North America.

To discuss these animals as chattel—that is, considered to be colonial property—in no way diminishes the horrors of some humans turning other humans into chattel through centuries of enslavement across the Black Middle Passage, nor is it tantamount to equating them and suggesting that they are somehow the same (e.g., Spiegel 1997; Kim 2011). Rather, juxtaposing them and thinking about these forced migrations together can help us better understand how carceral space, carceral logics, and carceral practices can impact both humans and nonhuman animals alike; it can help us understand how transforming human and nonhuman subjects into property and commodity follows similar carceral logics of entrapment, captivity, movement, exploitation, and death.

Human migration and immigration are long-standing, even foundational areas of interest within human geography, particularly in analysis of the ethics of border maintenance and control as well as the various 'push' and 'pull' factors that influence or cause human migratory behavior (some recent examples include Mitchell, Jones, and Fluri 2020; Bauder 2016; Hidalgo 2018). Such push-and-pull factors can be political, economic, or environmental—for example, related to those escaping ethnic persecution, poverty, drought, or hazardous circumstances and seeking places offering better conditions and opportunities. The methodological approach I am suggesting here will resonate more, though, with the material cultures of forced human migrations, such as those of the transatlantic slave trade. Artifacts collected at the African American Museum in Washington, D.C., and others, for example, such as below-deck stalls as well as chains, metal collars, weapons, and whips, offer evidence of the embodied human experience of tortuous capture of West Africans and transport to the Americas aboard the cramped and filthy slave ships—the parallel structures and tools used within the cattle carceral archipelago. Again though, making comparisons across these types of human carceral spaces and practices with those of animals is—for good reason— highly contestable, since it potentially reinforces the fact that some human groups have been (and continue to be) comparatively animalized and never fully brought into the status of 'human' (Wynter 2003; Ko 2016; Kim 2011, 2015).

An extensive literature in the natural sciences discusses migration and migratory behavior of a vast array of animals, from monarch butterflies to birds, fish, and land and sea mammals, within a vast array of global, ecological, and environmental contexts and circumstances (e.g., Milner-Gulland, Fryxell, and Sinclair 2011; Shea and Saxena 2016). This literature documents numerous animal species migrating over air, land, and water; over space and for various lengths of time; and migrating for various reasons, including to find food, shelter, breeding grounds, or more suitable climates. Animals migrate for survival, using myriad physical, physiological, social, and earth and atmospheric features to find their way. As Jorgensen (2015: 184) observes, within the biological sciences, animal migration is typically understood as an adaptation to resource availability. But Jorgensen, along with Wilson (2015) and others, calls for more attention to how human and nonhuman histories intersect in animal migrations—whether "forced or deliberately chosen" (Jorgensen 2015: 184).

Wilson (2015) tracks the widespread impact of humans on the migrations of a number of animals in North America such as elk, bison, and salmon, calling for more attention to this impact within environmental history. But the experiences of multitudes of animals, those forcibly caught within the practices and infrastructures of the American West carceral archipelago, are much more analogous to that of forced migrations not only of humans but also of many, many other nonhuman animals captured, transported, and relocated for human entertainment, sport, or food (e.g., Collard and Dempsey 2013) and the concomitant suffering under the sovereign and disciplinary ordering practices of exploitation, dominance, surveillance, and control.

The appearance and behaviors of bovine animals in North America within the colonial context has been a subject of considerable interest by historians, ecologists, and others. Much of the scholarship has tended to emphasize animals' agency as primarily ecological impact on the land, and in the case of the United States, consequently impacting the conquest of Indigenous peoples and dispossession of their lands. Environmental historians in particular have taken animals seriously as agents of historical change, especially during the era of European exploration and expansion. Crosby (1994, 2003, 2004) offers an influential analysis of animal agency via the ecological and environmental impact that animals made in the context of the Columbian Exchange; farmed animals were instrumental in helping Europeans establish colonies in other parts of the world, especially in North and South America.

Anderson (2004) details the role of farm animals—especially cows and horses—in the North American colonial project. Anderson maintains that these animals were "central to the plot" of colonization and were mentioned frequently in the historical-colonial record, particularly of that kept by early farmers. To Anderson (3–7), the process of colonization itself involved "two immigrant groups," human and nonhuman. Anderson describes how animals contributed to erosion, altered microclimates, introduced other ecological shifts, and compounded the difficulties Native peoples faced after colonization. "Because livestock tend[ed] to be discussed in terms of the ecological alterations they produced, the effects of their presence on people are largely indirect, mediated by the environment itself" (also see Specht 2016: 343–363; 2019; Sluyter 1996; Derby 2011). Anderson's framing of colonial animals as immigrants can help us understand them as colonial newcomers, but I would emphasize that their immigration was a forced one.

Bovine Mobility and European Colonial Seafaring

Colonial and imperial interventions by the English, Portuguese, French, and Dutch all included the introduction of farmed animals to North America. The bovine animals captive within the carceral archipelago at subject here were shipped first as part of the Spanish colonial enterprise via sailing ships to the

Caribbean. The first of these animals appeared along with Spanish explorers and conquistadors—Columbus, Cortez, Coronado, Pizarro, and de Soto all included agricultural animals in their colonial invasions. Stillman writes of horses who also arrived in the New World with the conquistadors: unlike horses, cows "were not heading home, although it did not take long for them to go wild" (Stillman 2008: 162). A number of scholars (e.g., Crosby 2003: 75ff; 2004; Specht 2016: 347; McTavish et al. 2013) make reference to Christopher Columbus bringing bovine animals on his 'voyages of discovery', the first to do so in the Western Hemisphere. He also brought horses, pigs, sheep, dogs, chickens, and goats, first to the Canary Islands and then to Hispaniola on his second voyage in 1493. Wherever Spanish conquistadors went after that, European domesticated animals followed, rapidly multiplying and supplying breeding stock for each step of Spanish colonial interventions (McTavish et al. 2013; Rouse 1977).

Yet nearly all scholarship on these animals focuses not on their journey but on their arrival and habitation patterns at their destination. The question of how the animals were moved, and their seafaring experiences of mobility, is an important one. What was this sea voyage like for them? As Tortorici (2021) observes, animal movement has been documented, recorded, and archived in highly bureaucratic and objectifying ways. Thus, accessing their experiences on ships is difficult since they tended to be documented in perfunctory ways, for example, "200 head of cattle loaded and transported"—often the only extent to which animal experiences are referenced in the Spanish colonial records. While animals *are* present in historical documents, their migratory status is often or typically documented only through their deaths—their transformation from living beings to commodities to be bought, sold, transformed, and consumed. Animal presence in archives, then, is predicated partly on their disappearance (Tortorici 2015: 82).

Kilgore (1983: 62) estimates that fewer than one hundred cows landed with Columbus in Hispaniola in 1493, and that very few additional shipments arrived before 1503, when Queen Isabella ordered that all ships thereafter carry livestock. Although Columbus kept a log of his second voyage, only very short fragments survive. Most of what we know of it comes from indirect references or from accounts of others on the voyage, especially about the journey and the important issue of conditions on the ship for both human and nonhuman animals. Jett (2017) discusses the perils of oceanic sailing in the fifteenth century—particularly that of the dangerous storms, winds, high seas, and adverse weather conditions. The scale, size, and type of watercraft structure impacted the experience at sea, of course, with Columbus's ship the *Niña* 55 feet long, with three large sails, and the capacity to carry 50–60 tons (2017: 153). Jett claims that Columbus and other voyagers actually preferred smaller vessels because they had more strength and maneuverability (2017: 160); the larger the size of the vessel, the greater the stresses from wind and waves. As Taylor (2017) describes this approximately three-week journey of the *Niña*:

> When the "Niña" left on any of her three voyages to the New World, her cargo hold was full of provisions, water, armaments. There were live animals ranging from horses, cows, pigs, and chickens. The four-legged animals were suspended in slings as the rolling motion of the vessel would have easily broken their legs. Needless to say, there was little room below decks for the 27 or so crew to sleep or cook. Cooking was done in a fire box located on decks in the bow of the ship. Sleeping was on the deck and was always uncomfortable as the ship was so loaded with cargo, her decks were always awash. A lucky few could sleep on the poop deck or find a coil of rope to sleep on to keep them off the deck a foot or so.

Crosby (2003: 68) points out that the transatlantic voyage was particularly "not an easy one for horses"—another among the large vertebrate livestock animals—from which we can extrapolate a bovine experience as well. The body of water between Spain and the Canary Islands, where almost all early expeditions stopped on their way to America, was known as the Golfo de Yeguas (the Gulf of Mares), situated in the Atlantic 'horse latitudes', so named because so many horses died and/or were thrown overboard to lighten ships' loads. The carceral experiences of animals crossing the Atlantic were thus not limited to bovines but were part of a larger pattern of carceral geographies at the time. Stillman (2008: 3–4) further documents the voyages of horses to the New World, also noting their presence on Columbus's second voyage in 1493, "held in place by slings and hoists." Stillman speculates that the animals could "only smell salt air mixed with the galleon stench" and "[hear] only the uneasy creak of wood as the giant brigantines hove[d] through the walls of water." Fifteen stallions and ten mares became the foundation stock for hundreds of horses that would serve in dozens of waves of conquest. Like bovines, they originated in the 'cradle of the conquistadors' north of Seville, Spain (Stillman 2008: 6–7, 25), and, like cattle, they first arrived in Cuba and other Caribbean islands and then migrated to Mexico and beyond. Thousands were shipped across the Atlantic from 1519 onward, with more than half dying along the way.

Anderson's (2004) study of the early English voyages to the eastern colonies offers additional insights into what these voyages would have been like for bovine animals. The *Mayflower* brought colonists to New England in 1620 but no farmed animals, although after a few years cattle were brought with colonists to Plymouth. The Massachusetts Bay Company transported cows to North America, and the Winthrop fleet in 1630 brought 240 cows, about 60 horses, and 700 humans. At that time, a ship crossing from England took 8–10 weeks, with people and animals in close quarters. As Anderson (2004: 99) explains,

> No colonist who left an account of the transatlantic crossing mentioned what it was like to spend eight to ten weeks in close quarters aboard ship with dozens of restive animals. Absorbed by their own anxieties, emigrants who described their voyages dwelled instead on the miseries of seasickness, the terror induced by tempests, and the relief occasioned by good weather. But the animals' passage could hardly have been less traumatic. Confined to dark, fetid stalls below decks, livestock struggled to keep their footing as ships rose and sank with the ocean swells. During storms, their terrified bellows and squeals added to the cacophony produced by lashing rains, howling winds, creaking timbers, and human shrieks and stammered prayers. A distressingly large number of animals perished at sea.

Anderson estimates that over half to two-thirds of the animals died during these early colonial voyages. Once on shore, many eastern colonists began to acquire their animals from the West Indies and Caribbean; they were one of the largest start-up costs of a new colony. Many animals died later from exposure in severe winters, ca. 1630s–1670s. Cows in the Chesapeake Bay Colony (in present-day Virginia) suffered from ticks, kidney worms, and parasites (Anderson 2004: 101–103) and fell victim to predators such as bears and wolves—to whom the colonists had introduced a new food supply. Bounties were offered to rid these predators, and they were the subject of frequent legislation. The harsh conditions meant that animals were being eaten, so it became a capital crime to kill any bull, cow, or calf, in addition to prohibitions against slaughtering them being introduced; this, whether the animal was privately owned or company owned. However, by 1650 there were more animals than colonists. Eventually these animals would populate the American South and intermingle with those animals introduced by the Spanish in the West—by the nineteenth century producing what we today consider the Texas longhorn.

The enormous difficulty in transporting large animals on long ocean voyages meant that fewer than one thousand individuals arrived in the West Indies by 1512 (Kilgore 1983: 62–63). The Spaniards shipped bovine animals to the Americas for about twenty years, but after 1512 these animals became an isolated group for the next two hundred years or so (McTavish et al. 2012). By 1512 the colonial infiltrators deemed further importation by ship unnecessary. No predators, no or few diseases, and year-round growth in vegetation left the animals to feed and wander freely, and they reproduced rapidly and prodigiously.

Transatlantic shipping of live cows as an American colonial import halted in the early sixteenth century; however, by the nineteenth century, seafaring

Fig. 1.1. A cattle steamer at sea. *Scribner's Magazine,* 5 November 1891.

by animals at the end of the cattle trailing period commenced with the brief moment of live transatlantic bovine export. Sherow (2018: 44) reports that the earliest recorded attempt to ship live cows and dressed beef from Chicago to London occurred in 1868. Fig. 1.1 illustrates a transatlantic voyage to Britain from the United States, offering another glimpse of what might have been the experience of such a crossing for cows. These animals, trapped and crowded shoulder to shoulder in cramped pens, appear distressed, eyes bulging, vomiting, or thirsting for barreled water just out of reach. Their efforts at vocalizing distress reflected their vain attempts to maintain their footing amid the wild sea currents. The *Scribner's Magazine* article and image shown in the figure (Gould 1891) highlight why cows often arrived at English ports in "rough shape" (Sherow 2018: 187).

By 1890, newly designed freighters had replaced the first steamboats that had transported live cows across the Atlantic. At the time, the National ship line's freighter, the *England*, held the record for the most live cows shipped across the Atlantic, departing New York City in September 1889 with 1,022 animals bound for England. The Anchor Line steamship company from Glasgow had dominated transatlantic transport of live cows and sides of refrigerated beef during the 1870s and 1880s. As Sherow explains, "This opened a flourishing 'dead meat' trade. By 1877, the company had outfitted six of its mail steamers with this technology, and each of the vessels could haul between 360 and 450 carcasses" (Sherow 2018: 44; also see 78).

Spanish Cattle, from the Caribbean to Mexico to Texas

The historical geographies of forced bovine migrants from southern Spain constituted a crucial element in settler colonialism of what is today called Texas. After their initial introduction into the Caribbean islands, cattle were subsequently introduced into Mexico around 1521, and within a few decades had moved north into what is now Texas and south into Colombia and Venezuela. The Spanish settlers largely allowed them free range in the unfenced wilderness. The biggest herds in Spain had numbered about eight hundred; just decades after their introduction that number was eight thousand in Hispaniola. Aside from being reduced to meat, hides, and tallow, the cattle were used mainly as draft animals in their new location, and subsequently traded— oftentimes for enslaved Indigenous people—beginning around 1527 (Jett 2017: 72). Kilgore (1983: 63) reports that in the early years of trade between Spanish conquerors in Hispaniola and those in Mexico, the exchange rate was eighty enslaved Indians for one cow—illustrating well that violence toward and exploitation of both animalized humans and animals exists on a continuum for any commerce, business, or industry whose design is based on carceral logics (Gruen and Marceau 2022; Morin 2018).

Kilgore (1983: 63) documents the shipping of cattle from the Caribbean to Mexico beginning in 1521 and the proliferation of the herds once there, describing the "explosive multiplication of livestock in the New World as one of the most astonishing biological phenomenon ever seen by modern man." As noted, year-round growth of vegetation and native grasses, as well as the abundant seed pods of brush plants and water along the river and stream beds, provided the conditions for this proliferation. Herds nearly doubled in fifteen months, "overrunning the countryside and destroying Indian cornfields." As the European population of Mexico built up and began to spread north, cattle ranching went along with it. "The penetration of Spanish cattle into the rich grass country of northern Mexico in the 16th century set off one of the most biologically extravagant events of that biologically amazing century. In 1579 . . . some ranches in the north had 150,000 head of cattle [and] 20,000 was considered a small herd" (Crosby 2003: 87–88).

Crosby (2004: 177–179) states that by the end of the sixteenth century, cattle herds in northern Mexico may have been doubling every fifteen years, with wild herds traveling farther north by the mid-1750s. Along the Rio Grande, Spanish rancheros acquired huge grants (Mercedes) from the king, stocked them with cattle, and supplied them with vaqueros who were themselves Indigenous peoples or mestizos (White 1991: 37). The Portuguese slaver and Spanish crown governor Luis de Carvajal (and first Spanish subject credited with entering Texas from Mexico), like Cortez and many other conquistadors, was also a rancher, and his grant from the king obligated him to introduce cows into his colony. Stillman (2008: 35) notes that this dynasty likewise bred the first horses in the conquered lands. The first bovine herds to enter Texas derived primarily from the lower coastal eastern plains, the area on the eastern Mexican plateau, today's Tamaulipas.

McTavish et al. (2013: 1389–1399) provides DNA analysis that shows that Texas longhorns of today are direct descendants of the first cattle introduced to the Americas. Although brought from Spain via the Canary Islands, the breed had an international heritage, with roots in the Middle East and India. These animals likely shared some ancestry with Northern African breeds of cows and thus may have included an indicine genetic component, via earlier gene flow from Africa to the Iberian Peninsula. Within the next four centuries, as McTavish et al. (1398–1399) found, natural selection drove the evolution of this group of semiferal herds for between eighty and two hundred generations (as opposed to the human-mediated artificial selection of European breeding programs). There were probably more cows in the Americas in the seventeenth century than any other type of large vertebrate animal because, according to Crosby (2003: 85–87), the Spaniards embraced the immense grasslands of the plains and drove cows onto them. Southern Iberia was the only part of western Europe during the Renaissance in which open ranching was common, although meat eaters formed only one market for beef, and not the most important market—more cows were killed for hides and tallow (for candles) than for meat during this 'age of leather'. (The fleet that crossed to Spain in 1587 landed nearly one hundred thousand hides in Seville, Spain; Crosby 2003: 86.) According to Butzer (1988: 29), cattle raising was small-scale and of subordinate importance in Spain, except in the estuarine marshland below Seville. Whereas the early colonial ranchers in Mexico originated from areas throughout Spain, their highly extensive management style appears to derive from the Marismas of Sevilla.

Crosby further explains that the techniques that would characterize ranching in America—the constant use of the horse, periodic roundups, branding, overland drives—originated with medieval Iberians. In other words, there is an important Spanish legacy to the carceral practices that made their way to North America. Spanish cows were considered adaptable, fast, lean, and, with their long horns, able to protect themselves from predators. Yet most were considered feral animals, retreating into the densest thickets and venturing out at night to graze on the prairie. Derby (2011: 605) maintains that the success of bovine and other animals had everything to do with their habitat. As they overgrazed areas and competition for grass grew, they ventured northward. Kilgore relates that the "record they created on the land indicates that substantial numbers of wild cattle settled beyond the Rio Grande much earlier than the Spanish who introduced them into Mexico" (1983: 63), with cows greatly outnumbering people. Thus, when Spaniards began a serious attempt to settle in southern Texas in the early eighteenth century, they discovered that wild cattle were there before them. Cattle then were the advance guard of colonial settlers (Crosby 2003: 88).

The history of Spanish missions in the New World also offers relevant background to the subsequent carceral or 're-carceralization' experiences of bovine animals in Texas. The first attempt by the Spanish to establish a mission among Indigenous peoples was led by Alonso de León, who drove the first cattle herd across Texas on his expedition and established a mission in 1690 but abandoned it three years later. When the French "intruder" Saint-Denis arrived in East Texas in 1714, his report indicated that "much of the country was literally covered with cattle and horses" (Kilgore 1983: 65).[1] (Saint-Denis was also to organize the first cattle drive east out of Texas, to Mobile, Alabama.) White (1994: 243) provides useful detail on the location of the Texas missions and herds, and the first ranches that developed with commercialized animals between 1750 and 1810. It was in these missions and on these ranches that the carceral practices of later western cattle raising evolved. By the late eighteenth century, more than fifty Spanish Franciscan missions held bovine herds in what is now Texas. Between 1750 and 1810, rancheros developed in three distinct areas of Texas: between the Rio Grande and the Nueces River, on the San Antonio River, and on the Louisiana border near Nacogdoches. It was on these ranches and on the missions that many of the practices of later western cattle ranching evolved (White 1994: 243). White (39) reports that into the nineteenth century, feral Criollo cattle from the mission herds remained largely limited to East Texas and the lands around the Arizona missions. After several generations in the wild, they could not be redomesticated. "They could only be hunted."

After Mexican independence in 1821 most clergy refused loyalty to the Mexican government, abandoned their missions, and dispersed their herds to local Native peoples or left them free to run loose, allowing wild herds to flourish. The latter of these became part of the public domain, considered abandoned, and ranching entrepreneurs began rounding them up, claiming herds of 300–1,000 as their own. Dobie (1941: 5) adds that at first the herds all belonged to mission ranches, but by the end of the eighteenth century, anybody willing to put up a house and locate a hundred cows could procure from the government a grant to a league (about 4,438 acres) or more of land to establish a ranch.

The Texas Cattle Ranching Frontier

Estimates are that 100,000 bovine animals roamed Texas by 1830, and just three decades later, on the eve of the Civil War, that number had increased to an estimated 3.5–5 million (Rifkin 1992: 68–70; White 1991: 220–225; Starrs 1998). Anglo settlers started moving into Texas in the 1820s, and many of these English-speaking colonists considered these animals as native to the land. As White (1991: 37) describes it, "Anglo Americans would not introduce a ranching culture into Texas. They would find a fully developed culture in place."

Davant and Herskowitz (2016) offer a detailed account of one family's immigration experience in the 1830s and 1840s from the U.S. Northeast to the Gulf Coast of Texas, and the transition in that locale from a primarily slave-owing cotton-and-sugar plantation economy and culture, ended by the Civil War, to a cattle ranching one—exchanging one carceral enterprise for another. Originating from a shipbuilding port town in Connecticut with traders used to doing business in the West Indies, the Richard Grimes family began to hear of trading opportunities at ports in Mexican territory, eventually immigrating to the Matagorda Peninsula and setting up cattle boats to trade along the Gulf Coast (Devant and Herskowitz 2016: 57–50).

When the Civil War accelerated the transition from plantation sugar and cotton growing to grazing land, veterans of the Texan revolution such as Grimes acquired thousands of acres of grazing land directly from the General Land Office in Austin in 1838, as well as by purchasing it from other veterans (Davant and Herskowitz 2016: 46). Grimes and his son started the WBG ranch, capturing wild cows, branding them, trading them via their boats to New Orleans, Havana, and the West Indies (33), and eventually herding them north on the Chisholm Trail to Dodge City, Kansas. In 1847 they saw "oceans of free range where thousands of unbranded cattle roamed . . . imagin[ing] profits on the hoof" (50). Steamships extended such businesses, such as the Morgan Steamship Line to New Orleans and along the Texas coast. Wharves and loading docks were added to accommodate ships that could carry live cattle to markets. The Grimeses also invented a cattle pen where animals could be more easily branded and sorted (54), and cattlemen came through their ranch to make use of the new pens.

At the time of the Civil War—the mid-1860s—the cattle trade in Texas transitioned from cattle import to export (Stillman 2008). Shillingberg (2009) outlines in some detail how the Civil War dramatically shifted the direction and movement of the emergent Texas cattle industry. Before the war, small allotments of Texas cattle had reached Kansas City and other Missouri river towns, with some going as far east as St. Louis and various Illinois border settlements, to New Orleans (then the largest market for them in the South), and to Mobile, Alabama. Those animals were either driven overland into Louisiana or shipped via flatbed or steamship from Galveston, Corpus Christi, and other Texas gulf ports. But the Civil War changed this. Most significantly, the war closed the Mississippi River to southern commerce. The Civil War had thus eliminated both the markets for cattle and the men who raised them. These were the 'untended' cattle who quickly reproduced.

By the end of the Civil War in 1865, longhorns formed the majority of the millions of cattle in Texas (White 1992: 253). When confederate soldiers returned to Texas, they found that their herds had doubled in size and were roaming the range, unbranded. After the war, transport of cattle to New Orleans resumed, with the first Texas cattle to travel the Mississippi River to New Orleans in 1865 (Sherow 2018: 50–51). Returning to the 'seafaring' carceral logic and animal experience described earlier, Sherow reports that animals in boats bound for New Orleans showed up in very bad shape, with those captive on steamboats and flatboats with nothing to eat but dry hay (*New Orleans Picayune*, 11 July 1865). Joseph McCoy, founder of the first cattle rail depot in Abilene, Kansas, said the motto of ship owners was, "The more cattle, the more dollars." He further noted that cattle were so densely packed on these boats that they had "to stand for from six to eight long days—the only way in which food could be given them being, to throw it over them and let one eat from the back of another—the only water that they got being such as could be thrown over them by the hose" (*Harper's Weekly*, 10 March 1883, p. 156; quoted in Sherow 2018: 176).

Such was the situation when the trade in cattle was to begin in earnest, when animals' lived experiences and mobilities within the western carceral archipelago would be fundamentally altered and broken—sensory and emotional experiences, bodily capacities, and social relations. I now turn to the larger-scale carceral processes that were taking place simultaneously with the arrival of European colonists and their animals: the fact of Indigenous carcerality writ large and the extermination of bovine buffalo herds that preceded and ushered in the trade in cattle in the first instance.

Indigenous Carcerality and the Emergent Cattle Industry

Settler colonial legal systems were created to dispossess Indigenous peoples from their ancestral lands and to designate land as property for the first time (Wolfe 2006; Kauanui 2016). When considering the foundational legal aspects and outcomes of the U.S. cattle trade, particularly that related to land law, it is important to acknowledge first a much larger-scale colonial-carceral process taking place simultaneously: land dispossession and the forced migration and removal of Indigenous peoples, and ultimately their confinement via the reservation system. This coincided with the extermination of their food source and basis of their livelihoods, that of the previous bovines in North America, the buffalo. As Wolfe (1999: 1–3) describes, settler colonies were not primarily established to extract surplus labor value from Indigenous people, but rather to displace them from (or replace them on) the land. In that sense settler colonies were premised on the elimination of Native societies and their animals— the colonizers came to stay and the Natives thus obstructed the colonizer's access to land and territory. Wolfe (2006: 387) calls this the "logic of elimination"; and as Kauanui (2016) adds, settler colonialism "destroys to replace."

The mass extermination of the buffalo, or bison (White 1994: 237), in North America is a crucial piece of bovine history and geography. Numbers vary, but an estimated 25 million bison roamed North America before widespread destruction of them began in the early nineteenth century. As has been well documented, this purposeful mass extinction was part and parcel of a violent Native genocide, land dispossession, and incarceration, which made the proliferating trade in cattle possible. Thousands upon thousands of buffalo carcasses littered the Great Plains in the mid-nineteenth century, killed for sport at the hands of tourists and travelers, at the hands of the U.S. military and railroad developers, and at the hands of settlers and land speculators, beginning around 1830 and continuing until just a few years before the cattle trailing era. White (1994: 249) reports that the buffalo were "already in trouble" before the real slaughter began, as early as 1840, due to drought, habitat destruction, competition from exotic species, and introduced diseases. With the expansion of the railroad network around 1860, white hunters would kill buffalo year-round, oftentimes shooting them directly from the train. Against Native resistance, professional buffalo hunters moved onto the southern plains in the early 1870s and killed an estimated 2 million animals the first year; the southern hunt peaked between 1872 and 1874, and by 1875 those herds largely ceased to exist. In all, the hide hunters killed an estimated 5.4 million buffalo during these three years (this was in addition to the traditional Indigenous kill of 1.2 million animals on the southern plains during this same period). White (1994: 247–249) adds that "the efficiency of the killing coupled with a staggeringly inefficient use of the carcasses left virtually all the meat to rot." The destruction of the smaller northern herds came later; they vanished by 1882–1883 as the Northern Pacific Railroad advanced into the area and army campaigns succeeded against the Sioux Nation and others.

In addition, early American colonial settlers exploited the independent movement of their cattle to expedite their encroachment on Native land. Anderson (2004) claims that it was essentially colonists' untended animals that displaced Native people and land as they progressed ever-westward seeking new tracts of available grazing land. This 'indirect' form of colonial dispossession of Indigenous land is depicted as an agricultural empire of increasingly domesticated animals as they encroached, overgrazed, and moved on. As Anderson writes,

> Concerned about feeding growing populations and committed to a style of husbandry that required far more space than they had anticipated, colonists could see no alternative but to appropriate Indian land. They often encouraged livestock to initiate the process by letting them move onto Indian territory prior to formal English acquisition.... Yet if livestock had been instrumental in dislodging Indians from their lands during the 17th century, the creatures also kept colonists on the move . . . seeking new territory on which to support proliferating herds. (2004: 10)

Spanish cattle also thrived and advanced into 'bison country'. For the two hundred years prior to the first direct attempts to destroy the buffalo, 1840–1860, the Livestock Census indicated that "wild native bison and wild introduced cattle encountered each other regularly" across the vast untamed North American continent (Cattle History in North America 2023). Records indicate that bison and longhorns coexisted for a time, and attempts were made to domesticate bison as they were eliminated in the eastern states in the early 1800s. Naturally occurring hybridization of bison and cattle was a well-documented fact, and more likely occurred since the first introduction of cattle into North America (Domesticating Bison for Survival 2023). Several accounts of hunters, travelers, and explorers reported seeing bison with white spots (implying interbreeding with cattle), including the Texas 'cattle king' Charles Goodnight, who mentioned finding a brindle (spotted) calf with his bison mother.

Horses of the Plains Indians were important in the buffalo hunt and in wars with the U.S. Army (Stillman 2008: 43–60), articulating a(nother) carceral continuum across carceral spaces and animal species. It was through raiding that the movement of animals—both cattle and horses—from European to Indigenous control and back again was tracked. Some animals escaped human control entirely, and both feral horses and feral cattle appeared on the margins of human settlements (White 1994: 237–239). As the bison were slaughtered on the range, the cattle were captured and enclosed, a process that led to the bison being geographically replaced by the feral longhorns who were eventually domesticated. In essence, the cattle were rounded up into the carceral archipelago and the bison were simply shot.

Another aspect of the carceral archipelago requiring consideration is the forced movement of cattle north from Texas across what was in the nineteenth century called Indian Territory, specifically the parts of the present-day panhandle of Oklahoma that were known as the "Cherokee Outlet" and the smaller "Cherokee Strip" through which ran the Chisholm Trail (Ludwig 2018: 118–119; Sherow 2018: 212–216). The various stories surrounding the namesake of the Chisholm Trail have been debated since the cattle trailing era (Ludwig 2018: 64)—the name itself, spelling of the name (Chisum/Chisholm), and Chisholm's identity, occupation, and origin (Texas? New Mexico?). Ludwig (2018) and others identify Jesse Chisholm, a "mixed-blood" Cherokee man, as an almost mythological figure responsible for laying out the Old Chisholm Trail from Texas to Kansas in 1865. The next year, the first large cattle herd was driven through the Cherokee Outlet from Texas to the railroad in Abilene, Kansas. According to Ludwig (2018: 64–71), Chisholm's father was a Scottish immigrant and his mother was Cherokee. He became a trader, slaver, and translator among white colonizers and Indigenous people, operating several trading posts in Indian Territory and southern Kansas. This Chisholm spoke 14 Native languages and was often called upon to translate.

The historical geography of the Cherokee Outlet centers on the forced removal and resettlement of eastern Indigenous communities to the cattle-raising region in present-day Oklahoma. Briefly, the Indian Removal Act of 1830 forced the removal (forced migration) of nearly 125,000 Native Americans from the southeastern United States, whose ancestors had lived and cultivated land there for centuries, to land west of the Mississippi River. The ensuing "Trail of Tears," people walking some 1,200 miles to a designated Indian Territory, resulted in the loss of thousands of lives and, ultimately, loss of control over an ever-shrinking portion of what became the state of Oklahoma in 1907. A census in 1835 had counted 16,500 Cherokee people living primarily in what is now northern Georgia. The Cherokee Outlet was a 60-mile parcel of land south of the Oklahoma-Kansas border, created by a treaty in 1836 with the U.S. government under which the Cherokee Nation was forced to cede to the United States all lands east of the Mississippi River in exchange for a reservation and this 'outlet' in Indian Territory, with a promised land patent verifying ownership (Treaty with the Cherokee 1835).

In 1880, cattlemen, mostly Kansans, formed the Cherokee Strip Livestock Association to manage a contentious situation in the Cherokee Outlet (Dykstra 1968: 344–354; Sherow 2018: 240; Ludwig 2018: 120–122). After the incorporation of the association in Kansas in 1883, the Cherokees negotiated a five-year lease of the outlet to the association for $100,000 per year. At the end of five years, the Cherokee Tribal Council put the lease up for bid, hoping to get a better price, and leased it again to the Cherokee Strip Livestock Association for $200,000 annually. The more than one hundred members of the Livestock Association (which included non-Natives) divided up the land, erecting barbed wire fences and corrals and building ranch houses. The association found an ally and mutual friend in the Cherokee Nation but was strongly opposed by homesteaders and the U.S. government (Cherokee Strip Live Stock Association 2023). Eventually succumbing to the effects of harsh weather conditions in 1886–1887 and the eventual 'sale' of the Cherokee Outlet to the federal government in 1891, the Cherokee Strip Livestock Association ended in 1893, the same year the outlet was officially opened to non-Native settlement.

Cattle drives would follow the Chisholm Trail, and numerous side trails, passing through the Cherokee outlet for the next 20 years. The Cherokee people raised their own cattle, as did the other of the 'Five Civilized Tribes' (Sherow 2018: 212–2210), and they also collected, albeit with difficulty, a tax per head of cattle passing through the outlet, anything from a penny to a dime per animal. The Cherokee Outlet was also often used to rest the cattle and let them graze and/or 'winter' before being sold to the buyers in the Kansas cow towns. Oftentimes the tax was taken in animals or other items. The Cherokees attempted to collect fees for grazing rights, which were approved by the U.S. Senate in 1878, but collection of the fees was difficult.

Many of the Texas cowboys and cattlemen who drove cattle through the Cherokee Outlet on the journey from Texas to Kansas wrote about their experiences (and that of their animals) as in the same category as other obstacles, dangers, and hardships they faced, such as blizzards, drought, hailstorms, and stampedes. Vignettes of approximately 350 cowboys, originally collected by George Saunders for the Texas Old Time Trail Drivers Association and later edited by J. Marvin Hunter into the monumental tome *The Trail Drivers of Texas* (which I cite as Hunter 1924), featured titles such as "Fought Indians on the Trail" (Hunter 1924: 37) and "Tells of an Indian Fight" (Hunter 1924: 769); they follow similar rhetorical structure and content although they vary by length and level of specificity. Most are memoirs written by cowboys that include details about being "attacked by Indians," "Indians stealing their horses," "trading with Indians," and animals and men being "killed by redskins." For instance, G. H. Mohle of Lockhart, Texas, wrote of a cattle drive in 1869:

> We camped about a quarter of a mile above the soldiers' camp (near the Republican River), and thought we were pretty safe from Indian attack, but one night about three o'clock we were awakened by an awful noise. We thought it was a passing railroad train, but instead it was our horses being driven off by Indians right along near our camp. As they passed us the Indians fired several shots in our direction, but no one was hit. We had sixty-three horses and the red rascals captured all of them except five head. (Hunter 1924: 42)

Though such are typical firsthand accounts, other, less dramatic, encounters with Native people were also recounted by these colonizing trail drivers. J. E. Pettus, of Goliad, Texas, wrote of an encounter on the way to Dodge City (n.d.):

> In making trips up the trail I was always happy when we crossed the Red River for we had less trouble with the Indians than with the grangers [a farmers' organization]. The Indians would sometimes come into camp and beg from us, demanding fat beeves, but we always managed to pacify them. But the grangers displayed a degree of animosity toward the trail drivers that was almost unbearable. (Hunter 1924: 526)

J. W. Driskill wrote of moving to Brown County [Texas] and attested (without any supporting detail) to helping "drive the Indians out of that country." He described an 1875 trail drive through Indian Territory: "I had to make a drive of ninety-six hours without water. I thought my time had come, but on the fourth day, just about sundown, I struck water and all the old trail drivers can guess how those cattle looked. I had about fourteen hundred and fifty head, drove them to Dodge City, with four men and myself and only lost one cow" (Hunter 1924: 708). It should be noted that farmer-rancher antipathy followed the cattlemen throughout the carceral archipelago (cf. Hunter 1924: 526), as farmers tended to resent the trampling of their crops by the incoming herds.

Moreover, 'mavericking' or 'rustling' of cattle from competing groups of ranchers and trail drivers was a common practice—that of acquiring already-claimed animals and branding them as one's own—and was not a practice uniquely occurring when crossing Indian Territory (Netz 2004: 12; Cox 1895: 62; Davant and Herskowitz 2016: 50). But more significantly, these reminiscences contrast with the much more hyperbolic racist and orientalist depictions of Indigenous peoples in post–World War II Hollywood westerns that featured cattle drives passing through Indian Territory. Short, dramatic sequences in these films played up the dangers and hardships encountered, with the white cattlemen typically portrayed as victims of bloody, unprovoked attacks by Native men, further amplifying the heroism of white cowboys taming and civilizing the West. In these and other ways the colonial and the carceral worked together to amplify, justify, and neutralize both settler colonial dominance and the bovine carceral archipelago that was an integral part of it.

Conclusion

This chapter introduced the notion of bovine animals' forced migration as a key aspect to centuries of European colonial intervention in the Americas as well as the empirical basis for the emergent cattle carceral archipelago that would subsequently take shape. The chapter focused on some of the most immediate carceral structures and practices that animals encountered and endured during this forced migration, particularly at sea, and opened discussion of the Spanish carceral 'template' that cattlemen followed in North America as well as the animals' subsequent feralization and prodigious reproduction in Mexico and Texas.

The multiple forces that facilitated the transition from a buffalo-bovine to cattle-bovine colonial western landscape was, moreover, a key ingredient to the development of the U.S. beef cattle industry. This transition illustrates the important intersection of the power of the colonial, the carceral, and the agricultural (Struthers Montford 2020: 278; also see Struthers Montford and Taylor 2020). This also amply illustrates the intersection of the ordering practices of sovereign, disciplinary, and biopower that Hodgetts and Lorimer (2020) evocatively outline; how these work (and worked) together in constraining animal mobility. Focusing on animal mobility offers insights into settler colonial power relations, the far-reaching physical, emotional, psychological, and social impacts on animals who were moved over long distances, and the impacts of control of them via developing carceral structures and technologies.

In the next chapter I elaborate on these ordering practices in discussion of bovine animals' immediate post–Civil War encounters along the carceral archipelago—their first capture and commodification via roundups and enclosure within carceral structures; the bodily modification tools used for their capture, control, and identification; and the legal infrastructure that enabled the carceral archipelago to take definitive shape via technologies such as barbed wire fencing and that prepared them for the cattle drives north.

CHAPTER 2

Enclosing the Range

CARCERAL TOOLS, PRACTICES, STRUCTURES

When industrial-scale beef production began to take shape in the middle of the nineteenth century, bovine animals caught within it were as yet feral, or semiferal, living in dense thickets and venturing out at night to graze on the prairie (e.g., Derby 2011; Kilgore 1983; Crosby 2003). This chapter employs material and other archival sources to understand these animals' lived experiences as they were first 'rounded up' from these wild thickets, corralled, separated, branded, and prepared for movement onto ranches and herding onto the cattle trails. A broad array of spatial and relational interactions among humans and animals took place in these carceral encounters, and from them stories of animal lives and lifeways can be derived. As the animals were gathered from the wild they were held in what were at first makeshift pens that at once enclosed them and turned them into individualized property of humans. Many western writers have described the roundup process of the nineteenth century (Hunter 1924; Cox 1895; Rollins 1922; McCoy 1874); my focus is on the accompanying disciplinary and biopolitical carceral practices of it. Although the specific animals discussed here were generations distant from those who first landed in North America under Spanish settler colonialism, the practices and processes described represent a significant afterlife of earlier colonial carceral practices and processes, perhaps what might be better labeled an ongoing 're-carceralization' of bovine lives within the cattle beef industry.

This chapter also explains how the early trade in cattle hinged on a weak legal framework of land law that enabled the initial carceral enclosure of these animals. The previous chapter helped situate the settler colonial legal system that accompanied genocide of Indigenous land, people, and lifeways, ushering in U.S. government control over land and gradual privatization of it into the hands of individual cattlemen, farmers, speculators, and others. The tension between how land came to be considered public or private, and the practices involved, which were considered either 'legal' or 'illegal' activities, were at the center of the rise of big ranching empires and the industrialization of cattle as food. Thus, we should first consider what it even means to think of capture of wild animals and enclosing them on what was ostensibly public lands in the United States as legal or illegal activities. If we can possibly put aside the foundational atrocity of settler colonialism's genocidal carceral logic writ large (Indian removal and the elimination of the buffalo), for my purposes in this chapter I want to consider what, if any, were the repercussions or consequences for cattlemen who fenced land without legal claim, and who acted in other ways that were 'beyond the law'. The evolution of U.S. land law, with its professed but unrealized legal remedies to resolving conflict among big-enterprise cattlemen and between smaller-scale farmers and ranchers, is an important (but not only) component of carceral logic, particularly in considering who was helped by such legal remedies and yet how these carceral spaces and practices impacted and harmed animals.[1]

The illegal enclosure of land by the emergent cattle-baron class in the nineteenth century, enabled with new technologies such as barbed wire and governments lacking the interest, will, or ability to challenge such enclosures, offers important insights into how carceral logic works in place, and the impact of these practices and institutions on animals. Barbed wire fencing in particular became a primary mode of seizure of public land and resources for the benefit of individual ranching enterprises, despite land laws prohibiting it but also with little repercussion for having done so. Certain legal as well as extra-government actions mediated human relations at the time, for example, the 'fence cutting wars' emerged as one human resistance to carceral enclosure. But an equally important part of the story lies in the carceral apparatuses mediating relations among humans (mostly men) and animals. In this chapter I bring to the foreground a range of historical-material artifacts that speak directly to past animal lives and to the kinds of bodily management practices, operations, instruments, and structures that cowboys, ranchers, and various other actors employed to capture and commodify animal lives in carceral settings—carceral apparatuses such as barbed wire but also tools and weapons of various sorts such as branding irons, ear cutters, and castration knives, and devices used for the control and restraint of animals such as the 'stock crush'. (These are not mutually exclusive.)

Archival documentary sources, photographs, newspaper articles, and narratives provide important context for the artifactual, offering firsthand human or eyewitness accounts of animal lived experiences, even if they many times only offer traces of historical animals' lived experiences as produced and filtered through human lenses. Skaggs (1973: 2) encapsulates the contents of numerous historical manuscript collections such as the Scotland-based Matador Land and Cattle Company in Texas to understand cattlemens' lives and the company's business operations. For example, one H. H. Campbell, in an 1884 letter from "Tee Pee City" [Motley County], Texas, reported on the scale of his operation, which at that time involved "the branding of over 21,000 calves, the gathering and bringing back into the range about 5,000 head of cattle that had drifted off it during the winter months, the separation from the other cattle, and driving into the beef pasture, which first had to be cleared of stock cattle, over 20,000 steers and the driving to the railroad over 3,000 beeves." Patents and agricultural or veterinary manuals also provide important documentary evidence as they fostered and instructed particular and preferred ways of handling animals in agricultural settings and normalized sometimes brutal practices of animal husbandry. Insights such as those of Cox (2015: 101–105, 110), who illustrates how veterinary archives are useful in writing the history of animals, help us to think differently about devices and objects such as fences, branding irons, ropes, and whips—at once considered ordinary and everyday tools and technologies of the beloved cowboy's life and trade—but which can also offer important clues to the historical experiences of captive animals under their control.

In this chapter I also begin to open discussion of the many re-narrations of the carceral archipelago found in cultural and historical museums throughout the carceral West. I focus here on the ubiquity of barbed wire and branding iron displays, displays that are at once useful in decoding what animal experiences of them might have been like, but which are also part of a larger discourse that casts such practices and tools as important discoveries, advancements, and inventions glorified in American expansionism across the continent made possible by cattlemen and cowboys.

Roundups and Stock Pens: The Spanish Legacy of Carceral Encounters

Various methods were used to capture the free-roaming cows who lived in the dense Texas thickets and ventured out at night to graze on the prairie (see fig. 2.1). A primary method of their capture involved sneaking up behind them at night in the thickets and catching them by their tails, throwing them off balance, and pacifying them by placing them with tame animals in the stock pens. Ludwig (2018: 36–37) offers a detailed account of how these animals

Fig. 2.1. Wild bovines in a thicket prior to capture. From J. Cox, *Historical and Biographical Record of the Cattle Industry* (1895, p. 141).

were caught: if in a dense thorny thicket, cowboys rode alongside them, pulling them by their tails—a practice called 'tailing':

> The rider maneuvered alongside the animal, reached out and caught it by the tail, and took a quick turn around the saddle horn or gave it a good yank, causing the animal to trip or somersault. The rider dismounted quickly and hog-tied the feet of the tailed animal before it recovered, gained its feet, and charged. Tailed cattle were left for several hours to calm down and then released near gentle cattle that were brought to act as a decoy herd for the wild cattle. Once among the decoys, the wild cattle could be driven with the decoys. If one escaped, the capture process was repeated and the offender tied to a tree or to another steer with a short rope so that its movement was severely restricted until it had settled; this was called necking. (See a similar firsthand account of tailing in Hunter 1924: 330.)

Use of the horse, periodic roundups, branding practices, and various tools all constitute an important Spanish legacy to the carceral practices that made their way to North America. Butzer (1988: 29) refers to this legacy as representing a "highly extensive management style" specifically characteristic to the region of Seville, Spain, as compared to small-scale ranching elsewhere. This area became the "heartland" of emigration to the Americas (Butzer 1988: 45). With this, the carceral continuum of Spanish, Mexican, and Texan capturing, roping, and pacification techniques helps emplace not only the experiences of nineteenth-century animals but also those who lived under much earlier carceral conditions—cattle but also other large animals, horses in particular.

The vaqueros of Mexico perfected on horses what we think of as most modern American cowboy tools and techniques (Bennett 1998: 317). Their practices had as a central ingredient controlling animals by first throwing them off balance. Stillman (2008: 57–58) observes that mid-nineteenth-century Texas was overrun with wild horses, and they were captured and exploited for use in extractive industries such as silver mining, in the calvary, and in the cattle trade business. Stillman writes that the lasso was the main instrument used to capture wild horses. Ropes were pitched over their heads, a saddle was thrown on their backs, and the horses would "snort and pitch until they stopped bucking, at which point a cowboy tied them up and beat them over the head and back with a doubled rope" (185).

Bennett's (1998: 313–320) study of horses also includes discussion of sixteenth- and seventeenth-century tools and techniques used to raise and control cattle in Mexico (also see Dalke 2010; Dalke and Hunt 2017; Stillman 2008). Bennett (314–316) discusses in detail, for example, the basics of the lasso, the lariat, and 'hock knife', all common among Spanish vaqueros. Vaqueros did not originally lasso the cattle, but brought them in with a type of iron-tipped lance meant to minimally damage the hide: "Its long blade was replaced by a lunate knife fixed transversely to the end of the shaft, the whole being known as a desjarretadera or hock-knife. The design of the hock-knife permitted the vaquero to bring a running steer down by hamstringing it, a practice that persisted into the nineteenth-century Texas cattle frontier.

> Gradually . . . the technique of snaring cattle with ropes began to catch on. . . .
> The tail of the rope threaded through a hondo [inner loop] create[d] a snare
> which [could] be thrown around an animal's neck, horns, or legs. . . . [The
> vaquero] draped the loop from a hook at the end of a lance. Galloping after
> a steer, the vaquero would swing the hook out over its horns and drop the
> loop over its head. . . . If he did not intend to kill the animal immediately, after
> roping it and throwing it down the vaquero (or his partner) would dismount
> and pierce its nose with his dirk. Then he would run the rope though the hole
> so as to guarantee that the animal would not pull too hard. He could then
> bring the steer home by lashing the line onto the fleshy part of the horse's tail,
> first carefully folding up the tail hair to pad the knot.

The roundups occurred in the spring and fall, and collected both branded and not-yet-branded animals. Often, animals were roped at night by moonlight, when they went onto the prairie to graze. The spring roundup was primarily for the purpose of branding and was mostly a 'calf roundup' after the vernal grass had come in, and the fall roundup was the 'beef roundup', which "gave forth kine fat for the abattoir, sleek cows and heavy steers" (Rollins 1922: 217). A cowboy named A. W. Capt of San Antonio (Hunter 1924: 363) wrote of roundups in the early 1860s: "In those days of open range and free grass, it was a custom practiced by the people to round up such cows as they were easily penned, regardless of ownership in most cases, and milk them . . . branding the calves in the cow's brand."

Philip Rollins, in his book *The Cowboy: His Characteristics, His Equipment, and his Part in the Development of the West* (1922), presents himself as a particularly dedicated eyewitness of range roundups throughout the 1880s to 1892. In the preface to his book he claims to report "truthfully what Western ranchmen, in the ordinary course of their business, said within his hearing and did before his eyes, and thus to recount accurately the every-day life of the old-time range" (viii). Rollins refers to bovine animals rounded up as "volunteers" who sought to join herds of animals already captured: "Stock quietly feeding would hear or scent the coming procession; would, for a moment, gaze inquisitively at it; and then, obedient to the instinct of gregariousness, would trot across country and fall into line" (220). But Rollins also comments on animals' behavior when they are being 'cut out' from the herd—to be sold, broken, or branded—where they appear to be anything but placidly 'volunteering' (225; also see McCoy 1874: 81):

> The cow-boys dash at [the animal] and before he is aware of it, is on the outside of, and separate from the herd; but no sooner does he discover the situation, then he makes a desperate effort to regain his comrades . . . which he tries desperately to do, and persists in trying so long as there is a shadow of a chance to outrun his pursuers. . . . But when he finds himself outrun and out generaled, he will toss up his head and look for the comrades which have been previously cut out, and are being held a few hundred feet distant. In the beginning of the cut-out, a few gentle cows or working oxen are driven a short space from the round-up and held, to form a nucleus, to which those cut out gather.

Other nineteenth-century eyewitness accounts confirm some of these practices. Another cowboy, C. W. Ackermann of San Antonio, wrote that in the late 1860s he would rope and brand

> eight or ten calves by myself in a day. Branding was not a very easy task, either, for we had to run the brand. We had no ready-made brands as now. Many times we had to gather the wilder cattle at night. When they went out

on the prairie we would sneak a tame bunch of cattle in with them and thus drive them in a corral. Sometimes we would build a stockade around water holes, leaving only one opening for the cattle to get in. Even with such a trap we were often unable to hold the wildest ones in. (Hunter 1924: 154)

Alongside the roundup were the infrastructural carceral developments of the cow pen or corral to hold the captured animals, from the early makeshift designs to those much bigger and sturdier. Alonzo Millett (in Hunter 1924: 816) described a rather rickety "old time rail cowpen" near San Antonio, Texas: "This pen was built before lumber came into general use. The posts were placed double and tied with rawhide, with rail ends between posts. Pens of this kind were frequently built large enough to hold several thousand cattle." G. W. Mills of Lockhart, Texas, described other approximately four-acre-sized pens into which the animals were herded (ca. 1874):

> As a matter of course these pens were built to endure and were very strong, as cattle in those days were wild, and in this exciting work none but well-built pens would hold them.... The material was largely Postoak rails ... [made of] fine cedar timber.... These corrals had to be much higher than the ordinary fence, as the infuriated longhorns would, in their desperation to be free, try to go over the top or break them down.... The subdivisions were divided into branding pens and horse corrals. (Hunter 1924: 229)

Oftentimes large numbers of cattle were cornered or blockaded in canyons or near water holes to facilitate a roundup or to enclose them for further purpose (cf. Hunter 1924: 154). This practice extended across the cattle carceral archipelago, from the open range to the ranch and cow town. A cowboy named T. J. Garner (Hunter 1924: 648) wrote that in 1877 Caldwell, Kansas, at the terminus of a cattle drive, his team

> drove the steers into a 15-acre pen located in a canyon which had been walled up at both ends, except a space of about twelve feet for an entrance. This space was closed by pole bars.... [At night during a hail storm] when the lightning flashed I could see those old steers run from one end of the corral to the other, but they could not get out. That was the only stampede I ever enjoyed.

A cowboy seeming to enjoy the panic and fear of a trapped animal alerts us to the callousness with which some responded to the suffering and pain of animals. But as will become subsequently evident, not all cowboys and not all ranchmen were the same in their sensibilities and treatments of animals under their control.

Fig. 2.2. Branding scene, LS Ranch (unknown date and photographer). Reproduced with permission of the Panhandle-Plains Historical Museum, Canyon, Texas.

Cattle Branding: Hot Irons, Burned Flesh

Branding, burning, or otherwise marking animal skin with symbols to claim ownership stands out as perhaps the most notoriously 'western' of western carceral practices that emerged with the cattle industry. Cattlemen competed with one another to claim the largest herds and largest spaces, and branding served to order, objectify, and possess physical bovine bodies within a context where virtually no other legal, economic, or recordkeeping policy was in place. Although marking bovine bodies as personal commodities would evolve with other technologies and more precise recordkeeping practices that paralleled claims to land, the mid-nineteenth century stands out as a particularly brutal moment in the marking as personal commodity formerly feral or semiferal animal agents.

Burning or otherwise etching into the skin a symbol, mark, tattoo, or number to claim ownership of another body is a common, taken-for-granted practice in carceral spaces throughout history and across space. No carceral practice seems more ubiquitous, yet also so cruel, violent, and presumptuous, than burning the skin to mark property ownership or to mark the other as killable—enslaved persons, concentration camp victims, those accused of crimes, and animals meant for slaughter. Searing a hot, heavy iron poker to mark animals as individual or group property of humans dates to the ancient Egyptians. Cooley (2022) offers a long historical perspective on branding and ways that it changed over time, as a way of ordering and objectifying people and animals. The practice coalesced in the "increasingly textual world" of the sixteenth century, where, she contends, property and status had to be "affirmed through records"; in this world branding emerged as a specific, valuable shorthand tool for correlating text and object while conferring commodification status upon it as well as possession (52–54). "The scope of the English term brand," Cooley explains, "hints at its legacy of conceptual blending through which burning, marking, ownership, and commodification came together." Horse breeders, for example, used branding to "render an animal's history, ownership, and characteristics clear at a glance . . . giving proof of the horse's value" (56–57) and enabling them to be easily standardized and taxonomized.

Many eyewitnesses to the early cattle trade commented on the hot-iron branding techniques of animals in the wild as well as those already corralled on ranches. Many described the restraining of frightened animals, whose eyes bulged, noses snorted, and mouths slavered, while the hot iron burned hair and seared flesh, producing an "acrid odor . . . strong, repulsive, no man ever likes it" (Arnold and Hale 1940: 92; also see Rollins 1922: 232–233, 244–247; Cox 1895: 62; Netz 2004: 19). Some early branding was drawn on hide using an iron rod with a curved end. These 'running irons' were used like a pencil, to alter 'legitimate' cattle brands on the range, but most western territories and states outlawed their use (Rollins 1922: 233–234). Ninety-five percent of branding irons were made of common iron, with wooden handles (that did not conduct heat), 2–3 inches thick and 4–8 inches long (Arnold and Hale 1940: 68–69).

Accompanied by Oren Arnold, the branding iron collector John P. Hale describes at some length branding animals on the free range, where a cowboy brought a branding iron with him by horseback: "You spot a yearling bull in the thorny brush. . . . He is unquestionably wild and frightened and not a little ferocious. . . . [After catching him with lariat and tying him down] you gather a handful of twigs, dry grass, cow chips, or whatever is near you that will burn. You build a fire. You poke your branding iron into it. . . . The crucial moment comes quickly. You run from the fire, slap down the iron—S-s-s-s-s-s ! 'BAW-W-W-W!' The hair burns, live flesh fries" (Arnold and Hale 1940: 16–17). "In the tenderfoot springs a horror," claim these authors, "then a feeling of abject pity followed often by anger" (91–92).

Rollins (1922: 244–246) describes the holding down of struggling and twisting animals being dragged toward the fire, who "slithered every few seconds, sliding on their sides, their backs, on any part of their anatomies, all of the beasts highly indignant." The branding of calves involved

> seizure of its ears, its head so twisted as to lie flat on the earth and to offer a seat of one officiating puncher. To effectually stifle any kicking, a second puncher, with one of his feet, pushed one hind leg of the squealing victim well forward, and, with both hands, pulled the other hind leg far to the rear. The little calf thus lay helpless, its bulging eyes wildly rolling, while still other cowboys, one with hot iron, the other with knife, made brands and cuts. . . . Then too, very frequently mature cattle, after being thrown by roping or tailing or bulldogging, had their legs (usually two hind and one front) fastened together by a short piece of line; whereupon the lariats, if any, were cast off. Thus "hog-tied," the victim was wholly impotent. As he was reached by the cowboys on their rounds of the prone animals, he received such treatment as he was to have, and then was released. . . .

> When the last estray had been cut out and segregated, when the beef cut had been completed, and when the last animal to be branded had emitted its odor of burning hair and singed skin, had scrambled stiffly to its feet and gone in search of maternal sympathy, there ceased all dealings with the original herd. It had, in technical language, been "worked." In other words, the job was done. . . . Other and long-since-branded animals, if showing contagious nervousness, would be cut out one by one and chased away; but, if reasonably placid, they would be kept as decoys to lessen the chance of a general stampede.

The U.S. Department of Agriculture explains in its pamphlet "Dehorning, Castrating, Branding and Marking Beef Cattle " (1929) that the two general methods of branding were 'casting and throwing' and chute branding, with the former giving way to the latter over time. Much of Arnold and Hale's observations about 'correct' branding comes from the advice of this government manual. The pamphlet admonished that deep burning is "cruel and unnecessary" and stressed the importance of making sure that the iron is neither too hot nor too cold "in order to make a proper imprint" (1929: 8). Arnold and Hale (1940: 86) describe the almost sadistic behaviors of some cattlemen, though: "We have seen incompetent branders hold an iron on and on and on, while the smoke curled and the flesh fried and the animal bawled in agony. We have also seen considerate, sensible men strike such branders with their fists; and a group of Oklahoma cowpunchers once branded a man named Ed Poole on his own rump because of his persistent cruelty to steers in branding." This aligns with the more salacious account of the folklorist Frank Dobie (1941: 154), who relates that "there is something almost refreshing in the lusty bawl of a big bull-calf being branded. The 'gosling stage' voice of a bull yearling was positively ridiculous. An old stag or bull, when wounded, would stick his tongue out a full foot and bawl so loud that cattle two miles away would turn to listen."

Arnold and Hale (1940: 93) ultimately attempt to place the branding process in terms of (albeit contradictory) profit-oriented human terms:

> After the burn . . . in a little while the animal always goes calmly on about its affairs, eating grass or chewing or dozing. . . . Most of it is fright. . . . No typical rancher would deliberately hurt any living thing save in the absolutely necessary process of extracting a living from nature. . . . The very dude or dudette who turned green and indignant at the branding scene will be the first to fork a filet mignon at dinner time. . . . A favorite—if barbarous—way to kill a beef steer is to knock it on its head with an axe. Often it will bawl and snort and bleed at the nose and stagger around miserably in the process of dying. But the filet, broiled to a juicy, bloody saltiness and served with sterling silver, Haviland china and imported crystal ware, plus swing music, is delicious indeed.

These authors' mention of privileged, wealthy consumers eating steaks off of fine china and linen underlines so much human contradiction with respect to animals: preferring not to acknowledge their suffering but participating in it and enjoying its benefits nonetheless (after Tuan 1984). And despite their eyewitness observations of such suffering, Arnold and Hale (1940: 71) defend the branding practice as not extreme or unnecessary, though, because the practice was no crueler than what "butchers or bankers or politicians" do (21) (and they had a point there).

Notably, a number of authors point to the differences between the branding of cattle and that of horses. Rollins (1922: 244–247) for instance, observes:

> During the progress of branding, the punchers often subjected cattle to the two humiliating actions from which horses were spared. Though a horse, when roped and thrown, was accorded the dignity of being held by lariats until all work on him had been finished, a calf was promptly deprived of the reata [long noosed rope] as soon as the infant struck the ground. . . . A horse was never hog tied, and rarely, save by accident, was roped on a hind leg. Doing either of these things might cause such a strain as permanently injure him for riding purposes. With any member of the cattle family, the rear legs were favorite targets for the lariat. A catch above one or both hind feet sprawled the beast out with ungraceful elongation, and deprived him of tractive force. After all, a horse was a horse, but a steer was only meat.

Arnold and Hale (1940: 86) add that "a rancher . . . may be able to burn a steer, hear the animal bawl with fear and pain, and see the ugly mark throughout its

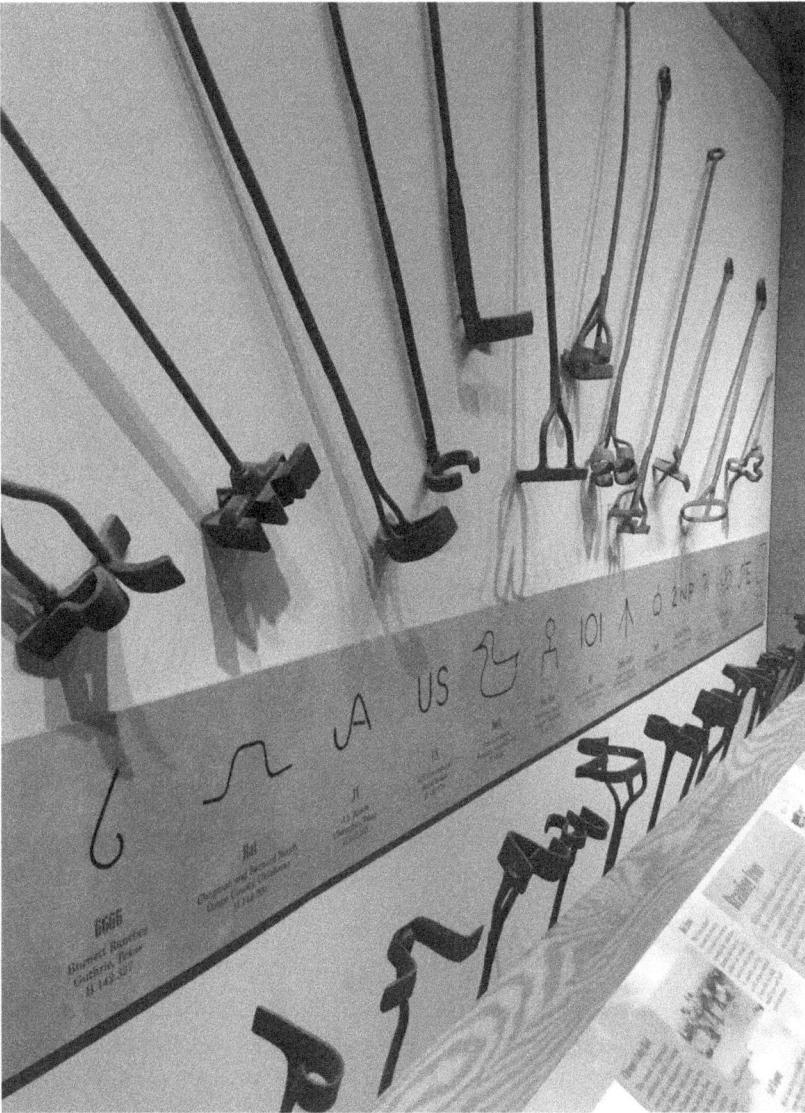

Fig. 2.3. Examples from the branding iron exhibit at the National Cowboy Hall of Fame and Western Heritage Museum, Oklahoma City. Photo by author.

life, and still feel no compunction whatsoever. But a man does not want his horses marred in the slightest. . . . A stolid steer or heifer has no future save to go off and graze and rest, but a horse must be put back in service tomorrow."

The above descriptions of the branding process in gruesome detail offers an opportunity to consider the pain and fear experienced by sentient beings thoroughly animalized and objectified through it. These discursive accounts can be triangulated with the material force of museum branding iron artifacts, and together invite us to consider the emotional, affective experience of animal suffering; the 'visceral knowing' of branding. Displays of branding irons belonging to various groups, ranches, or individuals are perhaps the most common feature of museums depicting the development of cattle ranching, the cattle trails, and cowboy life and experiences. Such displays primarily focus on the historical evolution and designs and meanings—that is, cattlemen's identification symbols—behind the individual brands. Much 'pride of brand' appears as part of the discourse, as designs oftentimes reflect generations of ownership and deep family and ranch histories. The National Cowboy Hall of Fame Museum features a special collection of branding irons and instruments used (and still used) to differentiate property claims made by various cattlemen (see fig. 2.3). The stamp irons, some now corroded with age, were used to apply a burn mark in one impression, typically about four inches in height. The Boot Hill Museum in Dodge City, Kansas, the Panhandle-Plains Historical Museum in Canyon, Texas, and the National Ranching Heritage Museum in Lubbock, Texas, all have such branding displays. The accompanying informational wall text at the National Cowboy Museum aligns with the details offered by Rollins's (1922: 231–251 description of the procedure:

> After calves were rounded up they were branded with the same brands and ear marks as their mothers. . . . One man sat behind the calf and pulled the upper hind leg back onto his lap as he shoved the lower hind leg forward with his foot, hooking the calf's leg with his boot heel. Another man placed his knee on the calf's head and held the upper foreleg while removing the rope from its neck. . . . The hot iron burned the hair and seared the hide deep enough to form a scab, which later peeled off to leave a scar [typically located on the left ribs or hip] where no hair would grow back. . . . [Eventually] branding cattle in corrals and chutes reduced the number of men needed for the job. The modern use of squeeze chutes made branding and doctoring chores even easier. . . . While calves are held for branding, other chores like castration, vaccination, and worming are usually done at the same time.

While this signage appears as straightforwardly informational, along with the presentation of material artifacts it conveys a message about the 'success' of the cattle ranching industry and cattlemen's empires, with the pain of carceral experiences hidden underneath the story of cowboy tools and their pride of using them under harsh conditions. The violence toward animals, in fact the animals themselves, are invisible and buried within such descriptions.

The brutality of branding must be one of the most taken-for-granted, seemingly ordinary practices of the carceral archipelago as well as a practice nearly glorified in its symbolism of big ranching empires and family histories. Photographers and artists of the period represented branding in all its mundanity (see fig. 2.2) but also in such glorified terms. William R. Leigh's painting "Branding JJ" (1945), for example, occupies a prominent position on a wall of the National Cowboy and Western Heritage Museum in Oklahoma City. This seductively beautiful painting depicts a spring branding, with the accompanying wall text emphasizing Leigh's ability as a painter of light and color, and rather ignoring altogether the subject matter—or, if there is a subject, it is the cowboys. Yet Leigh captures the animals fully alive and active—representing the fear in the eyes of animals about to be branded, and the cowboys' struggle to restrain them during the procedure.

Earmarking, Castration, and the Squeeze Chute: The Carceral Amplified

One of the carceral practices commonly associated with branding, occurring at the same time whether in the roundup, field, or ranch, was that of earmarking. Earmarking was (and is) the cutting off a portion of a branded animal's ears, in order to further differentiate identification and ownership. During a roundup, earmarks on animals were made with a pocket knife (see fig. 2.4). As Arnold and Hale (1940: 17–18) describe the process, "You drop the [branding] iron. You take out your pocket knife, operate, then move from the bull's rump to his head. Deftly you slit a design in one or both ears, actually cutting out pieces of the ear and throwing them away. . . . (Since it was a bull, remember you will also have castrated)." "The cartilage of a cow's ear is tough," these authors continued, "and the knife *must* be very sharp if a clean cut is to be made. Many ingenious marks have been devised by cattlemen: variously named 'crop, overslope, underslope, split, bit, swallow fork, steeple fork, oversharp, and undersharp'" (illustrated in Arnold and Hale 1940: 85). Cox (1895: 64–65) describes in detail the making of these various marks:

> A crop meant cutting about half the ear off smoothly, straight from the upper side; a half-crop, either upper or lower, was to split the ear from the tip, midway, about half way back toward the head, and cut off either half. If the upper half was cut off, it was over or upper half-crop. If the lower half, it was under half-crop. A split was simply to split the ear as above described and leave it thus. Under-bit or over-bit was to double the ear in and cut a small piece, perhaps an inch, out of either the upper or lower side, an inch in length and perhaps, one-third that in depth. . . . An upper and under slope, you may readily see, would make a sharp look by giving the ear a point. A swallow-fork was to hollow the ear length-wise, beginning half way back, cut at an angle of forty-five degrees toward the end. The result was a forked notch in the ear, called a swallow-fork. A grub was by far the most cruel mark of any, as it was

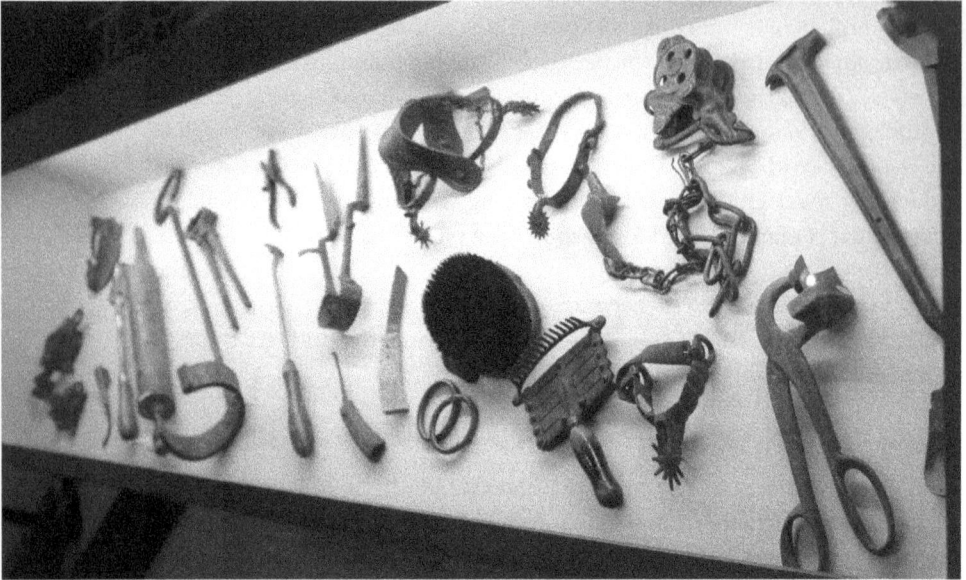

Fig. 2.4. Carceral instruments: animal control. Tool display, Boot Hill Museum, Dodge City, Kansas. Among the instruments are a cattle tie, nose rings, syringe, dental float, ear notcher, snout cutter, trimmers, and hoof cutters. Used for cows as well as sheep, pigs, and horses in the nineteenth and twentieth centuries. Photo by Daniel Olivetti.

to cut the ear off smooth to the head. None but very hard men ever used such a mark.

Indeed, Rollins (1922: 234) describes some of the crueler behaviors of cattlemen cutting ears and 'taking more than half' of the ear, and the fact that "various States required that not more than half of each ear be removed, that neither ear be whittled to a point, and that no cut or chipping made by one owner be altered or obliterated by a later proprietor."

Tattooing the ears with a special instrument was another method of marking cows' ears (see fig. 2.4). The instrument imprints characters, letters, or numerals in and under the skin of the animal's ear by means of a series of needlelike points that were dipped in a special indelible ink before applications (U.S. Department of Agriculture 1929: 10). The Panhandle-Plains Historical Museum's collection features a number of later devices for earmarking cattle, including an Ear Marking Machine, a device resembling a pliers that gouged a four-digit mark, with each digit changeable from a blank to nine, in the animal's ear, and the Jersey Bulletin Tattoo Ear Marker for attaching numbers to ears of registered cattle. When none such instruments were available, cowboys made do, however. The cowboy J. C. Thompson (Hunter 1924: 666) describes "chewing off" the ear of a captured 'maverick' with his own teeth in 1878 en route to Kansas from Texas:

> I was seventeen years old but was not a novice in the business by any means as I had been gathering, roping and branding mavericks all of my life. I remember on one occasion my brother and I caught a fine maverick one day and we had no knife to mark him with. Our mark was crop off one ear and underbit the other. Brother said if I would bite out the underbit he would bite off the crop. It took some 'chewing' but we did a fairly good job of it.

It is difficult to picture these two young brothers sitting or standing in a field next to a captured animal and chewing her ears off with their bare teeth. One wonders how long such a procedure took, what measures were required to restrain the animal while doing so, and the level of pain it undoubtedly caused. Marking animals' ears or branding their skin with hot irons to prove ownership were routine carceral practices whose logic requires a deep objectification of animal life and disassociation with it. Yet, and as with all the carceral procedures described here, there existed a range of human recognition of animal suffering, with these two brothers hopefully the exception even in a carceral space lacking any formal (or seemingly even informal) animal protections or governing rules.

As with earmarking, castration of steers—the cutting off of males' testicles to prevent reproduction, and thus ostensibly to develop in them a higher grade of meat—was done on the range with blunt instruments such as the common pocket knife (see fig. 2.4). Typically, castration was (and is) done on calves eight months old or younger, as according to ranching wisdom, the bleeding or hemorrhaging is too profuse in older animals. This practice, "while of greater shock to animals than branding, no doubt," argue Arnold and Hale (1940: 91–93), did not show signs of or cause extreme suffering (but see below). That said, these authors point out that "ingenious man in all the centuries has devised no more fiendish way to torture his fellow men than to burn them.... A second and almost as fiendish method of human torture ... is to mutilate a man by removing his procreative glands. This is held to be the supreme insult as well as a highly entertaining means of inflicting pain; a man's pride as well as his physical person can be tortured in that way." These authors report that castration nonetheless was "highly important on the range" (78–79):

> The meat of a steer is more refined, more tender and tasty and altogether better developed, and hence more valuable, than is the meat of a bull.... Unspayed or "open" heifers are slow to fatten properly, have less desirable meat than heifers that are spayed. Fat two-year-old heifers produce meat virtually as good as meat from steers of the same age.... As with branding, there are

> two main ways of handling stock for castrating and spaying: the animal may
> be roped, thrown and held firmly during the operation, or it may be placed in
> a "squeeze" chute. [Also see U.S. Department of Agriculture 1929: 4.]

Anderson (2004: 87–88) provides some background on such interventions in animals' reproductive lives. In colonial America, animals were typically categorized by color, to which were linked a number of behavioral characteristics. The principal method of restricting reproduction was castration of all but a few males, which controlled herd size and ostensibly reduced aggressive displays of dominance among those identified as prone to it. One bull was selected to reproduce with 60 cows. The castrated males were then expected to accumulate more body fat. The timing of reproduction was also highly controlled, with the goal of grazing animals born in late winter or early spring, so bulls and cows were enclosed together to mate in late spring.

The U.S. Department of Agriculture describes (1929: 4) the do-it-yourself incision method of castration, provocatively and viscerally enacted in one of the most searing scenes from the modern western film *The Power of the Dog* (2021):

> In performing the operation there are two methods of making the incision;
> one is to slit each side of the scrotum parallel to the median line. The incision
> should be made on one side and the testicle removed from that side before
> the incision is made on the other side. The incision should be made over the
> center of the testicle, and from about the top one-third to lower end. It is
> essential to extend the slit well toward the lower end of the scrotum so as
> to allow for proper drainage. The other method is to grasp the lower end
> of the scrotum and stretch it out tightly, cutting off the lower one-third. In
> this method the ends of both testicles are exposed. One testicle should be
> removed at a time, which may be accomplished by pulling or pressing the
> testicle out of the scrotum and cutting it off, allowing 3 or 4 inches of the cord
> to remain on the testicle. . . . Some cattlemen prefer to draw the cord tightly
> over the index finger of the left hand and sever it by scraping with the knife.

Various tools, called "bloodless castrators" or "emasculators," came into use in the early twentieth century, using methods of clamping to break blood vessels, crushing spermatic cords, applying constricting elastic bands on the scrotum, and others, still currently done without anesthetic. All such methods cause acute pain and distress to animals, as reported by the American Veterinary Medication Association in Castration of Cattle (2014). This work concludes by saying that while the new instruments make the procedure bloodless, "it is not painless. About four people have to hold down the calf while the fifth wields the vile instrument. The cries of the calf are something that you can never unhear. After the procedure, which lasts a few minutes, the calf continues to be in great pain for days." The authors elaborate, "Animals exhibit pain responses during and after castration; these responses include struggling, kicking the hind legs, tail swishing, foot stamping, head turning, restlessness, stilted gait, reduced activity, increased recumbency, abnormal standing posture, reduced interest in dams [sic] and each other and reduced grazing and feed intake. Pain response to castration in tandem or simultaneous with dehorning has been found to be additive." Arnold and Hale (1940: 80) add to this ghastly scenario by noting that "if done during fly season it is essential to apply some sort of fly repellent. Common in the warmer sections of the country is that also highly unromantic infestation known as screwworms or maggots, these being the larvae of certain flies."

The gruesome and so-called doctorin practices such as castration and dehorning would have required phenomenal skill in objectification, disassociation, and detachment from the affective results of these carceral practices on its subjects—as effects on these sentient creatures were obviously evident. Castration fits into a category of extreme disfiguration of animals, their complete loss of reproductive autonomy, and it must be underlined that a(nother) basic component of, as well as goal of, the carceral archipelago and emergent beef industry was that of producing increasingly 'meatier' animals. This intensive biopolitical formation and reformation of bovine bodies caused not only pain, suffering, and injury, but a loss of dignity to animals as procreative beings, the ethics of which must be rigorously questioned (after Gruen 2014).

To emphasize again, the carceral infrastructure and carceral spaces of cattle range, ranch, trail, and cow town, among many other biopolitical controls, severely restricted and curtailed bovine reproductive autonomy. The early reproductive control on the range is important to recognize as it occurred at a time that predated the more 'scientific' and institutionalized forms of reproductive control, especially selective breeding, that quickly became the norm in the twentieth century. This form of early reproductive control lays an important philosophical template for naturalizing the reproductive management of bovine animals in a carceral (and capitalist) system that was then reinforced and modernized through science and technology in short order. Moreover, as numerous authors such as Rosenberg (2016) have shown, the gendered heteronormativity behind this control over bovine breeding (and hence meat production) aligned with heteronormative gender controls over rural western human identities as well, enacted through and supported by numerous government programs.[2]

Branding and earmarking of feral or semiferal animals was done on the 'free range' when they were simply rounded up, claimed, and so marked as individual human property. But as they began to be confined in corrals and pens, such procedures occurred within cage-like restraining devices called 'squeeze chutes' or 'stock crushes'—procedures such as branding as well as a host of other carceral practices such as vaccination, deworming, castration, and dehorning. As the U.S. Department of Agriculture (1929: 7) explains, performing branding and other practices in the chute or stall provided "greater ease with which the operation can be done . . . the saving of labor, and the slighter disturbance of the cattle in the corral." The purpose of the crush was (and is) to restrain an animal in order to "minimize the risk of injury to both the animal and the operator" while work on the animal is being performed. As animals were encouraged to enter (or pushed into) the contraptions they were squeezed so as to be motionless and rendered helpless, and 'treatments' were thus administered (Arnold and Hale 1940: 21, 90). The U.S. Department of Agriculture's (1929: 8, 11) pamphlet instructs ranchers and farmers on how to build a squeeze chute, and provides detailed illustrations identifying dimensions, lumber size, elevations, and mechanical parts. The pamphlet explains that "it is very easy to crush a hip of an animal that is being confined in a powerful squeeze. For that reason the leverage of a squeeze should not be so great that the operator is likely to overlook the degree of pressure applied." In making a chute it is especially desirable . . . to have one side moveable so that the animal can be held snugly under pressure and without injury against the side of the chute" (see fig. 4.6).

Artifactual evidence of these contraptions at history and living history–type museums offer additional insights into their use and the role they played in the developing business of cattle ranching. A wall display at the National Cowboy and Western Heritage Museum explains that "branding cattle in corrals and chutes reduced the number of men needed for the job. The modern use of squeeze chutes made branding and doctoring chores even easier." The mechanisms squeezed the animal so that they stood "stock still, and locked their heads in place so that they could not see what was going on with their bodies." Such description implies an ever-improving technology in the cattle beef industry. Though commonly in use today on ranches across the United States, a nineteenth-century version of the squeeze chute from the Texas Panhandle can be viewed, along with numerous other ranching structures from the period (e.g., a railroad loading chute and corral, an old drift fence, and a 'wild cow corral and trap gate') on the 19-acre outdoor historical park at the National Ranching Heritage Center in Lubbock, Texas. The predominant message at the center is something of a celebration—ultimately emphasizing the successful scientific breeding practices of today that produce greatly improved beef.

Colonial-Carceral Infrastructure: Land and Law

All of the aforementioned carceral practices and instruments worked in tandem with and indeed relied on a government land office and weak legal framework that ensured the large-scale enclosure of the range in order to gradually capture and pacify wild bovine animals. Although disciplinary and biopolitical carceral power was increasingly expanded from the mid-nineteenth century onward—via initial enclosure, confinement, and bodily manipulation—recall that prior to this phase, these animals were highly mobile and largely independent as they migrated from Mexico to Texas. As previously noted, they practiced a free-range lifestyle; they foraged and fed themselves, found their own shelter, transported themselves to new areas, and cared for their young (Anderson 2004: 3–10, 83; Ogle 2013: 4–5; White 1991: 223; Specht 2016). The history of grazing 'rights' on western land tells us a great deal about the evolution of the carceral landscape under study here and the effect on animals in their territories.

A patchwork comprising the western American legal system together with technological innovations such as barbed wire facilitated the ability of some cattlemen to acquire vast personal land holdings. In the boom years of the 1870s and 1880s, the cattle barons controlled western public lands by declaring a simple right of sovereignty. An informal code of entitlement, range rights if you will, inhered if a rancher could claim to be the first to appropriate a local stream (legally "prior appropriation"). The aspiring cattle grazer could, by claiming the water supply, control the surrounding terrain. Thus, the first step in consolidating power over the herds was in gaining control over grazing land—grass for food—and water. Richard White describes cattlemen as "the most prone to violence of any economic interest group in the West," with their predilection for violence "largely result[ing] from the tenuousness of their own legal claims to the land" (White 1991: 344–345; also see Rifkin 1992: 100).

Legal ownership of the land was secondary to simply gaining access to it (which to a great extent remains the case today, with public lands so cheaply available to ranching throughout the West). Ranchers employed various means to graze animals on land to which they had no legal title. Most conflicts over land and grazing rights related to attempts to maintain illegal monopoly on public domain lands, and the ranchers' preference was to physically drive out the competition rather than fight them in courts. This weak legal framework, this lack of 'law enforcement' of the professed but unrealized legal remedies to resolving land conflicts, was not the only or main condition for carceral conditions to flourish in Texas—with or without the enforcement of land laws, the trade in cattle bodies would likely have developed. But this lack ensured that enormous cattle ranches and enterprises would develop, a cattle baron class would emerge, and carceral structures, features, and tools would expand into an industrial or factory-like system that would radically change food ways and cause untold, ongoing harm to animals.

Davant and Herskowitz (2016: 51–52) describe an informal code equivalent to law that operated in Texas in the early nineteenth century. Ranchers believed it was simply their right to make use of unoccupied government grazing lands without title or lease to it, and they adopted their own customs, rules, and regulations 'to which every cowman was committed'—the Law of the Open Range—or free access to grass and water. This became the foundation of the range cattle industry. As these authors describe, "Newcomers were thereby forewarned not to stand in the cowman's route to the ranges, not to block his way with towns and fields and—of all things—fences." A number of scholars have shown how the Wild West get-rich schemes of turning public land and other resources into private ownership was largely unregulated, and cattlemen sought control over vast acreages mostly by simply claiming them, as well as through manipulation of federal law such as the Homestead Act of 1862. Land fraud of various flavors was used to create large blocks of real estate under a single title, and involved an intersection of war widows, children, and family members working together with land agents and local politicians. In the mid-nineteenth century, Texas was particularly ripe for land schemes due to overlapping and contested Mexican, Texan, and U.S. sovereignty claims, but so were numerous other locations throughout the Great Plains and West.

On such illegally acquired land, animals could be fed for free, guaranteeing an enormous profit margin at the point of sale north. Thus, part and parcel of the American settler colonial project was this type of land acquisition—the process of turning the public domain into private property—yet the General Land Office, a bureau under the Secretary of the Treasury, was inefficient and ill equipped to handle the highly complex machinations of surveying, selling, and registering of public lands. This was particularly the case when prior appropriation or 'getting there first' bumped up against the complexity and overlapping nature of the 375 land laws passed by Congress from 1789 to 1834; laws adjusting the size of lots for sale, shifting the price per acre, altering the requirements for payment, and granting rights of preemption in specific regions. As Limerick maintains, 'first arrival' made the distinction between legitimate acquisition and theft a fine one. "In both cases, the act was similar—one simply appropriated something for one's own use—but, by a sometimes-subtle difference of timing, one act was honored and protected by law, and the other was punished" (Limerick 1987: 59–72, quote on 66; White 1991: 223). This would provide a basis for the carceral logic of the time and place. One of many notable examples involved one Bartlett Richards, who was indicted on illegal fencing of public lands in Nebraska and Wyoming. Bartlett fenced a vast acreage of 300 miles of public land (a total of a million acres when combined with his brother's) by 1899. By 1902 this amounted to over 6 million acres of federal land holding 350,000 cows. As Limerick (1992: 55) writes, "If Hollywood wanted to capture the emotional center of Western history, its movies would be about real estate. John Wayne would have been neither a gunfighter nor a sheriff, but a surveyor, speculator, or claims lawyer. The showdown would occur in the land office or the courtroom; weapons would be deeds and lawsuits, not six-guns." Again, acquiring physical control over land and herds was more efficacious for the cattlemen and cattle barons than seeking legal control over them. Those who were most successful at turning animal lives into personal property simply rounded them up, claimed them, branded them, and enclosed them. Sometimes whole herds would be collected through hunting and branding only wild calves (Netz 2004: 12; Cox 1895: 62; Davant and Herskowitz 2016: 50).

Barbed Wire: Carceral Space Perfected

One of the most significant instruments of carceral control within this hodgepodge of western land law was the revolutionary invention of wire fencing, which facilitated the enclosure of public land for private use. If any material artifact archetypally represents the carceral landscape, it was (and is) barbed wire—it is carcerality perfected. Not only did this technology allow for the widespread capture, control, feeding, bodily manipulation, transport, and killing of bovine animals, but it also wholly prevented, as an everyday matter, any sort of self-directed pattern and flow of physical movement on their part. Wire fencing provided control over animals for ranchers who had possession, if not the title, to large sections of land. Cox (1895: 352) notes that there were only a few fences in 1879, but by the mid-1880s they were "everywhere." The traditional wooden fence of the East or Europe would not be feasible in a landscape lacking trees for lumber; large-scale fencing only became possible in this region with the invention of barbed wire. (Contrary perhaps to accepted wisdom that iron wire became widely used in the West because trees were scarce, Cronon [1991] proposes that because wooden posts were required to hold the barbed wire in place, the new fences actually increased demand for timber from the North.) Many scholars have taken up the history and uses of barbed wire (Netz 2004; Bennett and Abbot 2017; Razac 2002; Lin 2009; Mayes 2020). As Cronon (1991: 221) aptly declares, "fences hastened the transition from prairie to pasture."

Netz (2004) argues for the critical importance of examination of this technology across species lines—and in the case of barbed wire, the violent enclosure and control of bovine animals during the colonization of the American West. Netz discusses the first experiments in wire fencing, designs by Henry Rose and exhibited at the DeKalb, Illinois, county fair. It was Joseph Glidden, though, who patented a four-point steel design in 1874 and opened a small manufacturing plant in DeKalb for its production. Washburn and Moen Manufacturing in Worcester, Massachusetts, took over large-scale production soon thereafter. More than 350 barbed wire patents were issued between 1875 and 1890, although it was the Glidden patent that came to monopolize the market and, indeed, is the fence still in use today.

The ideal wire purportedly prevented injury to animals—or at least purportedly did not cause open wounds that would become infected—and was aimed to increase a wire's visibility to humans and animals alike (including horses). Marketing of the wire fence was an important piece of advancing this carceral technology, as were improvements in iron and steel production. Glidden's 1874 patent (No. 157,124) is an interesting document of torture unto itself, declaring that unlike other wires that seriously harmed animals, "the double, machine-twisted strand of galvanized steel wire . . . prick smartly on contact and warning, but not wounding the animal" (Washburn and Moen Manufacturing, n.d.). This "perfect fence . . . borrowed from nature the principle of the sharp pricking thorn thus appealing to the sense of pain and danger that resides in the skin of the farm animal" (see fig. 2.5). Barbed wire was attacked by some as being harmful to animals, and a number of 'humane' wires with smaller barbs were developed as a result. Many of the other proposed wires caused too much injury and loss of animals; competition among wire makers thus focused on loss of one's property value rather than concern for animal welfare or suffering. The barbs were intended to domesticate or 're-tame' by shock an entire breed of animals through such immediate painful impact (Netz 2004: 38), but also ultimately served as an efficient biotechnology through which enclosed animals could be more easily bred, fed, and controlled. As Netz (2004: xiii–xiv) writes, the "history of barbed wire took place precisely at the level of the flesh. . . . The tool was created to control animals by inflicting pain on them . . . the simple and unchanging equation of flesh and iron."

Entanglements in wires, suffering open wounds derived from them (which led to insect infestation), and being stopped and trapped by fencing have been well documented by human observers. Cox (1895: 49) refers to the terrible destruction of stock caused from being torn first on the wire and insects "doing the rest." Many animals were seriously injured by the fences leading to open wounds, which easily led to screwworm fly infestation. As Netz (2004: 34) describes, when the worms emerged, they would "literally eat the animal alive."

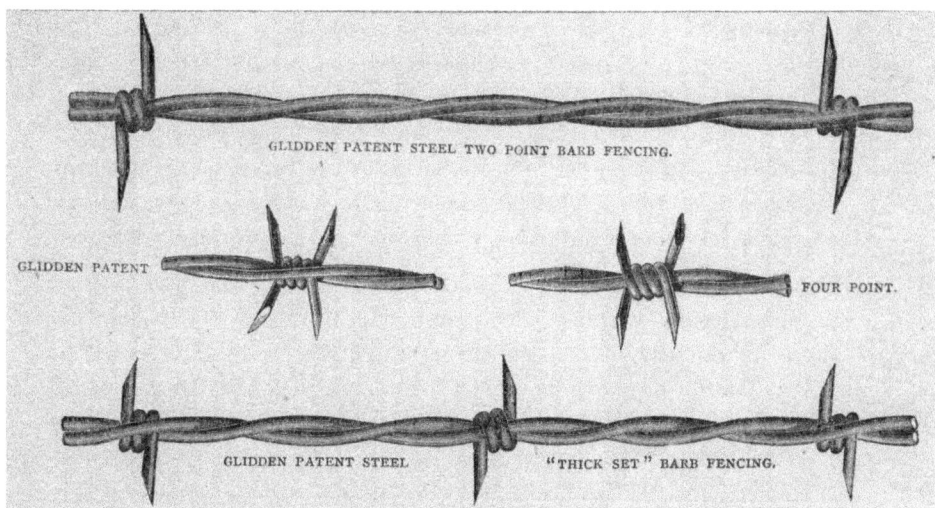

Fig. 2.5. Illustration from Glidden patent advertising brochure. Two-point and four-point barbed wire fencing: "Cheap, Staunch, Indispensable." Washburn and Moen M'F'G Co., Worcester, Mass. Used with permission of Dickinson Research Center, National Cowboy & Western Heritage Museum, Oklahoma City, Oklahoma (TS.271.g553).

White (1991: 223–224) details eyewitness accounts of the impacts of wire fencing during dangerous weather events such as droughts and blizzards. Harm to animals was one of the justifications for the "fence cutting wars."

One rather infamous early adopter of barbed wire in the Texas Panhandle, Charles Goodnight, fenced in over 3 million acres of public range with illegal fences while others followed suit, fencing land over which they had no legal claim (Rifkin 1992: 101–113; White 1991: 222, 345; Specht 2019: 68, 76). Also in the Texas Panhandle the Scottish-backed XIT Ranch oversaw its own 3 million acres, operating on a grant from the state with an estimated 6,000 miles of fence. Fencing provided greater control over animals for ranchers who had possession, if not the title, to large sections of land.

As with branding irons, seemingly all western museums that trace cattle ranching or cattle drive history feature some sort of wire fencing display and photographs, categorized by chronological or technological developments and changes, inventor, and type. The National Ranching Heritage Center offers signage explaining the ostensible four 'stages' of wire development while emphasizing safety to animals:

> Strands of smooth wire had been used as early as 1853 in New Braunfels, Texas. From this beginning, barbed wire went through four stages in its development: Early Varied, 1868–1877; Vicious, 1876–1880; Obvious, 1879–1884;

and Modified, 1884–1892. Inventors used single- and double-strand barbs, ribbon wire, twisted wire, clip-on barbs, machine-cut wire, wooden blocks and shorter barbs to improve this invention. Many cattlemen were initially skeptical of barbed wire due to the wounds it caused their cattle. Inventors redesigned barbed wire to win over cattlemen and prevent injury and disease among the herds. These innovations and improvements assured barbed wire's place as an important component in the ranching industry.

The Barbed Wire Study Collection at the National Cowboy and Western Heritage Museum also offers a useful entrée into barbed wire—by the sheer volume of variously pointed and strung iron and steel devices—as well as evidence of how an individual might experience their use. On display are 1,300 strands of barbed wire, among a collection of 8,000 strands, claimed to be the largest such collection in the world. The text accompanying this well-maintained and catalogued collection primarily emphasizes developments in wire technology, belying the pain and trauma inflicted by its samples. Animals entangled in wires, suffering open wounds derived from them, and becoming stopped and trapped by fencing are deemphasized in place of the re-narration of a much more valiant human past of design innovation and competition, and ultimately documenting the growth and development of cattle ranching empires through their use.

The Fence Cutting Wars and "Drift Fences"

Fraudulent or at best questionable fencing activities by the likes of Goodnight led to what has been called the fence cutting wars of the early 1880s, which pitted such large cattle companies that had illegally fenced thousands of acres of public lands against the smaller-scale open-range ranchers—many of whom were former cowboys trying to eke out a living from ranching—as well as pitting farmers against ranchers, the latter of whom argued that farmers should fence their crops to protect them from free-grazing animals (e.g., Holt 1930). Brown (1994: 393–403) also asserts that fence cutting was the major tactic used against the incorporating efforts of the cattle kings. Resistance surged in violence-torn central Texas during the 1880s and 1890s. In county after county, farmers and small ranchers cut the fences of the land- and animal-enclosing big cattlemen who were gradually forcing many of the small operators off the land or on to reduced holdings (Cox 1895: 45–50). Widespread fence cutting by the small-scale ranchers and farmers heightened in 1883–1884, with more than half of Texas counties reporting fence cutting and pasture burning, along with episodes of violence including gunfights and deaths.

The deleterious impacts on animals as their pasture grass burned amid the

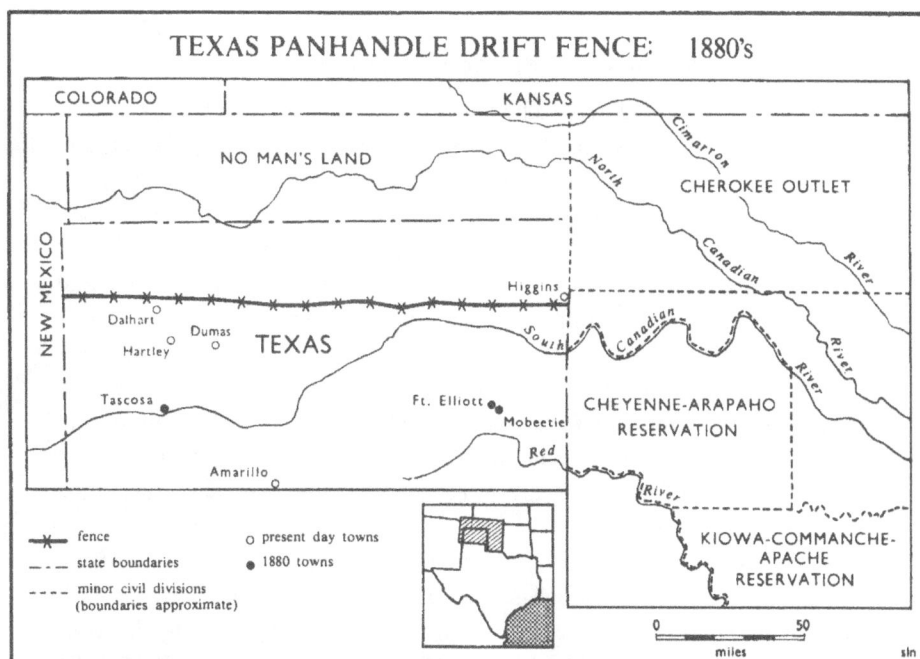

Fig. 2.6. Map of 1880s drift fence across western Texas. Reproduced with permission of the Panhandle-Plains Historical Museum, Canyon, Texas.

fence cutting wars proved calamitous. While human resistance to wire fencing at some level seems praiseworthy, as it was aimed against the bald corruption of the cattle kings, it was in the end largely focused on protecting small-scale ranching or other agricultural ventures, including those animals within them that represented valuable commercial assets—and not, likely, their protection or welfare as such. Local, state, and federal governments attempted to legislatively prevent fencing of public land. Angered by "unauthorized fencing" by cattlemen, many small farmers and ranchers wrote to the Secretary of the Interior, with their letters presented to Congress in 1884. The letters explicate the extent of large-scale and "fraudulent inclosures" of public lands by stockmen, including entire counties in Kansas. As Secretary of the Interior H. M. Teller wrote to Congress (Teller 1884),

> The cases mentioned in the reports and correspondence herewith submitted are to be regarded merely as indicative of the situation. I am satisfied from the information received that the practice of illegally inclosing the public lands is extensive throughout the grazing regions, and that many millions of acres are thus inclosed and are now being so inclosed to the exclusion of

the stock of all others than the fence owners, and to the prevention of settlements and the obstruction of public travel and intercourse.

The U.S. Congress finally passed a law in 1885 designed to prosecute anyone
who attempted to fence public land for private use. The large British and
American cattle companies suffered little repercussion from such legislation,
however, and continued large-scale fencing unabated through manipulation
of the Homestead Act (1862), the Timber Culture Act (1873), and the Desert
Land Act (1887) throughout the Great Plains and West, which awarded land
based ostensibly on building construction, planting trees, or installing irri-
gation (respectively); or they purchased land abutting the railroads and pre-
empted the public lands next to them. Estimates are that up to 7.3 million
acres of public land were fraudulently expropriated by cattle companies in
this way in the 1870s and 1880s. The endgame of this system of enclosure of
cows via fences, of course, legally or illegally, was their eventual death in the
northern slaughterhouses.

White (1991: 223–224) details eyewitness accounts of impacts of wire fencing during dangerous weather events such as droughts and blizzards. One
poignant example involved cows encountering and being stuck by the "drift
fences"—long continuous barbed wire fences—that the Texas Panhandle
Cattlemen's Association, working with large cattle companies in northern
Texas, erected in the 1880s, intended to control the number of animals traveling south for warmer weather and more abundant grasses (see fig. 2.6). Drift
fences were used most infamously in the Texas Panhandle from 1882 to 1887 to
control the winter southern migrations of animals. This fence was particularly
disastrous for animals during the winter of 1886–1887, when winter blizzards
and snow-covered ground drove tens of thousands of animals south and the
fences became "death traps" for perhaps two-thirds of the animals that ran
into them, piled up against them, and died by freezing or starving. Drift fences
were also built in Texas to prevent cattle from Oklahoma, Colorado, and Kansas from crossing into the state during blizzards. As a result of the 1887 blizzard, Texas in 1889 passed a law prohibiting fencing of public property, and the
drift fence was removed in 1890.

Many eyewitnesses reported 'miles and miles' of dead frozen bodies along
the drift fences in the later nineteenth century. Colling (2020: 21) writes, the
"consequences were devastating for the animals forced to walk miles to new
grazing areas. In a recurring tragedy drift fences barring northern cows from
southern pastures in Texas proved disastrous. . . . when thousands became
trapped and froze to death." Rollins (1922: 207–209) also states that the "drift"
was often tragic for both the animals and cattlemen; cattle were its usual

prey, for horses almost always had sense sufficient to avoid it, and to find shelter for themselves.

> The drift was the live stock's marching in wholesale numbers away from a particular locality, either to avoid the local conditions or to seek better conditions elsewhere. . . . Deep snows having covered the grasses . . . the beasts would march along for miles and until stopped by some insurmountable obstacle . . . huddling themselves in a compact mass. With the water from their eyes freezing, with long icicles hanging from their lips, and their back rime-coated, they stood, head down, moaning, hopeless. Abruptly, in sodden despair, with brain entirely dormant but muscles automatically working, some forceful steer started down leeward, and behind him, in like condition, straggled the staggering herd. Each animal, keeping true to the wind's course, fought on til the animal dropped; and where it dropped it died.
>
> The numbed brutes fell one by one, first the weaker calves, then the stronger calves, each little tumbling body causing the attendant, anxious mother to stop and wait and perish beside a diminutive mound of snow. . . until the final sacrifice appeared in the frozen bodies of some grand bovine monsters, lying piled before the impassable barrier of a high snow-drift, a deep cut, or a rocky wall.

John B. Connor (Hunter 1924: 379) recalled that in a trail drive in 1885,

> About sixty miles south of the Palo Duro River I saw the first dirt [sic] fence, which had been constructed to catch drifting cattle during blizzards. This fence ran east and west across the plains and served its purpose well, but occasioned heavy losses in some instances. As I journeyed on and when within about twenty miles of the Palo Duro, I began to see dead cattle every few hundred yards, and the nearer I approached to the river the carcasses seemed to increase until I reached the river, where there were literally hundreds of dead cattle scattered around over the prairie. I was told by the roundup men these cattle had drifted down to the dirt [sic] fence, where they almost perished for water, and when they came back to the river they drank so much water it killed them.

The numbers of these animals, and the scale of their suffering, are agonizingly grim. The incidences of animal suffering caused by barbed wire within the nineteenth-century carceral archipelago seem to exist at a scale of suffering all their own. The combination of the inventive application of iron and steel technology, human greed—and, as Netz (2004) so artfully describes, the wanton human infliction of pain to animals at the level of the flesh—all produced this most insidious of carceral inventions that remains the preferred mechanism of disciplinary and biopolitical carceral control today (Morin 2019).

Conclusion

Other historical carceral archipelagoes that obtain similar infrastructural 'improvements' and technologies like those described in this chapter have negatively impacted animal lives across historical time and space, and more are likely to be uncovered by animal studies scholars. Mayes (2020) shows, to take just one example, the impact of wire fencing in Australia in the 1840s, and its relationship to settler colonialism, indigeneity, and animal life there. Mayes describes the wholesale transformation of sheep lives through the development of fenced paddocks that were used to enclose, manage, sort, and reproduce them, what Mayes usefully refers to (after Foucault 2007) as "fencing governmentality."

The carceral conditions endured by bovine animals described in this chapter—the phenomenally successful set of carceral practices, tools, structures, infrastructures, and, above all, the carceral logics undergirding them—fed a growing American appetite for meat and set the stage for the cattle drives north. A number of 'push' and 'pull' factors shifted the cattle markets north following the Civil War, including the prodigiously growing numbers of Texas longhorns and the opening of the north for trade in them. These factors, along with the pull of northern town entrepreneurs who were set to profit enormously from such trade, people like Joseph McCoy of Abilene, Kansas, partnered with the railroad to build the structures that would enable transport of them to slaughterhouses beyond. As the next chapter outlines, the cattle trailing era presents a unique, albeit short-lived, period of bovine history in the United States unlike any other, wherein captive animals were coerced, for weeks and months at a time, into walking themselves to their deaths. Within this context I also follow on Rollins's sad recounting of the deaths of mothers and their calves in the drift fences—"each little tumbling body causing the attendant anxious mother to stop and wait and perish beside a diminutive mound of snow"—with an eye to understanding family or kinship relations provoked through captivity on the cattle trails.

CHAPTER 3

The Cattle Drive

COWBOYS AND CATTLE AT WORK

Six million Texas longhorns wandered wild and untendered by the end of the U.S. Civil War. After the Mississippi River blockade was lifted, Texans began shifting the direction of their longhorn trade to northern markets. Though the first documented overland cattle drive north was as early as 1846, when Edward Piper drove one thousand animals from Texas to Ohio, it was the year 1866 that witnessed the "birth of the great Texas cattle trail drives" headed north (Shillingberg 2009: 158–161, quote on 160; Rifkin 1992: 70; Wishart 2004: 162, 383–384; Dykstra 1968). In 1866 a quarter of a million cows crossed the Red River on the Texas-Oklahoma border (Cox 1895: 53). Estimates vary, sometimes very dramatically, but according to the National Ranching Heritage Center in Lubbock, Texas, in 1860 there were 31 million people living in the United States and 26 million cows grazing Texas. By 1866 an estimated quarter of a million of those animals were trailed to the northern cow towns, with that number swelling into a forced migration north from Texas of millions of animals over the next twenty years. During 1871 alone, 600,000–700,000 cattle were driven north from Texas. All told, until barbed wire closed the open range in the 1890s, as many as 27 million cattle were estimated to have been driven out of Texas to destinations east, north, and west.

Before the Civil War and the great cattle drives, the primary trail was the Shawnee Trail, which ran from central Texas to markets in Kansas City and St. Louis (Stillman 2008: 163). However, the 1,000-mile-long Chisholm Trail (or Old Chisholm Trail) was the main livestock trail from Texas north to Kansas.

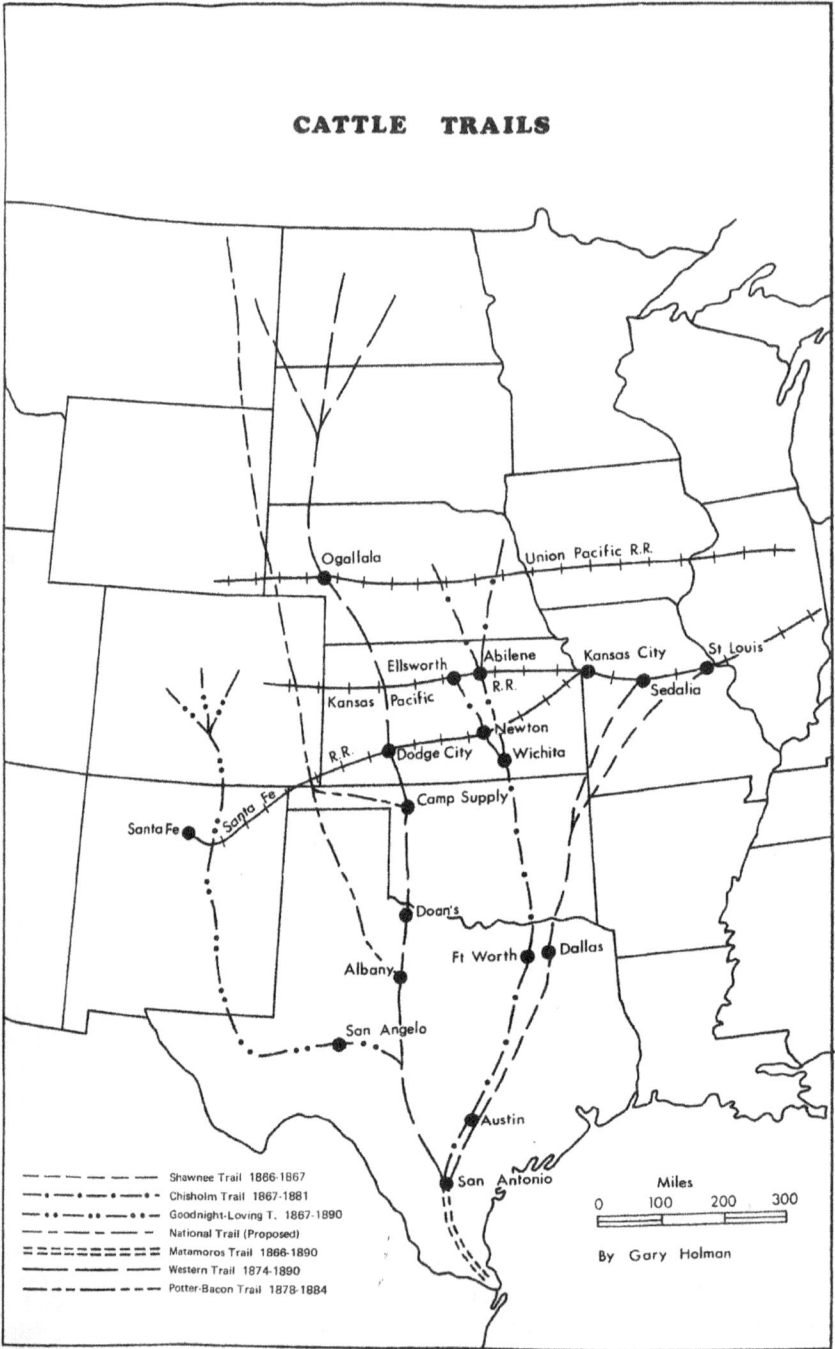

CATTLE TRAILS

Ogallala

Union Pacific R.R.

Ellsworth Abilene Kansas City St Louis

Kansas Pacific R.R. Sedalia

R.R. Newton

Dodge City Wichita

Camp Supply

Santa Fe Santa Fe

Doan's

Albany Ft Worth Dallas

San Angelo

Austin

San Antonio

Miles

0   100   200   300

By Gary Holman

— — — — — — — — Shawnee Trail 1866-1867
—·—·—·—·— Chisholm Trail 1867-1881
—··—··—··— Goodnight-Loving T. 1867-1890
— — — — — — National Trail (Proposed)
≡≡≡≡≡≡≡≡ Matamoros Trail 1866-1890
———————— Western Trail 1874-1890
—··—··—·· Potter-Bacon Trail 1878-1884

Fig. 3.1. Map of the main cattle trails from Texas to Kansas. From J. Skaggs, *The Cattle-Trailing Industry* (1973, opposite p. 6). Reproduced with permission of Oklahoma University Press, Norman, Oklahoma.

Later came the Western Trail or Dodge City Trail across the Oklahoma Pan-handle, with herds drawn to an active market in Dodge City, Kansas, then on to Ogallala, Nebraska, and then driven further to the northern Great Plains. So, although other trails appeared on the northern plains along several routes (Wishart 2004; 800–801; Dykstra 1968: 8–9; Welch 2017)—and other sites of cattle beef production existed in the United States at the time (Hoganson 2012 focuses on Illinois)—for reasons of their western iconicity as well as their integral role in the development of the Chicago slaughterhouses, I focus on the Texas–Oklahoma (at the time, 'Indian Territory')–Kansas route(s) and cattle towns that developed along them (see fig. 3.1).

The typical cattle drive took two to three months; after crossing the Red River, three to five weeks remained of the journey to Kansas, depending on circumstances. An individual cowboy would oversee the movement of 245–350 animals on a single cattle drive. In my discussion below I highlight the interface between mobility and carcerality, and the effect of this interface on the lived experiences of animals. The trail drive from Texas to one of the Kansas cow towns is one I describe as a 'carceral death march'.

The first week, they covered between 20 and 30 miles per day; in subsequent weeks, 12–15 per day—a schedule intended to alienate the animals from their former pastures, tire them to prevent activity such as stampeding at night, control their potential weight loss by moving them slowly as they pastured along the way (as they were eventually sold by the pound, not by the head), and overall 'break' the animals, ensuring that they became easier to handle as the days and weeks wore on. Stock breeding and domestication always have the effect of breaking animals and thus reducing their potential for resisting their conditions, even if they also then appear to be colluding with or somehow collaborating with their oppressors (Lambert 2018: 185–189; Fudge 2017; Cronon 1991: 217–224; Wadiwel 2016).

Along with Anderson (2004) and Ogle (2013), Specht observes (2016: 343) that cattle were ideally suited to nineteenth-century agriculture largely because the animals themselves performed much of the labor involved in beef production: "Animals are not simply inputs in our agricultural system, but key agents for creating and operating this system." He adds that

> Cattle are not sacks of flour. Cattle fought with one another and with their owners. They wandered off. When their young died on the trail they straggled at the back of the herd, trying to turn back. It was their ability to feed themselves on the range that was the origin of much of their value, meaning they were even performing a kind of labor. Though it is impossible to understand what the cattle-beef complex meant to them, it is important to recognize that the very possibility of this system depended on the fact that these ani-

mals were capable of moving, working, and in small ways, resisting. (Specht 2019: 17)

While we might easily accord these animals the position of biotechnological agent in developing a type a colonial agriculture, this ostensible agency led directly to the development of a carceral infrastructure that ensured these animals' torture, suffering, and deaths. Thus, it seems important to conceptualize the limits or extent of their labor and agency within the carceral context of the cattle trail.

Scholarly work has documented the lives of the cowboys (and the wranglers, cooks, and trail bosses that accompanied them); for example, they worked 12–18-hour days for two to three months at a time, making between $25 and $40 per month. Although cowboys (as well as ranchers) were, of course, not all alike, Cronon (1991: 218–224) challenges the relationship of their labor to their almost mythological status: "Far from being a loner or rugged individualist, [the cowboy] was a wageworker whose task was to ship meat to cities." Depictions of tough, heroic, or romantic cowboys in illustrated weeklies, photographs, paintings, and fictionalized western films highlighted the grueling conditions that both men and animals endured on the cattle drives—lightning storms, dust, starvation, stampedes, rustler attacks, and dangerous river crossings—and these conditions constituted the locations and conditions of their mutual work. I attempt to unpack how this mutual work was understood and experienced by these actors, the ways in which their work challenged taken-for-granted boundaries between humans and nonhumans, and the relative agency each was able to exercise within the carceral spaces of the cattle trails.

A focus on the cattle drive also offers an opportunity to consider one important and poignant aspect of animal experiences under carceral control—that of 'family life', including but not limited to that of kinship bonding and relationships between mother cows and their calves. The intersection of carceral geography, historical animal studies, and material culture offers insights into the noteworthy behaviors, norms, and relations of mother cows and their calves as they transitioned from free-roaming beings to those under conditions of captivity. Museum artifacts illustrate carceral tools used to speed independence of calves from drinking mothers' milk to foraging for grass, and human observers noted the pains of separation between mother and offspring, and the despair and anxiety mother cows expressed over losing their calves. Cowboys described mother cows' fierceness in adopting strategies to protect their young from the dangers of human carceral technologies and techniques, attempting to hide them and to position them out of harm's way. Cows' emotional responses of suffering, and many cowboys' shared grief witnessing this pain and loss, offer notable insights into life on the cattle trails that are quite distinct from the triumphal stories depicted in museums and tourist sites that re-narrate the cattle drives to contemporary audiences.

Although I do not examine the lives and experiences of horses, they were also important workers on the cattle trails, as many scholars have argued. Stillman, for instance (2008: 167–168), writes that in addition to the 6 million cattle and 35,000 men who traveled from Texas to Kansas during this period, a million horses did so as well, with an unknown number who did not survive. Stillman writes,

> The historical record does not tell us how many horses were used in the ac-
> tual drives. But considering that most of the thirty-five thousand men on the
> trails had not just one horse but several (a remuda, supplied by the owner of
> the cattle), and given that many of these horses died along the drives and had
> to be replaced, then, in addition to the million mustangs that were driven to
> market, there must have been at least half a million horses running up and
> down the old cattle trails of the central Great Plains. (168)

Thus, along with the cattle, untold numbers of other animals suffered and died within the carceral archipelago of the emergent beef cattle industry.

On the Trail from Texas to Kansas: A Carceral Death March

As noted, the trail drive from Texas to one of the Kansas cow towns generally took two to three months. Rollins (1922: 223, 253–256) describes how, during the first week of the drive, animals were "shoved" to the limits of their speed so that they would subsequently 'tire into submissiveness' and thereafter willingly keep to the course, with the cowboys hearing only the "bellows, lows, and bleats of the trudging animals" (also see McCoy 1874: 84). This is carceral logic and practice at work, and the exercise of human sovereign power and control over the mobility of recently free agents.

The animals ate their 'full meal' at night, when cowboys would sing to them to keep them pacified and not stampede—singing anything from known songs and hymns to texts on the labels of coffee or condensed milk cans (McCoy 1874: 99–101; Cox 1895: 54). Eyewitness accounts of the cattle drives nearly all mentioned the dangers or 'mayhem' of stampeding animals, one particularly gruesome outcome of the hidden carceral logic of the cattle trail and business (Cox 1895; Dobie 1941; McCoy 1874; Hunter 1924; Rollins 1922). As the iconic and all too ubiquitous portrayals of stampeding cattle in western films, descriptions of stampedes had much to imply about the nature, value, and lives of these animals, particularly in reinforcing them as animalized beings—they were wild, prone to losing control, and/or would 'stupidly' follow a lead animal or the rest of the herd. Meanwhile, stampeding animals presented a danger to the lives of their human 'caretakers' on the trail and offered them the possibility of restoring order following one. Stillman (2008: 175) adds that stampedes presented dangers to horses as well as the men riding them, and that one way that cattle were subdued was by shooting them through the horns: "a center hit caused enough pain to calm the steer. If the pith of the horn was punctured, the soreness kept the steer on his best behavior for weeks . . . [even if] occasionally a missed shot killed a steer. But the cows were cheap, and it was an advantage to get rid of the rebellious ones so they wouldn't cause more trouble."

Eyewitness accounts of the cattle drives by cowboys, newspaper reporters, and others consistently mention rain and hail storms, dangerous river crossings, freezing and cold conditions as well as that of extreme heat and fires, thirst and starvation, encounters with predators including panthers, wolves, and rattlesnakes, and the stealing/rustling of cattle from other herds (Cox 1895; Dobie 1941; McCoy 1874; Hunter 1924; Rollins 1922). A great deal of competition, dishonesty, and bribery characterized this journey for many. Some cowboys describe the whole endeavor as one of bribery and piracy, particularly related to dealmaking for river crossings and capturing animals of competing trail drivers (e.g., Hunter 1924: 544). One S. Brodbent (Hunter 1924: 593) asserts that there "was some dishonesty in trail driving," particularly in the practice of incorporating animals from other herds into one's own; "it is perhaps a surprising feature of the cattle drive that the owners of many herds that illegitimately increased the most on what they made a piratical journey north, went broke, and some of the most noted 'cattle kings' became herdsmen or dropped into oblivion."

Many cowboys describe the spectacle of animals' river crossings. Some portray a nostalgic heroism: "It was a wonderful sight to see a thousand steers swimming all at one time. All you could see was the tip of their horns and ends of their noses as they went through the water" (L. D. Taylor in Hunter 1924: 499, ca. 1869). Jerry Nance (Hunter 1924: 106) writes that "[the Brazos River above Waco, Texas,] was on the rise and it was so wide that all of the cattle were in the river swimming at the same time, and it looked as if I had no cattle at all, for all we could see was the horns." Most, though, recall animals drowning via treacherous river crossings when they got stuck in the quicksand-like river bottom or were overcome by rushing water. G. H. Mohle (Hunter 1924: 42–43) describes animals drowning on the trail:

> In April, 1869, I was employed by Black Hill Montgomery to go with a herd of
> 4,500 head of stock cattle on the drive to Abilene, Kansas. . . . On account of

Fig. 3.2. Headlong plunge of a thousand head of cattle into the Pecos River. Cover image, *Frank Leslie's Illustrated Newspaper*, 12 May 1877.

the heavy rains ... on the far side the bank was about six feet above the water and the going out place being only about twenty feet wide. We had trouble getting the cattle into the water, and when they did get started they crowded in so that they could not get out on the other side, and began milling, and we lost one hundred and sixteen head and three horses.

As Frank Dobie recalls (1941: 267–282), every trail herd had its dominant steer, which by instinct strode to the front of the bunch to lead the way. Good lead steers were particularly valuable when crossing a river because hesitant leaders would cause most of the others to stop. If a steer did the job well, he would not be sold; he would be brought home to lead the other herds north. Charles Goodnight owned such a valuable steer in "Old Blue." During eight seasons, more than ten thousand animals followed Old Blue to Dodge City—a one-way trip for them but not for him. Goodnight put a bell around Old Blue's neck, and the other steers learned to follow the familiar ringing (see fig. 3.3). Old Blue, according to range legend, "could find the best water, the best grass, and the easiest river crossings, and could even soothe a nervous herd during a storm with his reassuring bawl." After his last drive, Dobie recounts that Old Blue was retired to a permanent pasture and lived to be twenty years old. At his death, his horns, like those of many other longhorns subject to spaces of the carceral archipelago, were mounted in a place of honor in the Goodnight ranch office.

Many trail cowhands describe the experiences of losing animals and animal death in torrential storms, hail, lightning, and flooding along the cattle trail:

> One of the most perilous things encountered on the trail in those days [ca. 1874] was the electrical storm. Herds would always drift before a storm and we would have to follow them for miles, while vivid lightning and crashing peals of thunder made our work awesome and dangerous. Only one who has been in a Kansas storm can realize what it means. Sometimes several head of cattle or horses were killed by one stroke of the lightning, and many of the cowboys met their death in the same manner. (L. B. Anderson in Hunter 1924: 207)

Rollins (1922: 198–199) writes of sudden cloud bursts, with the downpouring of water so dense as to make breathing difficult, and the resultant desperation of drowning animals: "All of the deluge that fell upon the prairie, baked as it was like a tile, rivuletted into the main stream. In too few minutes . . . at some sand-bar or sharp angle, the floating cattle jammed. Into that mess, which was here writhing, moaning, wounded, here struggling but unharmed, there motionless and dead, cowboys delved with lariats and tugging ponies. Shots ended suffering. The next chapter was skinning of carcasses and drying of hides."

Water was the most important necessity during a drive, as an individual animal could drink up to thirty gallons of water a day. Without plenty of fresh water, the cattle became irritable and would stampede. Thirst and starvation were constants on the trail, with commentators describing animals nearly going insane with thirst, being driven days or scores of miles without water. Goodnight notes that on a hot night, "a steer that ran 10 miles might lose up to 40 pounds." Dobie (1941: 154–155) recounts the bawling and moans of thirsty cattle. "Cattle walking a fence in futile anxiety to get back to a range they have been driven from make the same distressful, relentless sounds:

> The mingled bawls and lowings, each of a different pitch and timbre, of a big herd of mixed cattle held forcibly while hungry and thirsty after a day of being ginned about, frantic heifers and headstrong old cows separated from their calves, calves in misery for their mothers, yearlings adding to the din in the same way that each of forty babies will go to crying if one opens up, steers bawling for their lost powers of masculinity or for the same reason that great Arctic wolves bay at the midnight sun or from some urge that only God is aware of, bulls bellowing at the memory of past combats or maybe without memory at all—all make a kind of music to many a cowman's ears, especially at a distance.

Sherow (2018: 180), drawing on an 1877 engraving from *Frank Leslie's Weekly Illustrated* (fig. 3.2), depicts thirsty cattle stampeding into a river. Sherow writes that "sometimes the herd found itself racing unaware toward dangerous steep stream banks. Those in front, unable to stop, pushed ahead by the momentum of the cattle behind them, would plunge over the side, straight down into the stream. Some lucky ones would manage to swim to the shore while many others would be crushed to death, gouged by horns or would suffer broken bones."

Many animals perished through sheer starvation brought about by both extreme cold and hot conditions. Thousands suffered from prairie fires during their trek north, which burned them alive but also burned their potential food, which led to starvation. Cox (1895: 50) observes that prairie fires presented exceptional danger and that frequently immense numbers of cattle were destroyed and "much larger numbers were driven to desperation." James T. Johnson (Hunter 1924: 761) describes that during the winter of 1871 and 1872, "I helped skin dead cattle on the prairies in Goliad, Victoria and Refugio counties, as the cattle were starving to death by the thousands, and very few grown cattle lived through the terrible winter. I have seen as many as a thousand head of dead cattle in one day's ride on the prairie near Lamar. Horses, cattle, deer and sheep suffering awfully during these times." John B Conner (Hunter 1924: 830) recalls, "I remember the summer of 1877 was so dry the creeks dried up and hundreds of cattle perished for water, and that winter hundreds of others died in piles, many of them being skinned for their hides." The *Leavenworth Times* (cited in Sherow 2018: 208) reports that in the Solomon Valley, where scores of herds had perished, workers dug a grave in April measuring forty feet long, eight feet deep, and eight feet wide. Into it they buried "several hundred poor Texas cattle."

Sherow (2018: 207) relates an 1871 freezing weather disaster near Ellsworth, Kansas, in 1871, when snow covered the ground several inches deep. Cattle scattered everywhere to seek shelter, especially in ravines, and reports filtered in to the editor of the *Ellsworth Reporter*: "Frozen carcasses filled those same draws. . . . The blizzard lasted for full three days and killed thousands of cattle, hundreds of horses, and several cowboys." Cold weather caused much suffering for these formerly wild animals from Texas who were waiting out the winter for shipment to slaughter or were caught in a drift fence and unable to reach warmer territory south. Rollins (1922: 193) relates that in terrifically cold weather the cattle's hoofs and horns sometimes would freeze, and thereafter the horns, "on thawing, would in some instances fall off." Sam Garner (Hunter 1924: 522) on his way with a herd from Kansas to Salt Lake City circa 1871 witnessed a great deal of hardship due to the cold: "Snow fell so deep that it covered the grass and our cattle and horses froze to death right in camp, and many of our cattle died. The old wild beeves became as gentle as work oxen, and we could handle them easily enough, but the extreme cold caused us much suffering. Our oxen would bog down in the snow just the same as if it was mud, and we frequently were compelled to ram snow into their nostrils to make them get up and move." J. C. Thompson (Hunter 1924: 667), during a cattle drive from Texas to Kansas in 1878, encountered a blizzard about forty miles north of Laredo, Texas: "A regular blizzard swept down upon us which had just been preceded by a very hard, drenching rain. That cold wind whistled all night . . . and the next morning we counted 180 head of cattle dead on the bedground." Thomas Welder (Hunter 1924: 293–294) in the early 1870s, en route to Kansas, declared that he 'made a mistake' preferring to trail the young steers rather than the old: "I soon discovered my mistake, for the young cattle, not being able to stand the hardship of the trail, soon began to give out, and I found myself with a lot of drags, as we called them. We were caught in a severe freeze on Gonzales Prairies."

The blizzard of January 1886 drew a great deal of attention to the Central Plains for both the nonhuman and human losses that occurred, including killing more than 100,000 grazing cattle: "The blizzard of 1886—a storm so terrible, it created a grim new business. For several years afterward it was a matter of common remark that one could have walked from Ellsworth to Denver, a distance of more than four hundred miles, on the carcasses. . . . Skinning those animals for their hides became an industry the following month" (Monster Blizzard 2019). Journalistic accounts of the period include tales of starving animals apparently committing suicide as well as the tricks new mothers used to conceal their calves from wolves (Specht 2016: 351). Frank Wilkeson, a rancher and journalist writing for the *San Francisco Chronicle* (1885), provides a particularly powerful description of abject starvation accompanying what appeared to him as animal suicide. To him, the conditions in Kansas were so terrible that cattle killed themselves to escape their misery:

> Four years ago I held a herd of Texas cows and steers in Kansas. . . . Fall prairie fires, [and then a] long winter set in, blizzards, storms, cattle grew weaker and weaker, their flesh seemed to wither away before the cold winds. Soon some of the half-starved animals were unable to rise in the mornings unless aided by the herders.
>
> Then a queer thing happened—not once but thirty times. A weak animal that had been helped up several times would suddenly and staggeringly chase the man who had aided it to rise with the sweet intention of impaling him on its sharp horns; and, discovering that it was too weak to catch him, would bellow with rage, and then stagger to the creek, and there deliberately throw itself into the cold water. . . . After they had been pulled out and set on their feet, they would be frenzied with rage and feebly chase the men who had rescued them, and then in many cases they would deliberately re-enter the water. If they neglected to do so at once, it was almost certain that they would go into the water the next day and die there. They were tired of life. They found it hard, cold, hungry. They were depressed in spirits. My belief is that they committed suicide.

Wilkeson's description validates in historical perspective the acute capacity for suffering, depression, and despair among bovine animals that have been documented by many animal studies scholars (e.g., Gillespie 2018a; King 2013). His narrative also illustrates a more specific animal similarity with humans in their exercise of agency for escape that characterizes suicide (e.g., Braitman 2014).

Such profound expressions of grief and despair were evidenced by other commentators as well. Dobie (1941: 155–158) offers witness to the grief and fear experienced by cows on seeing one of their own dead: when the wind was such that the leaders of a herd of cattle caught the scent of a cow that had been butchered during the night, they raised their heads,

> then broke out into a loud excited bellowing; and, finally turning, they started off at a fast trot, following up the scent in a straight line until they arrived at the place where one of their kind had met its death. The contagion spread, and before long all the cattle were congregated on the fatal spot, and began moving round in a dense mass, bellowing continuously. . . . The animal has a peculiar language on occasions like this; it emits a succession of short bellowing cries, like excited exclamations, followed by a very loud cry, alternately sinking into a hoarse murmur, and rising to a kind of scream that

grates harshly on the senses. . . . The performance of cattle by the smell of blood is most distressing to hear.

The animals that had forced their way into the center of the mass to the spot where the blood was, pawed the earth, and dug it up with their horns, and trampled each other down in their frantic excitement. It was terrible to see and hear them. . . . One of the memories I shall carry to the last is of cattle congregating around a blood-soaked cowhide that had been thrown, the flesh side up, over a pen fence. . . . They began to bellow. . . . By dark between two and three hundred cattle were milling and carrying on, bawling their lungs out and making such a to-do that we could hardly eat our suppers in the rock house a hundred and fifty yards up the hill.

Descriptions such as these help us understand the acute capacity for grief and despair among captive bovine animals. King (2013) has written provocatively on such animal grief and sorrow, although she is quick to point out that while animals feel sorrow, "goat grief . . . is not chicken grief. And chicken grief is not chimpanzee grief or elephant grief or human grief. The differences matter" (2013: 6–8). King's is an important insight, not because any one type of grief is more consequential or meaningful than another, but rather because the problematical human/animal divide can be reinforced when we say that forms of pain and suffering are the same or similar across species—with those whose are perceived as more 'human-like' taken more seriously.

Considering the firsthand observations of Wilkeson and Dobie and others, it does indeed seem, however, that these animals' expression of grief—"bawling their lungs out"—was not so different from recognizably human emotional capacities. Such is an important observation given that, as King argues, most species considered not 'like us'—and certainly those most animalized and commodified for food such as cows—typically can become even more vulnerable to violence and exploitation if their grief responses are not recognizable as such. Yet, many human eyewitnesses on the cattle trail observed and commented on the sentient experiences and suffering of the 'commodities' they trailed, and while evincing a wide range of human emotions themselves (more below), oftentimes required a deeply disassociative pattern of thought necessary for them to perform their work.

While naming the above experiences as occurring within a 'carceral death march' may appear hyperbolic, doing so seems apropos given what lay ahead for these animals at the end of the cattle trail. Some commentators mused about whether some animals might have been aware of this. Bradford Robbins, Richard Grimes's oldest son, who drove cattle from Texas to Dodge City and stayed there for two months (Davant 2016: 255), reflects on the most "rambunctious bunch of critters he ever handled" in all his experience on the

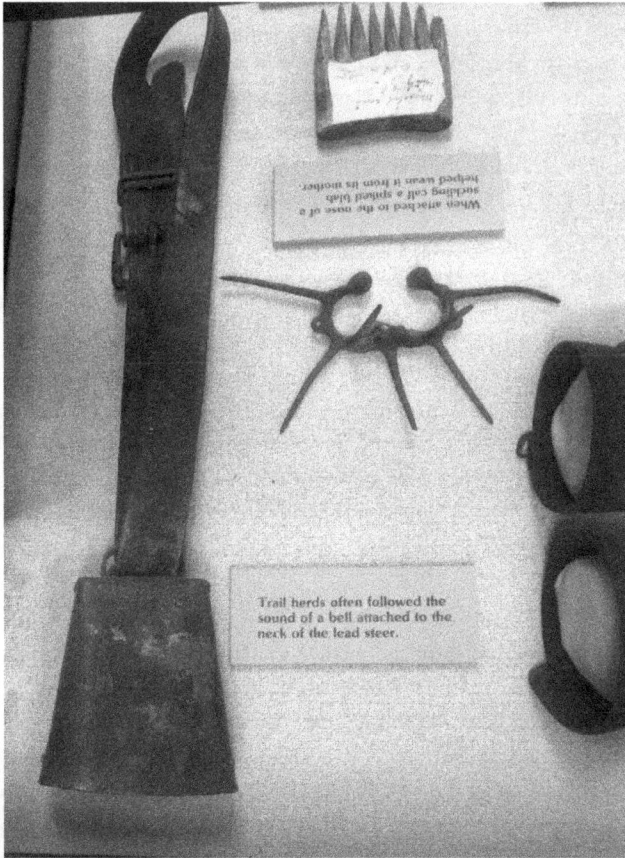

Fig. 3.3. Display case showing a spiked blab (center), a device attached to noses of suckling calves used to wean them from their mothers. Also shown, bell attached to the cattle drive's lead steer. Gift of Calvin Cook, Panhandle-Plains Historical Museum, Canyon, Texas. Photo by Daniel Olivetti.

range: "They stampeded nightly for six consecutive nights. . . . Just what got into those sea lions I don't know. Perhaps they knew they were headed for the end of the train that had no turning back."

Family Life on the Range and Trail: Mother Cows and Their Calves

Many individuals—from cowboys to cattle kings to local entrepreneurs—who observed and documented animal life during roundups, on the cattle drives, and in the pastures adjacent to the cow towns, commented on what could be called bovine 'family life' or kinship relations under carceral conditions. Both female and male animals were captured from their lives in the scrub and herded north in typically mixed groups of animals (cows, bulls, and steers). Cowboys in particular were close to and aware of the gender dynamics of the traveling herds and commented on them frequently, especially of the relations and behaviors between mother cows and their offspring as well as fighting among bulls and steers (Rollins 1922; Cox 1895; Arnold and Hale 1940).

On the range and during a cattle drive, as Rollins (1922: 193) puts it, "no oversight was given to maternity cases," and births occurred wherever the mother happened to be. Dobie (1941: 161) notes that "cows habitually went into the dense, tall grass of a certain bottom land to bring forth their young, and there they would keep their calves hidden until they were three or four days old." As one cowboy observes, calves "gave us a lot of trouble" (Hunter 1924: 742); they were considered more of a burden than a valuable source of commodity flesh due to their inability to keep pace with the rest of the herd during the cattle drive. John Haynes, a cowboy who recalled a trip to Kansas from Texas in 1872, relates that calves on the cattle trail slowed down the operation and were often killed (Hunter 1924: 246): "In a mixed herd many calves were born on the trip, and it was the custom to kill them before starting the herd each morning. Some outfits tried taking along a wagon for the purpose of saving the calves, but it did not pay." J. C. Thompson shares that on an 1878 cattle drive from Texas to Kansas (Hunter 1924: 666), "We would leave from five to ten calves on the bedground every morning, and the cows would have to be roped and hobbled to keep them from going back the next night to their calves, and this thing lasted until we reached the Indian Territory." Branch Isbell describes how this burden was dealt with in his experience in 1871 on a trip to Kansas (Hunter 1924: 573): "The herd we drove was half and half grown cows and steers, and that season it was customary to kill the young calves found on the bedground. I had a pistol and it was my duty to murder the innocents each morning while their pitiful mothers were ruthlessly driven on. It looked hard, but circumstances demanded the sacrifice, and being the executioner so disgusted me with six-shooters that I have never owned—much less used one from that time to this."

For those calves who survived early death, cattlemen employed carceral instruments to speed their independence from their mothers. One particularly insidious apparatus was a "spiked blab" (fig. 3.3), used to force-wean calves. Rollins (1922: 192–193) describes one type of spiked blab:

> There were inspection trips about the range . . . to discover the location and physical state of the scattered groups of stock. . . . On such ranches [were] "blabbed" calves . . . "blabs" on the noses of whatever baby cattle deserved the unsightly little board. Here and there about the Range would appear a lusty calf with an emaciated mother. If the calf were old enough, a thin board, six

inches by eight in size, was, at the centre of one of its longer edges, clipped onto the infant's nose. Thereafter he could perfectly well graze, but he assuredly was weaned. Blabbing was not always easy of accomplishment. The calf and his mater had to be chased so far apart as to permit the cowboy to rope and throw the calf, attach the blab, and remount his horse before there should arrive, head down and on the gallop, an irate and sharp-horned cow.

Many commentators provide considerable detail about mother cows caring for and protecting their calves, at least until approximately age four, and calves seeking help and care from their mothers. Cox (1895: 196–197) describes mother-calf relations on the prairie:

> I saw a little calf just taking his first steps on the prairie, and stopped to observe him. The cow ran away at my approach, but immediately came back and stood resolutely and defiantly by her young; indeed so wicked did she look, that the driver whipped up his horses and got away as soon as possible. . . . I am sure she was going to charge. . . . [The animals] run in families like buffalo, the cows keeping their calves with them sometimes until they are three or four years old. It frequently happens that the mother has under her protection sons and daughters larger than herself. The cow watches over her offspring, and when they disobey punishes them with her horns, to which they tamely submit, like well-trained children.

Dobie (1941: 153–154) asserts there is no wild animal, "or domestic either," that has as many vocal tones as the longhorn. The longhorn cow "has one *moo* for her newborn calf, another for when they are older, and one to tell them to come to her side, and another to tell them to stay hidden in tall grass." Dobie also asserts of the longhorn: "Moved by amatory feelings, she has a low audible breath of yearning. In anger she can run a gamut. If her calf has died or has been otherwise taken from her, she seems to be turning her insides out into long, sharp, agonizing bawls. I have heard steers make similar sounds. They seemed to be in the utmost agony of expressing something so poignant to them that the utterance meant more than life and would be willingly paid for by death." This range of vocalizations, and the emotional and other intentions behind them, aligns with research studies reported by Hanson (2020) and Hodgetts and Lorimer (2015: 288–289).

Determining ownership of calves for branding purposes was a common theme of discourse among cowboys, ranchers, and other observers. Arnold and Hale (1940: 20) note, "The mounted men will have determined ownership of the calves by watching the mothers they follow. . . . Even though all cows look much alike to men, they have individualities to each other. No calf ever mistakes its mother, if she is near (although in hunger will nurse another), and no mother ever mistakes her calf." During the 'cutting out' process (Rollins 1922: 225) when animals were removed from the herd on the range or in a pen, to be subsequently driven on the trail north, sold, branded, or slaughtered on the spot, mother cows were protective of their offspring, identified and lariated along with the calf and brought close to the fire so that her brands would be noticeable to be imprinted on her calf. During the process the mother cow would be the focus of the lariat because she could be expected to "sweep her youngster along with her in her rush." "No matter how great the confusion, the mother never would mistake the identity of her baby, although the latter might fail to recognize its parent." During cutting out and branding "came a constant and pandemoniac chorus from bleeting calves and bellowing mothers separated in the melee" (232). Rollins describes the angst of mother cows when her calf was being branded:

> When branding a calf, the group of men about it sometimes received a hurried visit from the little fellow's mother; which, unadvised that his wounds were so superficial as to lose their scabs within two weeks, and responsive only to his vealish cry for mama, eluded her human guards and arrived on the scene, head down and at considerable speed. If no readily climbable fence were at hand, escape was effected by a matadorlike wait till the strategic moment, by a handful of dust through into the charging animal's eyes, and by a coincident jump or roll out of her course. This dust tended not only to prevent the cow from dodging with the dodging man, but also to discourage her from promptly wheeling and returning the attack. (248)

Mother cows also protected their young from hazardous environmental conditions. Should the calf have survived long enough to be herded with his mother on the cattle drive, Dobie observes that "before entering a swift stream, the cow maneuvered to place her calf on the lower side, thus protecting it against the force of the current. She was cunning in hiding her calf, and even though she might be a gentle milk cow, her fixed purpose was to prevent anyone's seeing her infant before it was strong enough to run" (1941: 16).

Rollins (1922: 249–250) adds that mother cows seemed to be more 'aware' and responsive to their carceral surroundings than other members of the herds, both in their protection of their young and in everyday activities:

> The cowboy feared the Range cow more than he did any bull or steer. . . . She kept her eyes open, her mind on her job. She was exceedingly quick of motion, for all Range cattle were, for short distances, practically as fast as ridden horses. With horns in lieu of a broom, she went about her house-cleaning with considerable enthusiasm and thoroughly feminine persistency. The bull or steer, on the other hand, lumberingly moved himself into battle position,

horns to the enemy, roaringly advertised that he was about to annihilate, lowered his head, shut both eyes, and came on like a runaway coal-truck. The intended victim had merely to bide his own time, and, taking a short step to one side, to watch a blundering, conceited mass of flesh pound harmlessly by.

Wilkeson (1885) documents some of the most intriguing behaviors and characteristics of cattle on his ranch and on the open range, including on mother cows' 'animal intelligence' in protecting their young:

> The semi-wild Texas cattle display great intelligence in the care and protec-
> tion of their calves.... Hundreds of calves have been born on my ranch. I do
> not believe that any of them were killed by wolves. Cows about to become
> mothers leave the herd and seek seclusion in the tall blue-joint grass, or in
> plum thickets. A few hours after its birth the calf is strong enough to walk.
> The cows then lead them 200 or 300 yards away from the spot where they
> were born, and there they hide them. In some mysterious manner they con-
> vey to the calf the information that it must be perfectly still; that in motion-
> less silence is safety; that violent death stalks closely [nearby].

Wilkeson writes that when he happened to find a young, hidden calf on his ranch, "The entire herd rushed into the clover to do battle for the calf. What an uproar there was! Cows, steers, bulls, all calling loudly to one another in angry, excited tones.... The mother cows are willing to leave their offering out of the corrals overnight in a wolf-infested country, once they have hidden them and bade them be still." Wilkeson notes a further strategy of what he viewed as a practice to protect the young: "I have repeatedly seen a herd of stock cattle at-tack a wounded comrade and endeavor to kill it. These attacks were generally led by long-horned, agile cows that had calves by their side. I am satisfied that the cows knew that the scent of blood would draw carnivorous animals to the vicinity of the herd and the attack on the wounded animal was a measure of intelligent self-preservation."

These examples point to the extraordinary and profound kinship bonding that cows and calves maintained within the context of the carceral (as well as the human understanding and assessment of it). Gillespie (2018a) found with more recent examples that indeed the crying between mother cows and calves, especially over the distress of being separated at places like auction yards, is evident of an obvious strong emotional bond among animals. But the pain and suffering of such distress was not the only emotion observed and experienced in the carceral spaces of animal capture and enclosure.

Even in these spaces of threat, precarity, and violence, mothers and their calves displayed care, tenderness, and deep kinship connections for one another. Narratives of witnessing emotions and behaviors by cowboys and ranchers, placed alongside the carceral tools of disciplining and managing the mother-offspring relation, offer compelling examples of both the violent inputs and outcomes of the nineteenth-century carceral archipelago. Noting the fuller range of emotions such as between mother cows and their offspring (Wilkeson 1885; Cox 1895; Rollins 1922) brings insight into the capacities and experiences of these animals even within the fundamentally violent carceral settings in which they were trapped. Thus, in some ways, noting the tenderer emotions shines an even harsher light on what was necessarily lost among them as they reached their eventual destinations.

Cowboys and Cattle at Work

Although the nineteenth-century cattle drives have been abundantly mythologized in museum displays, films, paintings, and numerous other cultural artifacts as sites where American national identity was forged, particularly through the character and action of the cowboy, the cattle trail was fundamentally a location of work, for both cowboys and the animals they herded. As key connectors of other nodes along the early cattle carceral archipelago, cowboys and cows played an important role 'working together' in their biotechnological labors to move bodies—sentient, commodified bodies—from Texas to the awaiting rail lines in the cow towns. Although many scholars have established that much of the 'work' performed by animals during the early American colonial period as well as on the western ranches and cattle drives was in simply feeding themselves on pasture grasses and transporting themselves to awaiting railroad cars (Crosby 2003, 2004; Anderson 2004; Ogle 2013; Specht 2016), I want to consider this 'work' in its carceral context. To what extent can we understand the limits or extent of animal labor, agency, and oftentimes resistance to this work in the carceral spaces of the cattle trails? And in what ways did work on the trails create and sustain relationships between men and animals, as well as maintain—or lessen—the social and physical boundaries between them?

Blattner, Coulter, and Kymlicka (2020: 1–2, 7–11) argue that the largest, most exploited group of workers are nonhuman animals, especially in the central role they played in the development of both capitalism and colonialism. These scholars' broad-ranging analysis suggests, among other things, that animals might enjoy a sense of working or being part of a working relationship and that recognizing their work as such could be a source of meaning, dignity, or well-being for them. Among other observations, they assert that animals are competent actors who actively pursue their own interests and shape social relations, individually and collectively, and are not simply or merely victims who are acted upon. Of course, such shaping of social relations must be viewed in

context, and within the range of possible actions available. As Struthers Montford (2020) maintains, an understanding of historical animal lives requires an
engagement with both the *spatial* and the *relational* aspects of human-animal
interactions. The meeting grounds of interactions between humans and animals in carceral spaces—within the formerly wild, 'unclaimed' Texas pastures,
on the cattle drives, and in the cattle towns—offer glimpses into human and
nonhuman experiences, how humans and nonhumans existed and acted together, and their respective agency and ability to control their own behaviors
and choices.

As a useful framing for understanding the relationships across human and
animal labor, Fudge (2017: 270–271) asks, "What does it mean to work?" Specifically, what does it mean to a cow? She asserts that "animals' collaboration
at work is visible only when it is not obtained"—that is, when they resist (cf.
Nance 2015; McLean 2014; Scott 1998). Ordinarily, their work is invisible. As
Fudge writes, "The fact that we do not know what it means to an animal 'to
work' prevents us from seeing their consequences and imagining what they
could do with us." But we must also ask, what work would be in the animals'
interests? Fudge suggests that animals might wish to collaborate with humans, but this can be mistaken as pure instinct or mechanical reaction rather
than engaged participation. Perhaps collaboration is really just goodwill on
the part of the animal, in agreeing and obeying. And, of course, we must acknowledge the vast differences among nonhuman animal groups and individuals and thus their respective interests and capacities to participate with
humans (also a diverse category) in work.

Anderson (2004: 90) illustrates how the daily and oftentimes intense physical contact and proximity of farmers and their animals in seventeenth-century
America fostered an intimacy between them. She writes that "such closeness
could mitigate the exploitative potential of a relationship based legally and
theoretically on owners' absolute control. At the time, however, it could also
undermine the supposedly rigid boundaries between humans and animals."
These farmed animals received affection that we might more commonly asso-
ciate with dogs or other pets—they had names, lives, and relationships with
their 'masters'. In the case of the much more expansive nineteenth-century
western carceral archipelago, the close proximity of cowboys and animals
'working together' for months at a time on the cattle drive might have created
a similar sort of intimacy with humans and nonhumans experiencing many of
the same dangers, obstacles, weather, physical landscapes, lack of water, and
so on. Both humans and animals (including horses) transported themselves
through pastures, crossed rivers, and slept under the stars, in a sense working
alongside one another. This was their mutual work.

Examining the kinds of spaces that cowboys and cows shared and the work that each participated in tells us not only about their shared experiences of physical environments and conditions, but also about their relations with one another and the human-animal boundaries that were produced and/or maintained through those interactions. Historians of animals have contributed a number of important insights to understanding this boundary construction in historical contexts (e.g., Ritvo 1987; Few and Tortorici 2013).

Ohrem (2018: 135) contends that the West itself was less an actual place than it was a site of "transgression and experimentation, where one could work through the ontological ambiguity of what it means to be human and nonhuman." He offers some provocative ideas about the presumed animality of people on the North American frontier—human men made savage by close proximity to wild animals and the 'contagious' wilderness, but who ultimately tamed the wild into a domestic order à la Frederick Jackson Turner's "frontier thesis" (1893). The low social status of the typical cowhand or cowboy, uneducated and without means, frequently meant that cowboys were represented as sharing many of the animalized characteristics of bovine animals, particularly the longhorn; though praised for certain attributes such as toughness and their ability to withstand harsh conditions, they were also sometimes associated with a herdlike mentality, roughness, and stupidity, with such traits ultimately intended to be 'breeded out' of both men and animals. The low status of the cowboy mirrored the low status of the animal, both 'untamed' but with an opportunity to become domesticated. Yet, as I discuss in the next chapter, these men and animals are today re-narrated as national symbols of strength, independence, and endurance.

Focusing on the animality of men on the cattle trails who existed in close proximity to animals made the human-animal divide itself ambiguous, and allows us to challenge the very notions of animality and humanness. We are reminded that humans and animals are always co-constituted—one cannot exist without the other—with ontologies that are always relational, made only through difference and in relation to the other; that what are thought to be human characteristics are only conceivable through animals (and vice versa), even if the effects of this co-constitution have embedded within them asymmetrical relations of power (also see Creager and Jordon 2002; Tortorici 2015; Fudge 2002: 10). These power relations are foundational to the creation and sustainment of carceral spaces and practices: to state the obvious, unlike 'animalized' cowboys, the work of animalized animals on the cattle trails meant walking themselves to their deaths.

This animality of men on the cattle trails, in their close proximity to wild and untamed nature and animals, was a gendered construct, and the production of human bodies as masculine related closely to the gendered production of animal bodies with whom they appear in close proximity. It was also a racialized construct, with associated and presumed hierarchies of being. The Abilene, Kansas, entrepreneur Joseph McCoy complains with reference to cowboys that "the cattle are often shamefully abused on the cattle drive. Especially is this the case when Mexican help is employed" (1874: 86). McCoy's attempts at drawing distinctions between white and Hispanic cowboys and their relative animal tendency toward abuse must be framed within the larger context of McCoy's own contributions to the development of the industrial infrastructure for the capture, enclosure, transport, and slaughter of bovine animals, not least of which included the brutal chopping off of animal horns that prevented them from fitting into the railroad cars bound for Chicago abattoirs (see chapter 4).

Taking a broad view of numerous sites of labor, Coulter (2015: 23–29) argues that working conditions help forge human-animal relationships and influence both work performance and the forms of agency that humans and animals are able to express. Workers, she observes, are active social agents who can cooperate, question, contest, resist, and change workplace ideas and relations. Coulter outlines the many parameters that could impact the treatment of animals in the labor market, including the extent to which workers are on good terms with their bosses, with those on better terms treating animals better; and the material conditions of the job, pay, and overall job satisfaction, with those with dissatisfaction in these areas negatively affecting how they feel about themselves as well as their treatment of animals.

Cowboys' work on the cattle trails and that of ranch hands more generally—this hands-on, visceral, embodied work—was often devalued, poorly paid, often feminized, and quite precarious—contingent, erratic, and insecure (after Coulter 2015: 25)—with an obvious parallel to the slaughterhouse worker. Thus, a case could be made that one means by which the cowboy challenged his low status was to 'de-feminize' the labor with masculine actions and behaviors. However, mastery over animals might also manifest through emotional labor, that is, in aligning with the animals' plight, using varying degrees of kindness and force to accomplish human goals (32–35). Coulter illustrates with the example of the veterinary clinic, where emotional labor is continuously required; seeing animals hurt, sick, and being euthanized is a recurring part of the job. At the same time, Coulter (40–41) points out that many who work with animals do or did not have a choice about what work they perform(ed), especially in places with few employment opportunities (again, the work of the cowboy with parallels to the slaughterhouse worker)—in which case the job is just a job and a paycheck.

It is easy to demonize agricultural workers such as cowboys (Coulter 2015: 47), at least for their treatments of animals, but there are many differences among people and labor processes, different views of animals and feelings toward them, their work, and different reasons for doing their jobs—including that of the availability of opportunities in rural areas. Many cowboys seemed distanced from and disassociated to the pain and suffering of animals. Recall the cowhand who enjoyed watching the crazed cow running back and forth in a pen, panicked and frightened of the lightning storm (Garner, in Hunter 1924: 648). Dobie (1941: 154) expressed a rather savage delight in observing the suffering associated with hot iron branding—the "lusty bawl" and hanging tongue of an old bull being branded. And yet, as evidenced in the preceding sections of this chapter, these were not the most common responses of cowboys to animal suffering and pain on the cattle trails.

Cowboys and other observers who witnessed and described animals in distress firsthand seem to have approached their jobs more as tender 'care work', though knowing that they were keeping the animals alive only temporarily. Many understood the sorrow, grief, and despair of mother cows losing their calves (Thompson in Hunter 1924: 666), with one cowboy, referring to himself as an 'executioner' of calves on the trail, "murdering the innocents" (Isbell in Hunter 1924: 573) while their 'pitiful' mothers were pushed on. Dobie (1941: 154–55), in contrast to his cold witnessing of the branding scene, also occasionally softens emotionally toward the cattle, describing "frantic heifers separated from their calves, calves in misery for their mothers, [and] steers bawling for their lost powers of masculinity." Cox (1875: 50) notes the desperation felt by cattle caught by fire, and others note the torture of being burned alive; Johnson (Hunter 1924: 761) describes "cows suffering awfully" on the trail. Wilkeson (1885) observes the 'intelligence' of mother cows protecting their young, as does Cox (1895:196–97), the latter who describes mothers protecting their young and treating them like "well trained children." Rollins (1922: 248) mentions the anxiety of mother cows seeing their calves branded, and the calves "crying for mama." When Wilkeson (1885) describes what he considered bovine suicide, he writes that these animals were "tired of life. They found it hard, cold, hungry. They were depressed in spirit."

Cattle appearing in western films (see chapter 5) were almost always depicted in herds, negating the possibility that they possessed individual subjectivity with emotions, psychologies, desires, and interests, and thus reinforcing their status as killable commodities—in other words, validating the notion that their 'correct' placement was within the carceral archipelago. Cowboys' awareness of individual animal emotions, vulnerability, suffering, and anxieties on the 'real' cattle trail likewise did not challenge or reduce the carceral conditions of animals under their care. The intimate and close proximity of men and animals working together on the cattle trails offered unique and notable insights to human observers of animal life, and yet in the end, to the cowboy, the job was a job, and a paycheck.

Cowboy life on the cattle trail was challenging, difficult, and poorly paid—and, in fact, not paid until the cowboys reached the terminus of the trail in the cow town—in short, it was a job or experience that drew men with few other employment opportunities in the colonial (and colonizing) West. Following Coulter (2015), I surmise that despite the emotional care work involved, most of these were men with few other options and who aspired to 'become their own boss' as farmers or ranchers following the cattle drive and, hence, fully supported its carceral logic and structure as one with a personal promising future.

Animality, Agency, and Resistance

All of this being said, to what extent did cowboys and cows resist and challenge the conditions of their work on the cattle trails, if at all? Cowboys have often been portrayed as preferring the 'independence' of range labor to the grind of urban wage labor (Johnson 1996; Walker 1981; Tompkins 1992; Russell 1993). Stillman (2008) argues that both groups of workers are a kind of alienated labor often treated a lot like animals (and are similarly romanticized and objectified). The everyday life of the cowboy on the trail was one where the power relations with his trail boss and their differential social status oftentimes came into conflict. Cowboys' 'resistance' to the work of the cattle drive typically manifested as challenges to trail bosses' decisions and complaints about the type or amount of food and the harsh physical and environmental conditions, as well as other hardships such as sleeplessness and low wages (Sherow 2018: 135–136). One cowboy wrote of needing to put tobacco in his eyes to stay awake (Hunter 1924: 147).

Questions of agency and resistance to carceral conditions should also be posed with respect to how bovines experienced their labor on the cattle trails. Blattner, Coulter, and Kymlicka (2020) observe the long history of those who have no trouble seeing animal labor instrumentally, with animals as supposed willing participants in factory farms, labs, and circuses (cf. Fudge 2017: 270–271). Yet it would be hard to make the case that bovine animals would willingly work to collaborate in their own exploitation and eventual death via the cattle drive and other sites along the carceral archipelago. The cattle drive and cow towns were institutions of confinement where we find animal labor both producing and being produced as commodities; these are sites of animals working to transform their own bodies into commodities. Western films notably presented images of creatures who were without doubt willing participants in this enterprise and not resistant agents. But there is more to their personal stories.

Scholars notably have different ways of conceptualizing animal agency.

Some focus on defiance and resistance as agenic response to circumstances (Nance 2013; Hribal 2003; Wadiwel 2016), while others argue that animal agency can be manifested more broadly; even in the context of oppression animals contest, cope, negotiate, and/or care. All beings (human and non-human) are to a lesser or greater extent always limited in making their own choices, and moreover, and quite obviously, "self-reflexive intentionality is not a prerequisite to historical agency" (Fudge 2017: 262), as scholars of bovine animals have repeatedly articulated in their assessment of animal agency expressed as ecological impact (Crosby 2003; Anderson 2004; Specht 2016). Many scholars have also focused on increasing domestication, breeding practices, and carceral conditions as directly related to animals' capacity for, and indeed interest in, resisting their circumstances (e.g., Lambert 2018; Fudge 2017; Cronon 1991; Wadiwel 2016). Bovine animals clearly resisted the carceral practices and structures of the roundup, when they were first captured, confined, and declared human property. As the wild herds were gradually captured and declared property of individual humans, not only their status but also their lives and experiences dramatically changed.

Many scholars have focused on the basic property versus person debate in critical animal studies (e.g., Francione 2004, 2008; Wise 2000), but as Wadiwel (2015) observes, animals' status as property has had a violent impact on their lives but does not explain all the violence. Violence toward animals occurs whether they are 'owned' or not (consider violence toward wild animals, such as the vast extermination of the buffalo), even if carceral geographies tremendously facilitate it. Nor would having particular or different status within the law have likely changed much about their treatment; despite certain protections for certain animals within the law (then and now), the lack of bovine animals' legal standing simply made it easier to claim, buy, sell, and kill them. Violence to animals can occur with or without human ownership and/or property status, and at the same time, animal agency is not foreclosed by their status as property. However, carceral practices and geographies that turned cattle into property were, considered together, an act of tremendous violence, enacted in a systematic and structured way, that in turn impacted their behaviors, norms, and ability to resist.

Brown (2021: 11–14) provides a useful if broad overview of animal agency in his work on the animal history: "Human wills were shaped and constrained by what animals would and would not do." He continues, "Animals do things. . . . [They] have wills and intentions with which they shape the world. These intentions typically focus on immediate concerns—survival, food, water, shelter, sex, social connection, and avoiding suffering—topics that also occupy human minds to a great extent. Like human agency, animal agency (or more precisely, horse agency, dog agency, and so on) is constrained by structure . . .

[and] humans are a preeminent part of that structure" (Brown 2021: 13). Wadiwel (2021, 2016) also offers useful insights in returning to the question of how we might interpret an animal experience as one of resisting the suffering and pain of carcerality, recognizing that 'ordinary' violence toward animals, such as in horse racing or recreational fishing, carries with it a fundamental epistemic problem, which is that it is invisible; we live within a knowledge system that does not recognize such activities as violent. Much violence cannot be narrated by the subjects, as they have been so thoroughly silenced. Wadiwel notes that animals do reveal their noncompliance in many ways, although technologies are designed to conceal their noncompliance. A useful example he offers is the deceitfully ingenious design of the fishhook. It is designed so that the more the fish who is hooked struggles, the more painful the experience is. Thus, a nonstruggling fish can be 'misread' as compliant and not particularly suffering.

Colling (2020: 40) applies such insights to farmed animals, resonating with the earlier discussion on bovine family life, illustrating instances in which cows escaped their confinement to find their calves, being known to "travel long distances to find their stolen children." Many of the animal experiences witnessed on the cattle trails demonstrate pain and suffering, grief and despair—crying to see one of their own dead (Dobie 1941: 155–158) or despairing about lost calves and resisting confinement (and the inevitable backlash) in search of them.

We need to simultaneously ask, however (following Brown), what is in these animals' basic interests overall on the cattle trail? That is, to survive, to eat, to drink, to find shelter, and so on. Subjects might not be aware of their own confinement; they may understand their conditions as 'normal' and thus not resist them (Morin 2018). On the cattle drive, the basic interests of animals were likely eating, drinking, and resting. Surely, there are a range of differences and preferences among any group, herd, or species. Thus, we can acknowledge a great deal of resistance to structures of the carceral archipelago, including the cattle trail, but even where it is not found, it is important to keep in mind that social justice for animals is not just about the absence of these in any event. As Colling adds (2020: 59), if animals do not express or even experience misery and suffering, as with human beings, this does not necessarily imply that they enjoy their work, their circumstances, or their lives (and certainly not their deaths). I heed these scholars' admonishments that social justice for animals goes beyond relief from suffering and toward relief from human-imposed violence: ultimately, as Wadiwel (2016: 221) observes, a focus on animal suffering is not required to make assumptions about whether they are resisting their conditions or not; we only need assume that they would rather live than die (on a fish hook or in the slaughterhouse).

Fig. 3.4. Fort Worth "cattle drive," Fort Worth Stockyards, May 2021. Photo by Daniel Olivetti.

Conclusion: Re-narrating the Cattle Drive at Fort Worth

The "Great Die Up," the winter of 1886–1887, is regarded as the marker for the end of the 20-year cattle trailing period. The rural carceral archipelago terminated at the Kansas cow towns that would provide the means for railroad transport of animals to Chicago slaughterhouses and beyond. Overall, as Cronon eloquently observes, animals' lives had been redistributed across regional space: they were born in one place, fattened in another, and killed in still a third (Cronon 1991: 217–224; also see Rifkin 1991: 17). Many historical sites—particularly the cow towns themselves—serve as tourist 'living history' destinations that re-narrate the cattle trailing past to contemporary audiences. These sites offer archival and artifactual data, tools, and practices about historical animal lives that passed through them, but they also re-narrate a cattle-trailing past that symbolizes and celebrates men and animals as heroes that 'conquered the West' and established an American identity through hardship, toughness, and industriousness.

Before turning to these cow towns in the next chapter, I want to note briefly another sort of cow town operating today: the Fort Worth Stockyards National Historic District (a tourist area of the city of Fort Worth, Texas) offers today's tourist a type of re-creation of the Old Chisholm Trail, and the experiences of animals (and men) on it in the nineteenth century. The stockyards offer a twice-daily "cattle drive" using live longhorn animals (at 11:30 a.m. and 4:00 p.m.; see fig. 3.4). While obviously a 'Disneyfication' of the cattle trail experience, the daily cattle drives offer tourists a scene of longhorn cattle walking along on paved streets, herded by cowboys, and surrounded by all manner of mythological Wild West storefronts, saloons, shops, and hotels.

What, if anything, can these sites and these animals, highly exploited for the Fort Worth tourism industry, tell us about the historical animal experience? The objectification of these animals is tangible, and offers a good example of animal experience in carceral space; of being captured, 'driven', and held for others' use.

The Fort Worth cattle drives are particularly pathetic, with (probably older) tired animals slowly, and seemingly painfully, dragging themselves through the cement streets, hardly able to hold their horns up but constantly encouraged to do so by their handlers. In my observation the same was true for those subjected to the degradation of having tourists pay to sit on them and shout 'hee ya' for photo ops. These animals are clearly a big draw for the Texas tourism industry, and the price they pay with their bodies is perhaps only in escaping death by other means. Audiences do not seem to notice, or care, as they thoroughly appear to enjoy the 'Old West' atmosphere and the live-animal props accompanying it. While we can never know for sure whether the longhorns could be 'enjoying' their roles as tourist props to the rest of the town, their sluggish and downcast behavior certainly suggests they are indeed not. This sort of live-animal re-creation, again, is distinctly different from the exceedingly more 'upbeat' re-creations of the cattle trailing experience in the small Kansas towns I turn to next.

CHAPTER 4

Cow Towns and (Lost) Animal Lives

A NATIONAL CELEBRATION

A collective of people, places, and carceral logics and practices created the conditions for the intensive commodification of western bovine lives in the mid-nineteenth century. Small rural settlements known as 'cow towns' or 'cattle towns' appeared on the American landscape as terminal sites of bovine animals' walking journeys from Texas along the various cattle trails, nodal points where those trails met the awaiting railroad cars that would transport them to slaughterhouses in Chicago and other points north and east. The appearance and growth of these so-called cow towns in the mid-nineteenth century was enabled by a merging of carceral logics, structures, and practices, as well as a specific rural spatiality in the central plains that was fundamental to the nodal function the towns would play in the developing carceral archipelago. Infrastructural and technological developments at towns such as Abilene and Dodge City, Kansas, represent a singularly important carceral phenomenon of the nineteenth-century United States.

In addition to innovations in iron and steel technology that aided the production of barbed wire, innovations in transportation greatly advanced the development of the carceral archipelago via these cow towns. The railroad, specifically the "cattle car"—and, by 1881, the refrigerated car, which more cheaply hauled animal carcasses—was one of the most important technological developments that impacted and increased the trade in bovine animals and, indeed, that structured so much of cattle's' lived experience in the cow towns and beyond (see fig. 4.1). The companies that played a major role in de-

Fig. 4.1. Loading cattle on the Union Pacific Railway at Abilene, Kansas, 1870s. Reproduced with permission of the Kansas State Historical Society.

veloping the transcontinental railroad in the 1870s and 1880s were primarily British—the foreign 'cattle barons'—and they eventually also transported refrigerated cow carcasses to eastern cities and to Britain via ocean steamers. The central plains had already been benefiting from the railroad boom following the Civil War. As the Union Pacific's Eastern Division, later renamed the Kansas Pacific Railroad, continued pushing westward, negotiations ensued as to where to locate cattle shipping points. Entrepreneurial cattlemen and town builders who were set to profit enormously on the cattle trade attempted to garner political support for themselves and worked out agreements with railroad industrialists to develop their rural towns as shipping depots. Railroad development and sitings in the cow towns included an array of ancillary infrastructural (carceral) developments that impacted animal lives—railroad stations with telegraph facilities, supervisory personnel, and company-owned cow pens and stockyards.

Embedded within these infrastructural and technological developments was a shared carceral logic, underlying a number of other shared legal, political, and economic commonalities of rural agricultural areas that provided conditions for the carceral archipelago to take hold. Cattle towns shared a specific rural spatiality that diffused in specific ways throughout the rural American landscape in the nineteenth century, but most famously (or perhaps infamously) in the state of Kansas. Specht (2019) observes that whereas pigs in nineteenth-century North America were 'city' animals, cows were country animals. Thinking about the cattle trailing West as a carceral archipelago gives us an enhanced understanding of rurality itself—particularly the relationship of rurality and rural places to animal husbandry practices and agricultural industrial development, and the impact of these industries on small-town life and communities. It is the case that specific and 'distant' rural towns, with their unique histories, features, and laws, made them attractive nodal and developmental points in the production and commodification of bovine animal bodies and lives.

This chapter focuses on the location and nature of small Kansas cow towns, the empirical realities of animals' lived experiences in them, and how these experiences are symbolized and presented to modern audiences as tourist attractions. One of the most important things to recognize about the cow towns is that those in positions of influence were and are able to represent the treatment of animals as part of everyday animal husbandry; or, if not that, represent the animals as participants in an American past to be honored and celebrated. In this chapter I specifically discuss the towns of 'Old Abilene' and Dodge City, Kansas, focusing on how longhorn cattle became important cultural symbols of the towns and how their lives are re-narrated in museums and other sites. They are presented to contemporary audiences as somehow important players in the American past, as participants in the heroic conquest of the West, as a hearty breed whose characteristics are closely tied with American national identity itself. Part of my analysis rests on study of the afterlives of longhorns—re-presented as taxidermied animals in museum dioramas—as well as replica statues, such as the "El Capitan" monument that is a tourist centerpiece in present-day Dodge City.

As I focus on the importance of longhorn cattle as central symbols to cow towns' history, legend, and lore, this inexorably leads to particular attention to the longhorn *horns* that are highlighted in these museums. I juxtapose the animals and the symbolism of their horns against the 'reality' of the business problems that the horns posed to town builders and the cruel, painful practice of horn removal—a contradictory practice in that while the horns were (and are) celebrated for their magnificence, they were (and are) at the same time subject to erasure. The impressive horns of longhorn cattle became part of the cattle drive lore, but it must be noted that their lived, tortuous experiences of 'dehorning' was a carceral practice that arguably originated in these cow towns. Yet, most artifactual evidence in the cow towns, including that of horn displays, re-narrates to contemporary audiences a version of the mythical and grand Old West—a sort of re-carceralizing of the animals on an ongoing basis.

Carceral Structures and the Cow Town Past: Abilene and Dodge City

The emergence and growth of cow towns were considerably enabled via the spatial and geographical characteristics of rural places in the mid-nineteenth-century United States. The combination of 'free' land, 'free' animals, and 'free' grass upon which to feed them, combined with the entrepreneurial agenda of men in rural areas through which the U.S. railroad was beginning to pass, converged into an intensive carceral archipelago.

A number of authors outline the rich historiography of rural studies over the past several decades that offer insights for the present study (e.g., Argent 2017, 2019; Woods 2009; Cloke, Marsden, and Mooney 2006). Woods (2009), for example, argues that the social meanings that have been ascribed to rural places oftentimes emphasize their mythologized or romantic pasts. Meanwhile the 'real' places are made invisible by the predominance of state-sponsored simplifications of monocultural agriculture focused on a single outcome, oftentimes a single crop or industry (Scott 1998). Rural America is also oftentimes associated with putative antimodern concepts and attributes (Immerwahr 2023), yet is dominated by distinctly modern corporate influence that nonetheless remains hidden.[1]

In the case of the cow towns, we see this especially with the surging railroad industry as well as rural land laws that only loosely governed the creation of localized infrastructural and technological carceral developments such as barbed wire fencing of grazing lands, which together enabled the cattle industry to rapidly flourish. The rural towns in this case, then, places like Abilene and Dodge City, Kansas, were economically vulnerable to the maneuverings of exploitative legal and political entrepreneurs that contributed to industrial violence in the form of meat processing in the United States on a scale today that would have been difficult to imagine in the nineteenth century.

The cow towns were specifically sited locations for the railroad infrastructure as well as sites where a wide array of carceral tools and practices were emplaced to modify, discipline, and control bovine bodies. In addition, a number of local enterprises sprang up to support and profit from the demands of the growing population of people and animals—those related to consumer goods and services, dry goods and retail outlets, hotels and boardinghouses, saloons and dance halls, banks, doctors' and attorneys' offices, laundries, barber shops, drug stores, and blacksmith and livery shops, as well as realty and contractor offices. The first cow town along the Chisholm Trail was Abilene, Kansas. Other Kansas towns would quickly follow in the 1870s and compete with it: Ellsworth, Wichita, Dodge City, and Caldwell (see fig. 3.1). (Dykstra 1968 offers a constructive overview of the sitings, development, and competi-

Fig. 4.2. First railroad shipping point for Texas cattle, Abilene, Kansas, 1867. Alexander Gardner's photograph of the stockyards, loading ramp, and rail cars shows the facility shortly after it had opened for business. Courtesy Library of Congress.

tion among these towns, and Specht 2017 focuses specifically on the town of Ellsworth, where little 'living history' is available to today's tourists.)

Local politics in places like Abilene and Dodge City centered on conflict between critics and defenders of the cattle trade. Critics were most often farmers who feared their crops would be trampled by the incoming animals or feared infection of their domestic herds by the 'Texas fever' that longhorn cows carried. Dodge City, located on an offshoot of the Chisholm Trail known as the Western Trail, owed much of its success in the cattle trade to the shifting westward of a quarantine line that prevented tick-infected cattle from entering areas of Kansas (Ogle 2013: 18–19; Skaggs 1973: 73–77; Strom 2010; Specht 2019: 153–160).

Community sensibilities about capturing the cow town past have changed over time—with those in the present moment attempting to (re)capture this Old West past and re-create it, overshadowing previous attempts to cosmopolitanize and modernize in the post–World War II period (Hook 2021). Much of the lore of these towns focuses today on the stories of the men (and some women) responsible for the emergent cattle industry and Old West mythology, the likes of Joseph McCoy, Wyatt Earp, and Wild Bill Hickok (the one-time marshal of Abilene who seems to be known primarily for accidentally shooting his own deputy).

The primacy of the Kansas towns in the cattle trade ended when the railroad trunk lines moved south to Texas and animals could be shipped directly from there (Wishart 2004: 800–801). But the early development of the railway in the cow towns and information about anticipated animal experiences within it are worth noting. The trains bound for Chicago or Kansas City purportedly stopped every ten miles to let the animals off to eat and water (McCoy 1874). Cox (1895: 198), citing a Texas cattleman writing for the *National Live Stock Journal,* advises,

> The cars for transportation should be well bedded, and food for the entire trip transported with the stock. Arrangements should be made for a through trip when starting. Food, water, and careful watching by the herdsman will land them at the place of disembarkation but little damaged by the trip. Care should be taken not to crowd too many in one car. Thirty head can be taken if they are properly cared for. . . . After reaching the terminus of their journey by rail, a week's rest, in dry lots, should be granted them, with the same kind of food as before shipment.

The writer states that if these and other measures were taken, the animals "can be imported and acclimated at not exceeding a loss of ten per cent." These admonitions make sense within the context of protecting one's speculative assets; receivers paid for animals in advance, which was to McCoy much like "gambling on the future price or value of stock" (1874: 298–299). That said, much evidence suggests that such procedures were not remotely adhered to. Rollins (1922: 262–264) observes that upon arrival in the cow town, animals were "delivered . . . into the purgatory of foodless, waterless miles of a bumping railway journey." Commentators often remarked on the brutality of the animals' railroad journeys, for example, by describing the brutal sawing off of horns if they did not fit into the railroad car (Hook 2021; Specht 2016; Dobie 1941). In such cases the experience of the cattle car would have been one of crowding and extreme pain and probable bleeding.

One of the earliest and most successful Kansas entrepreneurs to link the cattle trails with the railroad was the dealer and town promotor Joseph McCoy, who built stock pens near the rail depot on 250 acres of land in Abilene to hold cows awaiting shipment north on the Kansas Pacific Railroad (see fig. 4.2). As Rifkin observes, "cattle stepped over the divide and onto the railcars, thus changing the course of America's history." William Hawks, self-described 'historian of the plains', wrote to George Saunders, the president of the Texas Cattlemen's Association (Hunter 1924: 1025–1026):

> I have spent 30 years gathering true data of the good old days, when men
> were men, and would offer you everything they had, even to their lives, and
> they thought it was right. . . . The Chisholm Trail, the Old Shawnee Trail,
> Middle or West Shawnee Trail from Red River north to Abilene and Baxter
> Springs. . . . Joe McCoy started his yards in Abilene, KS, July 1, 1867, and sent
> WW Suggs down to pilot the herds to the new shipping place. . . . The first
> cattle shipped out of Abilene was on September 5, 1867, and there were 36,000
> shipped from that point during the balance of the year.

McCoy convinced the railroad to construct a rail siding for a cow pen at the
Abilene depot, and then pay him a commission on every carload of animals
shipped. The trip from Fort Worth to Abilene was five hundred miles (about
a two-month journey). As Hawks notes, the first twenty-car shipment of cows
from Abilene to Chicago was in September of 1867. McCoy (1874: 52) outlines
this shipment of animals in the twenty cars; by 1871 Abilene was processing
700,000 longhorns annually—with a total of five million animals over five
years driven through Abilene, all bound for the abattoirs in St. Louis and Chicago. This north-south cattle complex expanded in the 1870s, as the demand
for beef, tallow, and hides greatly expanded amid post–Civil War prosperity.
(McCoy was eventually financially ruined due to competing town conflicts
over the quarantining of animals carrying the Texas tick.)

The cow pens at the terminus of the cattle drives were central carceral
structures in the cow towns. Picking up from the previous discussion of the
pens originating on the range, these early cow pens represented significant
developments in carceral logic and technology. McCoy (1874: 221) comments
on the use of these structures, in which the animals confined in them were
fattened before transport by rail to slaughter. Taking some evident enjoyment
from witnessing the cruel outcomes in tying the animals by neck chains in
stalls for feeding, he shares:

> Being tied up, they become clumsy and almost lose the use of their limbs.
> So it is common to let them out in an enclosure once or twice during the
> two or three weeks previous to shipping them to market, and let them run
> about and recover the proper use of themselves. It is amusing then to see the
> dumb brute, rejoiced at regaining his liberty, and to get once more into the
> sunshine. He attempts to kick up his heels, which usually results in falling
> headlong on his nose; then he will look foolish, and walk about the yard care-
> fully but awkwardly, until he regains his confidence, when he will spurt off
> at some tangent only to be again hopelessly discomfited by tumbling down.

A distinct structural continuity can be seen across these early corrals and the
development and design of the earliest slaughterhouses. Historical and histo-

Fig. 4.3. Old Abilene Town today. A tourist brochure advertises "Gunfights, Can-Can Dancers, Stagecoach Rides, Old Time Photos & MUCH more!" Photo by Daniel Olivetti.

riographical studies of the expansion of animal slaughterhouses in the United States are abundant, from the early twentieth century onward, including studies of their structural, infrastructural, and technological developments (Giedion 1948; Pacyga 2015; Rifkin 1992; Pachirat 2011). Study of the animal slaughterhouse proper is beyond the scope of this study, but it is worth mentioning that the increasing carceralization of the western U.S. landscape was built on the basic designs of early cow pen structures.

Today's Old Abilene Town (fig. 4.3) is a re-creation or replica town, focusing a great deal on Joseph McCoy and the millions of cattle that would eventually be driven to and through it. The town features a replica of McCoy's Great Western Cattle Company, as well as many of the fabled Old West structures such as a general dry goods store, saloon, hotel, stagecoach, railroad depot, cattle loading pen, settler's cabin, carriage house, and a grave marker for an anonymous Texas cattle driver "who died in a stampede on May 1, 1869," among others. The town offers daily main street 'gunfights' in season, and the cattle trailing experience is visually captured in a museum that describes a typical cattle drive that included ten cowboys, a trail boss, a cook, a horse wrangler, and a lead steer in a triangular formation around the herd. Another building houses a 1:24 scale model of the nineteenth-century town, which features, among other tools and artifacts, a mounted longhorn skull with enormous horns. According to the Old Abilene Town curator (Hook 2021), "The longhorn was bought by Roger Watt in the 1990s from a ranch in Oklahoma. He raised it like a pet. Never had plans for using it for meat. So when it died, he kept the skull and horns."

Of the towns that developed along the cattle trails, no place is more iconic than Dodge City, Kansas, the 'Queen of the Cow Towns'. Dodge City, a site that had served as a center for the trade in buffalo hides from 1872 to 1874, subsequently flourished within the Texas cattle market from 1876 to 1885. The town was founded in 1872, but within just three years, the buffalo herds were essentially gone. Cattle driving quickly took over as the city's primary source of income, and at the height of the industry, 500,000 cattle passed through Dodge City in a year. The first longhorn cattle drive arrived in Dodge City in 1875. From 1875 to 1886, millions of animals were driven from Texas to Dodge City along the Chisholm, Western, and Santa Fe Trails. Net prices were averaging $30 per animal, which brought millions of dollars in return for cattlemen (Shillingberg 2009: 287).

Although Dodge City's popular depiction was formed via Old West Hollywood, Wyatt Earp, and the popular television show *Gunsmoke*, it became a major tourist destination as a major shipping port for cattle. Today, Dodge City's reconstructed history primarily focuses on cowboys and cattlemen— the big personalities. Dean (2021: 227) notes that such public history displays are common, with animals serving as mostly backdrops or 'sidekicks', albeit important ones, to human dramas, as commodity, specimen, or symbol. Yet, Dodge City offers Old West and cattle driving history that far surpasses in scale that of Abilene or the other towns, perhaps because the excessively large (40,000 animals plus) cattle feedlots of the National and Cargill companies surround the town of Dodge City today, complete with 'scenic' overlook sites to the feedlots, though the original stockyards have been paved over.

The town also offers an elaborate replica village circa 1876, the expansive Boot Hill Museum with thousands of artifacts including of barbed wire (and a 'Fencing the West' display), branding irons, and numerous other carceral tools and instruments (see fig. 2.4). Extensive maps are available to find one's way around, following the statuary and information about the outsized human personalities; a Boot Hill Cemetery; and a still operating (so I am told) longhorn park zoo near the regional airport.

There is much going on symbolically in this cow town, so in the next two sections I dissect a bit more about the Dodge City of today and the ways it offers an important window into how the history of cattle as symbols of American national history and identity has been created and maintained there. This, via 'taxidermied' animals on display in its Boot Hill Museum, as well as more generally its centerpiece longhorn statue of El Capitan, both of which add important re-narrations to the carceral past though through quite different means and materials.

Dodge City Taxidermy as Carceral Condition

In comparison to sites where one can glimpse real longhorn animals today, such as at the Fort Worth live 'cattle drive' where we see slow-moving, pathetically and painfully objectified animals, much more seemingly animated representations of longhorns, though now long dead, appear at sites such as the Boot Hill Museum of Dodge City—in taxidermied form. One specific type of museum artifact, the taxidermied animal, helps us think further about the tension between carceral logic and archival historical evidence, evidence that is presented as both thematically popular and 'authoritative'.

Museum studies and scholarship on collections of material artifacts such as those found in natural history museums, particularly those that focus on the practice of taxidermy, offer important insights into past animal lives (Alio 2018; Haraway 1993; Patchett 2008). Although I do not develop a biological (cellular) profile of the afterlives of nineteenth-century cattle in this work by examination of veterinarian tools à la Cox (2015), Cox's astute observations help us question where, today, if anywhere, do we find historical cows' biological remains—that is, skin or other body parts of these animals. Study of carceral instruments, spaces, and technologies should arguably include a study of taxidermied animals; these animal bodies or body parts, not ending up as human food or products such as leather, seem instead to remain as a seductive symbol of a mythologized American past.

Dean (2021), in her work on public history, posits that museums—even those devoted to the study of animals, such as natural history museums—are actually 'empty' of animals, empty of animal stories. Even in these museums animals appear only as objects and commodities, specimens, or symbols associated with human dramas, absent from their own histories and stories. This is the case in the western cow towns that celebrate their historical human celebrities such as Wyatt Earp in Dodge City, a town whose celebrity was nonetheless based on the emergent cattle trade. To Dean, the truly historical animal, the individual who is the subject of their own life and story, is only beginning to appear on the margins, such as in artistic provocations, in small museums, in temporary exhibits, and in social media (e.g., Gustafsson and Haapoja's *History According to Cattle* exhibition, 2015).

A small number of taxidermied longhorns appear as representational icons from the mythic western past in cow towns and other sites along the cattle carceral archipelago. Two taxidermied animals are on display at the Boot Hill Museum in Dodge City, featured within an elaborate cattle drive diorama that

Fig. 4.4. Taxidermied longhorn situated in a diorama of the Texas-Kansas cattle drive. Boot Hill Museum, Dodge City, Kansas. Photo by Daniel Olivetti.

also includes accoutrements of life on the trail for cowboys (fig. 4.4); and in the Natural History Hall of the Panhandle-Plains Historical Museum in Canyon, Texas, which features a large glass-covered diorama with a longhorn as centerpiece. These dioramas contain the remains of animals who were living individuals. Thus Dean's (2021: 230) insights inspire questions about whether these taxidermied animals are offered any backstory, any history that makes of them individuals? Do they have lives, experiences, locations, or deaths?

According to the Boot Hill Museum curator (Bell 2021), the light-colored longhorn (fig. 4.4), on loan to the museum, was "cape mounted"—meaning that the real animal's neck to the shoulders is included as well as the head. The other, a black longhorn, was purchased for the museum. Only a few archival notes are available about them: "[The] large brown and white long horn steer head is cape mounted. He [lived at] the Dodge City Long Horn Park [established in 1996] near the Dodge City Regional Airport. He was shot [in 2007] because he exhibited aggressiveness. . . . The only thing we know about the black long horn is it was a purchase [around 2020]."

Taxidermy is a way of ordering and representing the world, particularly the relationship between humans and animals. Alio (2021) helps explain how the connection between realism and the emergence of taxidermy was related to the subjugation of nature and the colonial objectifying of nature. Along this line, Haraway (1993) contends that taxidermied animals whose material remains in western museums are important colonial artifacts (indeed, they are important colonial-carceral artifacts). Haraway (1993: 242) discusses the iconic display of gorillas at the Museum of Natural History in New York City, explaining that the animal skins, placed within the story of the diorama, were used "within a masculinist eugenic moment" to both conceal the human-animal relationship and fulfill an idea of manhood. Taxidermied animal skin can also represent loss, abuse, subjugation, and mourning. Zivkovic (2021) proposes that the skin/hide is the starting point to examine the interaction and relation of humans and nonhumans. The mutilated, stuffed animal is more than a symbol; it is a tactile object, and museum dioramas transform these animals into spectacles. In the right arrangements, dead animals in dioramas may seem alive and engaged, just on the point of movement, and thus, through their bodies, are made to 'co-constitute' spiritual or cultural stories (after Mize 2021).

Alio (2018) notes that taxidermy, once the province of natural history and dedicated to the pursuit of lifelike realism, has recently resurfaced in the world of contemporary art, culture, and interior design. Drawing on what is known as the 'speculative turn' in philosophy and recovering past alternative histories of art and materiality from a biopolitical perspective, Aloi theorizes what he calls "speculative taxidermy": a powerful interface that unlocks new ethical and political opportunities in human-animal relationships and speaks to how animal representation conveys the urgency of addressing climate change, capitalist exploitation, and mass extinction. Taxidermy in this way operates as a powerful interface between humans and animals, rooted in a shared ontological and physical vulnerability, offering animal skin in the gallery space as a productive opportunity to rethink ethical and political stances in human-animal relationships.

Patchett (2008), too, provides a useful overview on how we might understand the afterlives of animals, a way to recover taxidermied animals within the context of material geographies (even though her empirical focus is more on the practices of taxidermy than on the animal lives behind them). In her work she also faced a situation much like the two longhorns on display at the Boot Hill Museum: little documentary evidence was available to piece together how a roomful of tigers' heads (mounted at a museum in Scotland) was brought into being. Though she helpfully illustrates that there is a lack of fixity of meaning to any diorama or taxidermied animal, we must ask what the animal is meant to represent; in the case of the tigers, 'archetypes of British aristocratic adventure' or trophies of the British colonial enterprise. The lived histories of the animals disappears, and in their place the wall mounts are a means of taking possession of them historically (21–22). The animals retain both aesthetic and ontological ambiguity, yet their skins and traces remain a 'shadowy presence' of real prior lives, framed by human desires. Ultimately Patchett tacks back and forth between the representational and the nonrepresentational, arguing for the complementary use of, for example, photographs to understand killing practices and engaging in a type of 'restorative ethnography' involving contemporary animals (after Lorimer 2006).

Ultimately, neither of the taxidermied longhorns in the Boot Hill Museum diorama appear to have names, ages, or particularized stories; they are meant to represent composite identities and are presented in majestic, hagiographic terms. Yet right beside their bodily remains are cases and exhibits of material carceral objects—for example, branding irons, barbed wire, and an array of tools used in their capture, enclosure, forced movement, and death (see fig. 2.4). It seems incongruous at best to position these animals, with their enormous, beautiful horns, alongside these gruesome carceral tools. Yet what emerges in the exhibit hall in its entirety is a seamless mythic story about these animals' co-history making efforts in the grand western colonial adventure in the Old West. This is but one example among many of how the materiality of bovine lives and bodies have been deployed to smooth over colonial-carceral encounters and more specific historical geographies.

El Capitan and the Longhorn as Cultural Symbol

Rather than the taxidermied animals such as those at the Boot Hill Museum, who were once live animals with individual experiences, most sites narrating the cattle trailing and cow-town past feature some sort of statuary or replica longhorn animals. Both serve similar symbolic purposes, though, in narrating a particular heroic and nationalistic version of the American past. As Halley (2012: 5) observes, "Cows hold a central, symbolic place in a national U.S. story of origins. . . . The story of the meat industry mirrors the story of national economic development." The "El Capitan" sculpture in Dodge City serves as a good example of this symbolic importance: it is the centerpiece and most famous landmark of Dodge City. Unlike the 'background' cattle that become filler to cowboy and cattlemen stories and history, El Capitan is placed center stage on Wyatt Earp Boulevard, and is explicitly aligned with human identity and characteristics.

El Capitan is not intended to represent a real individual animal that lived in history; rather, the depiction serves as a collective symbol for all of the superior longhorn steers who led and essentially managed other animals on the cattle drive from Texas to Kansas (Bell 2016; M. 2019; "El Capitan" 2019). The statue is a life-size bronze sculpture of a Texas longhorn steer (that is, a castrated male),[2] situated in a park-like space above a sidewalk, which gives an impression to the viewer of even greater size and fierceness. The sculpture was created by the Tempe, Arizona, artist Jasper D'Ambrosi and erected in 1980. The statue's inscription reads, "This statue commemorates the Texas Long-horn that gave Dodge City its place in history as 'Queen of the Cowtowns.' The Longhorns are descendants of Spanish cattle brought to Mexico in the 16th century. Between 1875 and 1886, over 4 million head were driven up the trail to the Santa Fe railhead in Dodge City."

Cows and cattle as features of the heroic conquest of the American frontier are common components of cow town museums, with displays and artifacts oftentimes focusing on horns of the animals, including real horns from real animals, such as that displayed in Old Abilene Town, as well as artifacts and objects (including chairs) fashioned out of the cow horns. This focus on the horns is a way of representing the special longhorn breed of cattle, with the horns themselves representing a type of fierceness and intelligence not found in other cattle breeds.

While Texas longhorns were considered a distinct breed of cow in the nine-teenth century (White 1992: 252–253), as McTavish et al. (2013) found, they were related to but not exactly the same as the Spanish animals of earlier cen-turies; instead, they are a mixture of Mexican and Anglo-American breeds that had long existed in the American South. Anderson (2004) observes that cattle were relocated to the eastern colonies by British settlers, with a Durham short-horn breed arriving as early as 1783 and, according to the National Ranching Heritage Center, followed by Herefords in 1817 and Angus in 1873. The Durham shorthorn illustrates well a type of biopolitical power focused on the modifi-cation and modulation of aggregations of animal bodies and their collective properties such as that found in selective breeding programs (Hodgetts and Lorimer 2020: 15). Many scholars have noted that after the Civil War, the Texas longhorns began to be mixed with English cattle moving westward or brought to Texas earlier by Anglo settlers, 'breeding up' or 'breeding out' the lean long-horn characteristics, particularly as they wandered woodlands and forests in semiferal herds with uncontrolled feeding, reproduction, and movement (Crosby 2004: 171–195; Kilgore 1983; Anderson 2004: 120–24; Specht 2016).

Many eyewitness commentators described the general characteristics of longhorns in stunningly hagiographic terms. Wilkeson (1885: 6) states that Texas longhorns are self-reliant and intelligent: "Almost all men who have han-dled stock firmly believe that [these] animals have well-established methods of thought and an undetected system of communication. I have seen cattle do things where cause and effect were clearly reasoned out." Dobie (1941: 143–147) comments on longhorn bulls' fighting (and again, their vocalizing):

> They sharpened their horns purposefully against trees and brush to prepare
> for fighting. . . . [One] not only gored the earth but thrust his horns into the

tough stems of a cenizo bush and, jerking and twisting his head from side
to side, broke the bush to stubble. . . . It is impossible to convey sounds in
print—the wild, raucous hair-raising sounds made by the old range bulls;
their growls; their threats loud and deep that seemed to blast the earth; their
uplifted notes carrying like the finest coyote bark; their expressions of pride
and fury. . . . Some other bulls are quick . . . but none of them can bawl, bellow,
mutter and rage like the bulls of Spanish breed and none can move with such
swiftness.

Citing Dobie's journalistic accounts of the Texas longhorns, Specht describes
these animals as 'hardy, independent, intelligent, wild, tough, proud, ornery,
and with high endurance' (as compared to domestic cattle, which Dobie says
"are stupid"; Specht 2016: 350–351). And to Charles Goodnight, the first cattle
king to move longhorns into the Texas Panhandle, on his JA Ranch in Palo
Duro Canyon in 1876, "the longhorn can go farther without water and endure
more suffering than others" (quoted in Worcester 1987: 60). Goodnight and
others believed these animals were fit and able to survive severe snow storms,
droughts, starvation, fire, and the fiercest bands of wolves. Such hagiographic
descriptions are economically aspirational; they belie the experiences of the
animals within carceral spaces that constrained and affected the range and
norms of their behaviors. That said, the discourse around breed shifts over
time, such that Texas longhorns were initially regarded as hearty, superior
cattle with pedigree but eventually became the subject of a registry invested
in an altered heritage identity and mixture with other bovine breeds.[3]

Holloway et al. (2009: 395) discuss the concept of breed itself as emerging in the late eighteenth century and institutionalized into breed societies
and organizations that championed, catalogued, and promoted particular
breeds. Ritvo (2010: 132–156) offers useful insights on historical human-
animal boundary maintenance related to domestication and breed. Ritvo's *The Animal Estate* (1987) illustrates how animals, particularly cows and
sheep, fit into the 'hierarchy of being' prevalent within the British empire—
human-human hierarchies as well as human-animal hierarchies. As human
attitudes toward animals changed in the nineteenth century—from beings
with agency to beings becoming mere property—it was particularly domesticated animals, including the horse and dog, that set the minimal standard
for obedience, higher levels of cooperation, and devotion (1987: 21; also see
Derry 2003: xvi, 198).

Ritvo traces how notions of social class were projected onto classifications
of domesticated animals in nineteenth-century Britain. The magnificence of
white, 'purebred' cows in Scotland, the 'Wild Cattle of Chillingham', became
linked with certain aristocratic humans and thereby reified British notions of

race, descent, and pedigree: "an almost totemic conflation of the bovines with their owners" (Ritvo 2010: 133–135; also see Ritvo 1987: 45–52). Any calves not conforming to the ideal type were immediately killed in order to maintain that association. Thus, Ritvo argues that when people celebrate the pedigree (origin and identity) of their animals, what they are really doing is 'exalting the prestige of their own ancestry' (2010: 6).

The paintings of the elite or purebred bovine animals that Ritvo studied (1987: 58–59, 74) depicted them within the aesthetical setting of the quaint, pastoral English countryside of the early nineteenth century, often devoid of humans. They were evocatively portrayed with enormous rectangular bodies and tiny heads with short horns that endorsed a particular taste of their bodily meat—that is, one with a higher fat content than were typical of those in the United States at the time. Pawley's (2016) discussion of cattle portraiture of the first half of the nineteenth century shows that to a growing community of breeders, lithograph and woodcut portraits of cattle became very popular in broadsides, catalogues, agricultural journals, and manuals, praising those with big rectangular bodies and tiny legs, showing how American breeders committed themselves to British animals and British theories of inheritability. This knowledge conveyed through portraiture would thus change bodies themselves (Pawley 2016: 40–42).

Ritvo's focus on British paintings of 'elite' cows is paralleled by a virtual mini-industry of such paintings and drawings depicting cattle drives and cattle ranching in the United States. In the historical American context, the paintings and sculpture of Frederick Remington (1861–1909), Charles Russell (1864–1926), Frank Reaugh (1860–1945), and other western artists provide similar examples of such hagiographic representations of bovine animals (which also appeared in illustrated magazines). At the same time, a phenomenally large number of so-called folk artists provided similar examples of representations of western bovine animals.

It was, however, actually the appearance of the cowboy in American art that brought cows into the frame. The first image of a cowboy was featured along with cows in a drawing by Alfred R. Waud for *Harper's Weekly* titled, "Drove of Texas Cattle Crossing a Stream" (5 October 1867; reproduced in Goetzmann and Reese 1983). Cows in such painters' works are depicted impressionistically, typically within dramatic or melodramatic scenes, with the artist attempting to capture the sounds and smells and sights of the earth moving, the routine as well as the extraordinary efforts required by cowboys to maintain the cows, and with a pronounced focus on the effects of light, using a limited range of soft colors.

Both Remington and Russell favored mounted cowboys thundering through a cattle town at the end of a long drive (Goetzmann and Reese 1983;

Gerald Peters Collection 1988: 59). The artist Frank Raeugh was nicknamed the "Rembrandt of the Longhorns," and about two hundred of his watercolor paintings of longhorns are held at the Harry Ransom Center at the University of Texas at Austin. The exhibit of Reaugh's painting "Approaching Herd" at the Panhandle-Plains Historical Museum in Canyon, Texas, alerts the visitor that this was probably Reaugh's masterpiece: "They were beautiful animals. They were very wild." Reaugh's animals appear bathed in warm light and soft grass, and oftentimes seem to be looking directly at the artist—as if mutually participating in the scene, knowing and relaxed. Such romanticized renditions of the longhorn cattle, from taxidermied animals to statues, paintings, and sculptures, belies the carceral reality that these animals experienced.

Taking a cue from Ritvo (1987, 2010), we can see how the 'magnificence' and array of other longhorn traits highlighted in the cow towns and by commentators of the period—particularly traits of independence and toughness—associated the cow towns with a uniquely American past that parallels not only the social hierarchies of the cattle barons, cattlemen, and other successful town builders, but more generally an American mythical conquest of the frontier by the humble but heroic cowboy and his animals (after Turner 1893; Heffernan and Morin 2021). Woods (2017) helps clarify this relationship between breed and national identity. Though focusing on Hereford cattle (not longhorns), she demonstrates how the breed of the animal, especially a breed that can be cast or represented as 'native', is often associated with national identity. Woods compares this to colonial belonging and legitimacy, and to the empire project itself: being native intersected with ideas about nationhood and citizenship (2017: 4, 12).

In the case of the longhorns, certainly one of the main themes suggested in the Kansas cow towns is that they are part of the American historical fabric: they are native to American history and destiny. Such mythology also compared longhorns to the buffalo and their disappearance, which made them seem ever more indigenous to North America rather than imported (forced) migrants.

Though the longhorn traits were ultimately bred out in industrial preference for the meatier British animals, they would remain part of cow town history as well as a symbol of Texas pride and statehood itself; a symbol of a simpler historical time focused on the romantic cowboy and enterprising cattlemen (Specht 2016). But there is something deeply contradictory and troubling about the mythologizing of the longhorn breed, particularly with respect to their remarkable horns, which requires analysis. That is, the contradiction between the celebration of the longhorn horns and the everyday reality of horn removal due to the business problems that they represented to cattlemen and others when the animals were enclosed and confined. In the next section I take up a most cruel of carceral practices that also arguably originated in the Kansas cow towns, that of "dehorning."

Dehorning: Carceral Barbarity

The Texas longhorns are so named, obviously, for their magnificent, extraordinary 'long horns'; horns that have been the subject of numerous recorded observations, reports, studies, and stories (e.g., Cox 1895; Dobie 1941; Specht 2016). One Texan whose ranch covered thousands of acres in south Texas in the 1880s and 1890s, George West, describes one of his prized steers this way: "Born on the West ranch in Live Oak County in 1883, [this 16-year-old steer had] not a drop of improved blood in his veins, and he weighed close to 1700 pounds. His horns had an upward curvature, and when he stood at rest their tips were over eight feet above his hoofs. They measured seven feet and nine inches straight across, and about nine feet following the curves. . . . [It was the] noblest specimen of the type [I] had ever owned" (as quoted in Shackelford 2015: 34). Dobie devotes an entire chapter of his book *The Longhorns* (1941: 203–220) to the horns themselves, describing numerous competitions for the longest stretch of horn from tip to tip, their curvature design, material composition, and dimensions. "The natural twist of horns," he writes, "nature's curves, give them far more character, interest and beauty than mere length" (205). Dobie describes Champion, a family animal who he says was 'the best known steer in the world' and whose likeness appeared for forty years on postcards and in magazines, newspapers, textbooks, and trade books: "To scratch the root of his tail with a horn-tip [Champion] had but to turn his head slightly" (205–206). Like other wild and domesticated animals with horns, longhorn cattle use them to protect themselves and their offspring against predators, for fighting, scratching, obtaining food, clearing the way to move through rough terrain, and so on. These animals, 'left to make their own way' in the wild, developed hardiness, fleetness, and self-dependence. They grew horns to fight off wolves, to hook down succulent mistletoe out of trees, and to sweep out of the way thorned branches protecting sparse tufts of grass on the parched ground (215).

Such observations are noteworthy not only because the horns are useful physical appendages that also carry significant symbolic portent, especially for Texans— those from "the Longhorn State" (Specht 2016)—but also because the lived experience of animals with such prodigious horns were threatened by singularly hostile repercussions in carceral spaces. Though dehorning would become a practice associated with concentrated ranching operations throughout the cattle West, it was a practice arguably originating in the cow towns, with bovine animals' first encounters particularly with the railroad cattle car. One appalling and common practice in the mid-nineteenth century was the sawing off of horns of cattle who did not fit into the railroad cattle box cars in Abilene and elsewhere (Hook 2021; Specht 2016; Dobie, in Cox 1895). Specht (2016: 351) writes that "the horns, useful when cattle walked to market, were dangerous when the animals crowded onto train cars." Dobie (Cox 1895: 210) describes the 'serious problem' of getting a steer's head through a railroad car door that was smaller than the 5–8 foot doors of today: "Some steers simply could not be loaded before the horns were chopped off"; he relates problems associated with loading the animals as well as the subsequent problem of getting their horns stuck between the railroad car slats. Thus "men accompanying shipments sometimes took saws so that if a horn got inextricably fastened, it could be sawed off and the animal thus *liberated*" [my emphasis].

The longhorns' horns brought numerous other business problems to ranchers and cattlemen seeking profits from longhorns' bodies, including that of 'wasting space' when the animals were fed in stalls and pens, their inability to eat in confined locations, the tendency to injure one another, getting caught on fences and other confining materials, and being generally more aggressive—more difficult to discipline and control—than those without horns. Arnold and Hale (1940: 80–81) assert that shipping of horned cattle invariably resulted in bruised carcasses, and "bruises on meat greatly lowered its money value at the market. In general, de-horned cattle bring from twenty-five cents to seventy-five cents more a hundredweight on the market than do horned cattle of similar quality and condition." (In the twenty-first century, that number is approximately $1.50 to $2.00 more per hundred weight—"a $1 loss for every animal slaughtered or total loss to the nation's beef industry of 24.5 million" [Dehorning Calves 2004: 6].)

Thus, within the nineteenth-century cattle beef carceral archipelago, the common and exceedingly painful practice of dehorning, or cutting off the horns, was justified by ranchers and cattlemen so that they could more easily enclose, control, move, and commodify bovine animals. Dehorning controlled animals' behavior upon capture and in stock pens, enabled easier loading into railroad cars, and became a standard practice simply because ranchers believed that hornless animals would fatten better. Common wisdom held that steers had longer horns than bulls, since as castrated animals they were better able to 'send their energy' to horn production rather than use it for reproduction.

If a simple saw was not employed for the dehorning (U.S. Department of Agriculture 1929: 1–2), other instruments were designed for the procedure, such as that shown in fig. 4.5, an approximately 5-foot-long (47 inch) dehorn-

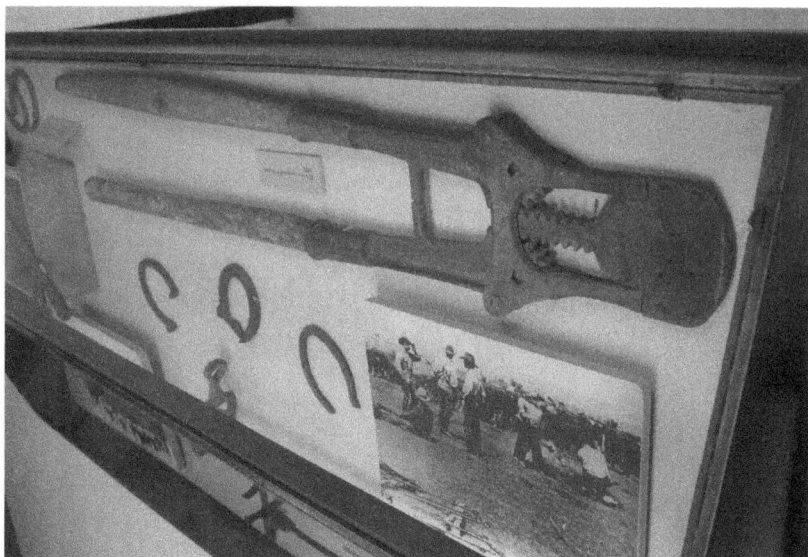

Fig. 4.5. Dehorning tool (No. 1976-168/1). Gift of V. L. Simpson, Panhandle-Plains Historical Museum, Canyon, Texas. Photo by Daniel Olivetti.

ing tool, this one an artifact displayed at the Panhandle-Plains Historical Museum. This apparatus appears to be a grotesque instrument of torture from the Middle Ages, and yet, such instruments are still in use today. This dehorning implement was patented in 1892 (No. 480,246), by A. C. Brosius and manufactured by M. T. Phillips of Pomeroy, Pennsylvania. The description of the tool on the patent reads:

> The dehorning implement consists of a pair of knives, a solid frame for these knives, a follower, and operating-handles. . . . In dehorning stock the handles are opened, thus separating the knives, leaving an opening between them when the horn is passed through the same. The handles are then brought together . . . and the horn is quickly and easily cut from the head of the animal. [A] powerful pressure is brought to bear upon the movable knife. . . . It is simple in operation, durable, and cheap to manufacture.

The U.S. Department of Agriculture Farmer's Bulletin No. 1600 (1929: 2), while describing the various methods and illustrations of dehorning, castration, and branding, features the gouging of horns of an animal trapped in a squeeze chute on its cover (fig. 4.6). Should the dehorned area be infected by screwworm infestation, the agency instructed, "For destroying the maggots in a wound, nothing better than benzol has been found."

Veterinarians concede the intense and extreme short-term pain as well

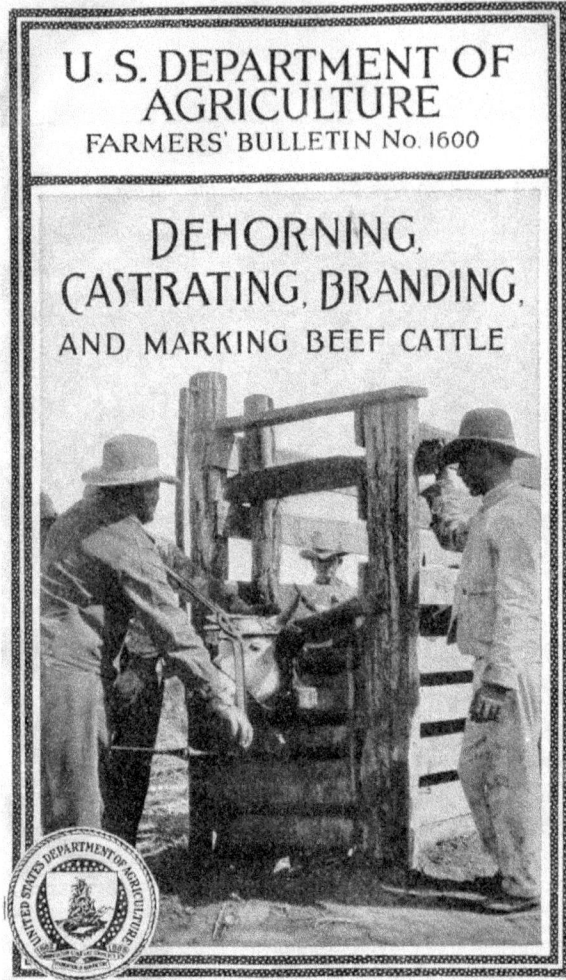

Fig. 4.6. Dehorning a cow with head restrained in squeeze chute. Cover image, U.S. Department of Agriculture pamphlet on dehorning, castrating, and branding cattle, 1929.

as long-term pain that dehorning causes (Dehorning and Disbudding of Cattle 2014: 3–4). Avoidance as well as acute distress responses and behaviors evident of the painful effects have been documented; these include tail wagging, head movement, tripping, rearing, head rubbing, head shaking, neck extension, ear flicking, tail flicking, increased numbers of transitions between lying and rising, reduced rumination, increased risks of sinusitis, bleeding, prolonged wound healing, damage to nerve endings, and infection. The pain causes "altered behavioral and physiologic states," and one might surmise that this is under 'modern conditions' and not the likely cruder practices aboard the railroad cars in Abilene, circa 1860–1880.

The dehorning tool on museum display and shown in fig. 4.5 is presented informationally and factually alongside numerous other carceral instruments with text that simply describes their use and value. Thus, unlike other types of 'dark tourist' museum artifacts that highlight the macabre, hauntings, suffering, and death; that invite audiences to be entertained by reenactments of others' torture, pain, and suffering—sites such as ghastly or notorious prisons (Walby and Piche 2015)—cow town historical museums and other museums that feature such carceral instruments seek to diminish if not completely erase the possibility that the instruments represent distress, fear, and torment to sentient beings.

As it happens, the carceral archipelago made horns—a physical animal body part—obsolete. Cox, writing in 1895 (211–212), notes with detail that this 'weapon of defense' for the animal became completely unnecessary:

> Cattle frequently injure each other unintentionally with their horns, and, moreover, a great deal of space is wasted by these excrescences. Now that stall feeding is gaining ground in Texas, the value of space is being felt materially. . . . Hornless steers can be housed with much greater economy, and it is also found that two or three more beasts can be placed in a [railroad] car with less difficulty or danger when hornless than with horns. . . .
>
> The Texas cattleman has often been written up as cruel and heedless in regard to inflicting pain on his stock. It is significant, in view of these criticisms, that for every man that gets rid of the horns on his steers by means of saw and other tools, at least five or six expend hundreds if not thousands of dollars in introducing the blood of hornless varieties, and thus gradually removing the objectionable articles by a more costly but much more merciful, and of course, permanent process. . . .
>
> It is a very small matter to dehorn a calf or a yearling and to do a nice job by simply removing the small young horn from the head with a sharp knife, which can easily be done and without much difficulty. . . . [Thus] there is no reason why even three or four-year-old animals cannot be dehorned without positive injury, by clipping the horns off right at the edge of the hair, and separating them from the bone of the head right down at the roots of the horn. Cattle may be run into a chute, their heads fastened in a socket, and their horns clipped off with a dehorning machine without any difficulty, or without much serious inconvenience to the animal, and they will go right along gaining in flesh, and will not lose a feed from this mode of operation.

> The way cattle are dehorned sometimes . . . where there is a stub of horn left an inch long on the head, is cruel and barbarous, and requires a month or six weeks for him to regain his appetite and get on feed. . . .
>
> There may be, and probably is, a necessity for cattle to maintain their horns when grazing on the Western prairies and ranges, where they are attacked often by wolves, and where a cow may have to fight for her calf. In such instances it is absolutely necessary for the animal to have horns.

Today, dehorning with tools, or 'disbudding'—removal of the horn 'buds' on calves either chemically, by use of a hot iron, or physically excising them, is performed on restrained animals and is disturbingly unregulated and not required to be performed with anesthesia (Dehorning and Disbudding of Cattle 2014; Hemsworth et al. 1995: 174). A quick Google search produces numerous questions and answers about how to stop the excessive bleeding that accompanies dehorning, even today with 'modern' methods including those used by veterinarians. Physical methods of dehorning include use of embryotomy wire, guillotine shears or dehorning knives, saws, spoons, cups, tubes, and high-tension rubber bands. When cattle have large horns, they are sometimes 'tipped', a procedure that removes the sharp end of the horn but leaves the base (Dehorning and Disbudding of Cattle 2014, Dehorning Calves 2004, Hemsworth et al. 1995).

Disbudding removes the horn bud and growth ring attached to the skull via cauterization with a hot iron, a knife, or, once the horns start to grow, a surgical cutting wire ('cup dehorner'), saw, or caustic dehorning chemical paste, depending on how much the horn has grown and the growth ring developed. Animals are enclosed in a contraption like a squeeze chute with their heads held in a head gate; or their head is restrained with a dehorning table or chin bar. "Be prepared to stop bleeding after dehorning and to care for two large, open head wounds for a period of time," warns the Tennessee Agriculture Extension Service (Dehorning Calves 2004: 6). After dehorning a calf, "the calf should be released into a quiet, shaded environment so its blood pressure will go down. This is an important step in reducing bleeding."

The practice of dehorning bovine animals produces a host of detrimental carceral effects on and in their bodies—physiological, psychological, emotional, and social. The practice illustrates a textbook concurrence of structural, technological, and experiential components of carcerality: instruments designed and patented for easier commodification of animal bodies; structures and techniques developed to ease the human exercise of disciplinary and biopolitical power over the animals; the broader operations in carceral spaces that were designed to make animal horns not just obsolete but inconvenient and unwanted; and, finally, the experiential aspects of injury, pain, and abject suffering. *That* is the story to be told.

Conclusion: A Carceral Continuum, Chemical Delousing Vats

Many miseries plagued the animals on farms located near the cow towns as they awaited transport to slaughter, from the terrible and dramatic to the more prosaic. W. F. Cude (Hunter 1924: 216) describes the agony of biting flies on such a farm in 1869:

> Sometimes we would get farms to put the cattle in at night and the farms were stocked with cockleburs and the cattle's tails would get full of burrs, and when the buffalo flies would get after them they would lose their tails fighting flies. Their tails would become entangled in small pine trees and there they would stand and pull and bellow until they got loose. You could hear them bawl a mile. Some of the cattle would run off and lay down, crazed with misery, and it was hard to drive them back to the herd.

The carceral structures, infrastructures, and technological developments in cow towns described in this chapter were in a sense a culmination, or at least the end of the line, of the rural carceral archipelago that developed in the mid-nineteenth century for bovine animals. While I have described numerous carceral practices, instruments, and structures of the cow towns, their impact actually extended to a continuum of many others not explicitly detailed here, since others have amply addressed them, particularly those detailing the economic and business history of the cattle industry (Skaggs 1974; Dykstra 1968; Sprecht 2019; Rifkin 1992, to name just a very few).

My concentration on animal experiences and material culture in particular shapes a different kind of history, but notably also includes other carceral inventions and practices that were directly related to cow town carceral logic and reality. One worth mentioning at least briefly were the chemical "delousing vats" that arose, particularly in the South, as a response to political and economic pressures from the cow town leaders that attempted to prevent cattle infected with the Texas tick from entering their territory, and subsequently establishing constantly shifting quarantine lines to control their movement (Strom 2010; Specht 2016; McCoy 1874; Sherow 2018). In fact, one of the few ostensible impediments to the development of the carceral archipelago from Texas to Kansas in the mid-nineteenth century was the infestation of the Texas cattle tick, which evidently did not affect animals from Texas who had become immune to the fever but impacted other animals in the North. Ticks were picked up on grasses and pastures on which infected animals had previously tread. White (1992: 252–253) describes the tick as holding "all these profits hostage," as animals spent a year or more fattening on the central and northern plains before being shipped free of the fever (and then, according to White, it was a hard freeze that eventually killed the ticks).

Tick infestation damaged hides and caused cattle to lose weight; they produced sickness, suffering, and death, and their eradication was most certainly an outcome of the carceral state, designed to make animals profitable and marketable. Havins (1948: 147–148) describes the effects of the ticks on animals, symptoms that included "contracted muscles, dry skin, with hair on end, sunken eyes, murrain . . . in one word, a scourge." Strom (2010: xx) documented the tick fever attacking the cow's red blood system, causing high fever, anemia, listlessness, trembling, delirium, staggering, and grinding of teeth, with animals typically dying within 8–10 days of infestation.

Chemical vats filled with arsenic were introduced into this carceral landscape to rid animals of the ticks. Locational impacts, town politics, and competition over quarantine lines have been covered elsewhere (e.g., Dykstra 1968), but the vats that presumably killed the ticks are important to recognize as at least indirectly a product of the carceral archipelago, with detrimental impacts on animal experiences. Said another way, political and economic resistance to Texas cattle in the cow towns resulted in their torture in these southern deticking vats. Many writers of the period describe the deticking apparatuses and provide instructions on how to build and use the vats (e.g., Cox 1895: 199–200). Cox's instructions include how to drive animals into a small pen first, 8–10 at a time, and then prodding them along a platform to the chute at the end. One by one they stepped onto a trapdoor and were plunged into the vat, thus submerging them completely in the harsh chemical. Again, these were animals who had not developed immunity against the ticks and who thus suffered—one way or another—under a significant outcome of the forced migration of Texas animals in the first instance.

CHAPTER 5

Cattle-Drive Westerns

CARCERAL SPACE AND BOVINE ACTORS

The Oscar-nominated Coen Brothers film *The Ballad of Buster Scruggs* (2018) features six vignettes that depict, via the Coens' signature dark humor, the hyper-violence, lawlessness, lucklessness, and vigilante justice of the nineteenth-century American West. One of the vignettes features an outlaw (played by James Franco) who, after having robbed a bank and survived a near-hanging by vigilantes who are themselves killed by stereotyped blood-thirsty Comanche warriors, joins up with a stock-rustling cowboy who invites the outlaw to join him stealing cattle to drive them to Abilene, Kansas, for sale. As is typical in western films, the animals in *Buster Scruggs* serve as important background fixtures and signifiers of rugged, undeveloped land, while the main plot focuses on human interactions. The cows provide the film a romantic backdrop, walking calmly and steadily along the horizon line. Although the concept of stealing cattle in this context remains unproblema-tized, of course—all of them were at some point 'stolen' by someone, some-where, albeit through various means—the film's bringing forward the cow town of Abilene, Kansas, to twenty-first-century popular audiences is worth noting. The mention of Abilene suggests how foundational that site remains in western American history and, by extension, to the vast exploitation of bovine animals and the origins and development of the U.S. beef industry.

Another recent award-winning western, Jane Campion's *The Power of the Dog* (2021), illustrates (among other things) a continuing western carceral landscape. The story centers on Phil (played by Benedict Cumberbatch), a

1920s Montana ranch owner whose repressed homosexuality links to a gritty portrayal of toxic masculinity. Jumping to one particularly gruesome castration scene, Phil instructs those handling a calf to "keep that leg stretched out . . . [to] grab his head," with a soundtrack featuring cows loudly bleating and visuals showing Phil cutting the testicle sack with his knife and then brutally pulling out the testicles barehanded. (Film dialogue establishes that 1,500 calves were castrated that day on the ranch.) Yet what the audience is actually seeing in this scene is unclear, with hands and arms and ostensibly animal muscles all viscerally crowded into a close, intimate camera shot. Notably, this hands-on procedure for making castration cuts was that advocated by the U.S. Department of Agriculture in the early twentieth century (1929).

These examples attest to the resilience and longevity of the western film genre over the past century—the heyday of which was the Hollywood western of the post–World War II, mid-twentieth century, whose stories, though, focused on people, places, and events of the nineteenth century. These films played an important role in solidifying national American identity in the post–World War II era. As many scholars have argued (Aquila 1996; Johnson 1996; Walker 1981; Tompkins 1992; Russell 1993), these films played an important role in solidifying national American identity in the postwar era; they focused on some version of the colonial conquest of the western frontier—the so-called American Manifest Destiny of establishing justice and freedom in the wild frontier—while inventing the rugged cowboy as a national heroic icon.

They also featured, importantly and significantly, if obliquely, bovine animals within what were made to seem the 'natural' carceral spaces and practices of the nineteenth-century cattle trails and towns that have been outlined in previous chapters. The extraordinary popularity of western films, particularly those with the common setting and plot centered on the cattle drive—one of the most popular themes of westerns—was arguably the single most important avenue for American audiences to learn about the carceral archipelago and the cattle beef industry while also narrating a national past that perpetuated popular myths about the American West, cowboys, and bovine animals. They thus helped neutralize the historical carceral landscapes and practices that they represented; they encouraged audiences to think about bovine animals as important participants in the American past as well as exploitable and killable food commodities. As I argue in this chapter, this normalization and neutralization of the carceral in these films encouraged audiences to not only accept but even enjoy images of the carceral.

As Falconer (2020: 3–4) relates, westerns accounted for 20–35 percent of Hollywood feature films from 1935 to 1952, with approximately one hundred made each year during that period. This golden age of the western represented a nineteenth-century nostalgic past that helped to justify the carceral conditions and intensive commodification of bovine animals. These fictional portrayals of animal experiences were highly influential in how audiences ostensibly came to 'know' bovine animals and their shared environments, itself requiring the linked processes of their animalization and their exploitation as a nutritional, wholesome food source. These filmic portrayals infused American culture with meat eating itself as a patriotic act (after Specht 2019; Rifkin 1992). Aided by new technologies and intensifying agricultural practices, the swift and sharp rise in beef consumption is notable during this period; the number of beef cattle consumed in the United States rapidly increased from 12.5 million animals in 1920 to 45 million by 1975 (Earth Policy Institute 2012).

The quintessential film in this genre, *Red River* (1948), is a fictionalized account of the first cattle drive along what became the renowned Chisholm Trail, a film saturated with potent and iconographical images of the West, bovine animals, and futuristic visions of turning them into beef: "beef to make [people] strong, beef to make them grow," as John Wayne's Tom Dunson character declares. "The orchestral music swells, the dust rises, the adrenaline starts to pump, and that classic sequence from how many cattle-drives in the movies begin, with cowboys yelling 'Hee yaa. Hee yaa. Whoopee. Yahoo. Yaa Yaa', as they ride herd and head for open range" (Kowalewski 1996: 1). One of the first sequences of the film depicts Dunson's order to brand his fledging herd, a scene complete with sounds of animals' sizzling flesh; "burn it deep" he orders, explaining how by simple declaration his ownership of this new commodity emblazoned on cow skin would take place. The trail crew eventually overrides Dunson's commands and shifts the herd onto the Chisholm Trail toward Kansas rather than toward Missouri, and prevails through scenic pastures as well as dangerous stampedes, cattle rustlings, river crossings, and other iconic trials of the cattle drive. Ultimately the film celebrates the heroic men and animals who endured the hardship of the trail, terminating in the film's final scenes of their triumphal entry into Abilene, Kansas, amid joyful cries of the townsfolk and railroad entrepreneurs doling out cash payments to cowboys.

In addition to *Red River* (1948), other well-known mid-century films whose subjects were cattle drives and towns include *Dodge City* (1939), *Cattle Drive* (1951), *The Longhorn* (1951), and a number of Gene Autry films including *Barbed Wire* (1952) and *Cow Town* (1950) (many others followed in the 1970s and later). In this chapter I consider the extent to which human representations of the lives of cows in these films invented ideas about them that were subsequently used to produce certain kinds of bodies and foodways. The shift in focus to blood and pedigree in animals became an enormous influence in the United States by the late nineteenth century and greatly influenced dietary habits. Such representations are consequential on many levels, including also carrying implications for the imagined identity of ranching dynasties and of the class associations of the cowboy to the animals who have been romanticized in westerns. Dalke's (2010) work on mustang horses in the U.S. West helps frame such study. She writes that these horses evoke conflicting responses as historical icons, from being pests to beautiful cultural symbols, images constantly shaped by culture, technology, nature, and people—animals that can be wild and tamed and carry positive or negative associations based on their use. It is therefore important to ask, what were (and indeed are) the purposes and motivations behind the images of bovine animals in western films—economic, political, cultural, and social?

The western films under study here are ostensibly about cows and cattle drives, yet the animals themselves have no stories of their own; they serve only as backdrops or props to the human dramas unfolding. Thus, in no more foundational visual, performative, or cultural lenses do cows appear as both central to the plot of the heroic winning of the West and as totally absent from it at the same time. They are absent presences. Yet much of what is shown on screen indeed appears to be outright animal cruelty or danger to animals common in real carceral spaces—for example, branding, castration, stampeding, and crossing swift flowing rivers. For this reason, study of these films can also enhance understandings of the material carceral artifacts and practices enacted on animals during their production.

In this chapter, rather than scrutinize and unpack western films as such, I bring to the foreground the role that cattle have played in them, a subject heretofore completely absent in the study of animals in film. These 'cinematographied' animals were at once animalized (after Wolfe and Elmer 1995) as a food source, and also gendered as masculine, heroically helping claim and tame the American frontier—figured as they were within the successful practices and processes of the emergent carceral archipelago. The portrayals are of humans and nonhumans working, relating, and sharing spaces along the cattle trails and in the cow towns.

Mid-twentieth-century western films thus offered an important entrée into how the gendered constructs of men (cowboys) and animals provided the justification for the U.S. colonial-carceral project. This chapter thus ties together the hagiographic mythology surrounding the heroic cowboy to that of the cows themselves, as a necessary backdrop and integral to colonial conquest. The material, social, and symbolic production of animals in such spaces, as shapers of land and life, relates quite closely to and perhaps even mirrors the production of that of the cowboy (to some extent conflated with the rancher) (after Tortorici 2015: 6; Johnson 1996; Walker 1981; Tompkins 1992; Russell 1993). As Russell (1993: x) argued, "The myth of the cowboy . . . represents physical freedom and spiritual solitude, individualism, and a closeness to nature in all its rugged, soaring magnificence." But what is hidden behind the myth of the cowboy is that his association with, affection for, and perhaps intimacy with animals rested on his (carceral) domination of them. His cattle were protected so that they could be killed at the end of the trail. And so the gendered nature of this relationship is both hegemonically masculine and masculinist as well.

Although the main subjects of this book are bovine animals caught in the carceral archipelago developed for the nineteenth-century emergent beef industry, later in the chapter I pause to muse about their twentieth-century counterparts who 'acted' in western films and thus re-narrated their experiences to future generations. What might it have been like for them to become a part of a Hollywood experience, as herds crossing rivers, stampeding in the night, or as individual animals pulling wagons, being branded, and so on? Burt (2002: 15) offers a good starting point for thinking about how animals appear in film, and among the many aspects of western films worth noting must be the role and treatment of the real animals used in their creation. As it turns out though, the 'real' and the 'fictionalized' experiences of bovine animals are not much different. Animals appearing in these films were generally living under the carceral conditions of then-operating ranches of the mid-twentieth century—a carceral continuum of animal experiences on ranches dating from the previous century. Study of the bovines and other farmed animals in feature films is a rich, unexplored area of research.

Animals in Film Entertainment: Brief and Selective Background

'Animals in film' covers a wide range of genres, from naturalistic documentaries that take the viewer into otherwise inaccessible places to fictional blockbuster movies centered on animal stars, with many genres in between. My focus in this chapter is on fictionalized Hollywood westerns that depicted bovine animals in cattle drives and cattle towns, with the purpose of highlighting how intertwined their portrayal or representations were to narrating a particular version of the American colonial past, as well as depicting them as animalized animals in order to supply exploitable and killable bodies for the developing beef industry.

Although much has been written about animals captive within the extensive human entertainment industrial complex generally, from zoos to theme parks to circuses (e.g., Urbanik 2012; Acampora 2010; Nance 2013; Collins 1993), bovine animals largely have not been considered 'entertainment' and thus have been excluded from this analysis. Moreover, cattle have not been discussed in the literature on film entertainment specifically—even though, as noted, in the case of Hollywood westerns, many of the most iconic ones centered on stories of cattle drives and cow towns. Much greater attention has been paid to other animals in westerns; for example, horses. The use of horses in films, especially the harm and killing of them in westerns, has been an area of considerable focus by scholars as well as oversight safety groups. Stillman (2008: 196) argues that horses 'built Hollywood' as they were America's first movie icons, "serving as the backbone of Hollywood in the burgeoning new genre of westerns." Horses being driven off of a 70-foot cliff in the film *Jesse James* (1939) and a 'trip wire' invented to cause horses to fall prompted the American Humane Association (AHA, today's main oversight organization of animals in film) to intervene and led to contracts between Hollywood and the Hays Office (which oversaw the more general Motion Picture Production Code [PCA] until closing in 1966), and giving the AHA the right to review scripts and secure representatives on film sets to supervise the filming of animals (Burt 2002: 153). The relative success of this organization in doing so is debatable, though (PETA 2022).[1]

Drawing on and triangulating with other postwar cinematic portrayals of animal-actors with individual identities and 'personalities', such as the dogs Lassie and Rin Tin Tin (e.g., Collins 1993), famous horse stories such as Black Beauty, and those centered on bears, chimpanzees, or other animal 'stars' in classic films and television shows helps frame what at least some of their experiences might have been, what their portrayals of nineteenth-century carceral spaces meant to twentieth-century audiences, and how particular kinds of performances were produced and motivated from them (Wolf 2014; McLean 2014; Genzert 2014; Collins 1993).

One characteristic feature of post–World War II films and television shows (as well as other entertainment venues, such as the circus) was the portrayal of animals as sharing human goals. The heroic canine adventures of the film and television star Lassie were a particularly anthropomorphic version of American postwar heroism; Lassie performed dangerous stunts to benefit humans, such as swimming in flooded rivers, scaling high fences, jumping off bridges, and defusing bombs (Wolf 2014). Such animal actors have names and identities and are treated as individuals faced with moral and ethical dilemmas they share with humans; they are humanized animals. Heroic dogs like Lassie are physically strong and beautiful; they are emotionally available and tactful and tutor people in addition to saving their lives and reconciling their differences (after McHugh 2004: 109). As Cronon (2009: xv) adds, "Such narratives depicted animals behaving in ways that reinforced the gendered family roles idealized in 1950s sitcoms, increasing their appeal to middle-class American audiences." Moreover, Lassie's star image promoted a type of breed purity; as Wolf (2014) argues, Lassie becoming a wartime hero ushered in the image of the purebred collie as an ideal pet, and 'pure' blood itself as an indicator of prosperity, tied directly to a system of reproductive manipulation and the history of eugenics (Wolf 2014: 117–118; Haraway 2008).

In her wide-ranging historical study of the cultural, economic, and social lives of circus animals, Nance (2013: 5–13) shows how consumer capitalism, particularly within the entertainment business, obscured the 'backstage realities' of the production of animal behavior, agency, and resistance. Nance argues that elephants do not do things that they know are dangerous, yet they were forced into many such activities, with menagerie owners and trainers presenting themselves as animal lovers, not unsentimental traffickers in living property (41–46). Elephants were portrayed to circus audiences as if they wanted dominance and affection from their owners, but meanwhile managers were using techniques such as hooks, ropes, and pulleys (cf. Bennett 1998) as well as behavioral modification methods to control them and make them do things against their will. Elephants, many of whom were strong willed, often resisted the conditions of their captivity; they exercised a type of agency that helped them respond to managers and trainers and survive captivity even with no real power to challenge their captivity (175–176). But such resistance led to even more rigid training and transport routines, which in turn caused the elephants to increasingly put people and property in danger. Behaviors such as rocking to stay calm and survive their captivity within carceral spaces were a response to being unable to satisfy their "hardwired urges to walk, fully explore their surroundings, browse for food, and interact with others" while in captivity.

Nance's insights about circus elephants help us understand both the means and measures by which animal behaviors were (and are) controlled and managed in order to present a particular version of animals as entertainment. Additionally, keep in mind that restrictions exist to (ostensibly) protect animals used for human entertainment via the AHA. Burt (2002: 141) explains that the creation of regulations for animal film imagery brings into play a whole series of codes, which make cruelty dependent on the framework in which it is presented. "Certainly different genres of animal films (family stories, adventures and safaris, natural history documentaries, medical films, animal rights topics, experimental and avant-garde films) have different criteria by which to judge what might be considered acceptable or unacceptable imagery. Animal death, for example, is treated differently in these different types of films." All such codes and rules rest on facts such as the intended audience consuming the violence within the images (for example, whether the intended audience is children). This then becomes a question of acceptable norms and venues of violence for the purpose of entertainment. Many have written about the invisibility, distancing effects, or acceptable 'proper place' of animal violence to occur, in entertainment and elsewhere (e.g., Pachirat 2011; Elder, Wolch, and Emel 1998). As Burt (2002: 137) explains in the case of film, "Animal film imagery can highlight the making visible of violence. For a society that does not so much conceal violence as attempt to restrict it to its proper place, this unavoidable visual attention to its mechanics is inevitably problematic. This is reflected in the fact that from an early period legislation for the treatment of animals in films attempted to cover both the production process and the final imagery."

Studying the performances of bovine animals who appeared in Hollywood westerns presents a unique opportunity to consider how these animalized animals, lacking any individualized star power or personalities, helped usher in a foodway into the American diet perhaps unmatched by any other. Concern and understanding of them shapes up quite differently than that for their more humanized counterparts who have received much greater attention in study of animals in film.

The Western Film Genre: Bovine Animals and Carceral Space

The carceral logic of westerns is one that validates bovine captivity and portrays these animals' existence as lacking emotions, psychologies, or stories. To understand this cinematic carceral logic, it is important to ask what we see animals doing in films, where they are doing it, and how and why certain animals develop (or not develop) identities and personalities in films. As Hodgetts and Lorimer (2020: 13–14), drawing on Burt (2002) and Lippit (2000) argue, the usefulness of film in the study of animals is particularly valuable because film can uniquely capture animal movement. Though perhaps they did not specifically have westerns in mind, it is worth noting that in western films we primarily see cows moving—walking along a cattle trail, crossing rivers, pasturing, and stampeding. Western films about cattle drives and towns thus centered on their captivity within and controlled transport through carceral spaces—spaces that were represented as normal and necessary to commodity production.

Cows are almost always and only portrayed in western films within herds, an important aspect to keep in mind since this tends to negate the possibility that they have individuality and thus subjectivity. Few and Tortorici (2013) argue for the importance of examining the lives of particular animals in the historical record, and Nance (2015: 9) concurs that historical animals have always been individual animals with unique lives, with individual reactions to particular circumstances. Unfortunately, though, animals such as cows—unlike the many animals in films who became beloved stars—enjoyed no unique identities or personalities in film; depictions only as anonymous parts of a herd tended to thwart any potential for fostering or encouraging connections with audiences. This carried tremendous ramifications for creating a context for the killability of real animals whose fictionalized portrayals were represented on screen, and moreover must be regarded as a cinematic choice: historical eyewitnesses noticed and documented cows as individuals, such as mother cows nurturing and protecting their calves from harm during cattle round-ups and on the trails. And yet, just as these undifferentiated herd depictions in films contributed to the normalization of bovine carceralization in the American mindset, even in 'real life' cattle drives wherein cowboys described and emotionally sympathized with individual animals, this did not result in attempts to reduce their carceralization. The job of the cowboy was, as it turns out, just a job, and hopefully a short-term one at that (after Coulter 2015). Still, it nonetheless seems the case that only depicting animals in undifferentiated herds, lacking individuals with interests, desires, suffering, and so on, would almost guarantee that large film-going audiences would simply be permitted to animalize them further.

One film that provides inspiration for this chapter is Ilisa Barbash's and Lucien Castaing-Taylor's *Sweetgrass* (2009), a 'visual anthropology' of present-day Montana sheepherding. In this unsentimental look at modern-day herding we see herders overseeing sheep during their summer pasture in gorgeous mountain wilderness, and herders caring for animals they do not particularly like and even scorn. It is a film that displays in some respects the sublimity of caring for sheep—such as the incredibly quick and elegant process of sheep shearing—yet also the profound exploitation, objectification, and violence of such 'caring'; the shearing, for example, leaving these animals without the protection of their coats in the cold early spring air, standing motionless huddled together. As one *New York Times* reviewer claimed, however, there is something about this film that "belongs" to the sheep, as they gaze directly into the camera (Dargis 2010). Such an example of farmed animal subjectification on film, if you will, is rare. Moreover, it is unlikely that audiences enraptured by American westerns (then or now) recognized the cattle or sheep or other farmed animals in such scenes as captives, or the spaces through which they were forced to move as carceral spaces. How could a lovely pastoral landscape be equated with a prison? (after Moran, Turner, and Schliehe 2018; Morin 2018).

As noted previously, the use of horses in western films has drawn much more attention and oversight than any other species of farmed animals (*American Humane Association of Hollywood* 2015). Horses figure prominently in westerns—oftentimes appearing as romantic actors themselves, with lives and stories of their own and performing dangerous and heroic feats alongside their riders (yet oftentimes injured or killed in the process), such as Gene Autry's horse Champion. Not so with cattle. As a general observation, western films normalized carceral spaces, practices, and technological equipment related to the emergent cattle industry, such as in featuring puffing locomotives, cows crowded into pens adjacent to railroads, and auction yards at the destination cow towns. Such films tend to either begin and or end with dramatic images of the railroad coming to town, such as the Errol Flynn film *Dodge City*, with obvious implications for animal commodification. Publicity for *Dodge City* featured the actors riding the railroad to the actual Dodge City, Kansas, for the film's premier.

Images of cattle on the trails and towns include infrequent and very brief animal facial close-ups à la *Sweetgrass*—particularly during stampede scenes—but much more common are the long shots of herds moving, grazing on the open range, or crossing rivers—always accompanied by rousing majestic music signifying both heroic deeds and a pastoral ideal of the American western landscape. Yet, many films ostensibly about the cattle trails and towns contain barely any footage of animals (e.g., *Cattle Drive*). The story of *The Longhorn* centers on an attempt to bring a herd of cows and a herd of steers together to start a new breed of animal that would combine the stamina of the open range longhorns with the more captive, fattier, and meatier Herefords. It is not until forty-nine minutes into this seventy-minute film that a herd of Herefords from Oregon appears briefly on screen. The scenes of animals are so incredibly brief that the viewer cannot tell what is being shown; mostly it is men on horses, with cattle present only a few seconds at a time—an imagined animal, if you will. A camera shot at the end of the film lasting a few seconds depicts the merging of herds so tiny and distant onscreen as to be unrecognizable (and I did not detect any animals with horns)—and again, an imagined new breed to be produced.

Practically every western film about cattle drives features a stampede scene. The spectacular footage of the stampede in *Red River* is notable for, among other things, the many dead animals left behind. In such films a clumsy or clueless cowboy typically causes the still night to explode into chaos, such as the drunken cowboy precipitating the stampede in *Dodge City*. *Dodge City*'s stampede shows homesteaders who accompanied the cattle drive taking cover under overturned wagons with spliced footage of cattle running amok overhead. The stampede in *The Longhorn* is the longest scene of animals in the film, and eventually in *Cattle Drive* a lightning storm ignites the animals' uneasiness over thirst and chaos ensues. "Cows get as thirsty as these when their tear glands dry up," declares a cowboy, and the party finally finds water at a place called Paradise Canyon. In later western films that began to reframe the plots and aesthetics of westerns (Kowalewski 1996), such as *The Culpep-*

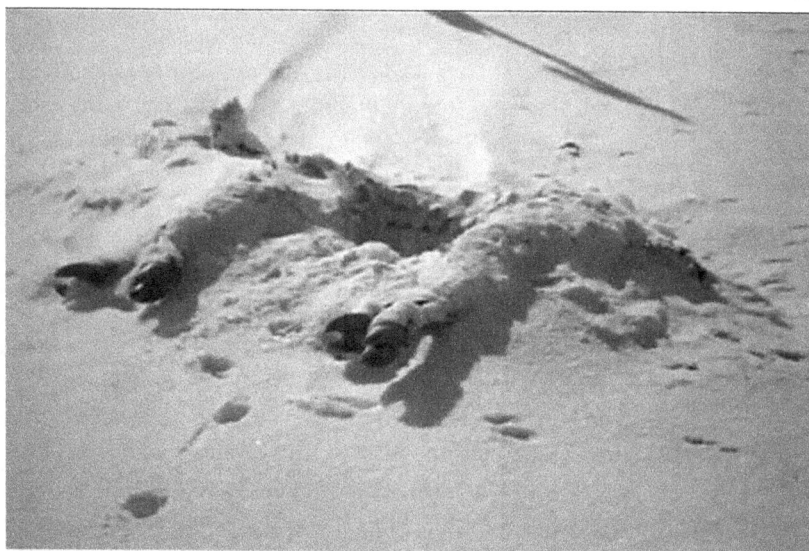

Fig. 5.1. Cattle caught in snow drifts, freezing to death. From the Gene Autry film *Cow Town* (1950).

per Cattle Company (1972), a villain provokes a stampede as part of a cattle-rustling scheme.

What are we to make of these stampede scenes? What message is intended about the cattle trailing business and especially the nature, value, and lives of these animals? One takeaway is the reinforcement of the animalization of bovine animals, who are not worth caring about. Stampede scenes also reinforce the notion—a notion true of most animalized animals—that captivity is the correct approach to handling the animals and that human intervention is necessary to control them and restore order. The power dynamics depicted on-screen thus emphasize the animality of those incarcerated in order to validate enclosure and captivity to viewers, yet what is invisible to the film-going audiences is that these carceral spaces produce the animalistic behavior in the first place (Wolfe and Elmer 1995; Morin 2018). In other words, a stampede is only a problem within the context of the carceral.

Dead animals appear strewn about in the dark, bleak landscape of *Red River* following a stampede. Other films feature dead animals—such as in the slaughtering of animals for food (*The Culpepper Cattle Company*), or as victims caught in barbed wire. Dead animals appear prolifically in the Gene Autry film *Cow Town*, a movie that seems to promote and illustrate the dangers of barbed wire to animals—scenes depicting frozen, starved, or mutilated animals (fig. 5.1); never mind that other Autry films showcase the benefits of the wire.

The carceral practices and places of branding cows also figure prominently in these films. I have already noted the branding scene in *Red River* with its gruesome images and sounds of sizzling flesh. Likewise, in *The Cowboys* (1972), a story focused on 'turning boys into men' through their work driving cattle north, cowboys rope and brand the leg of a calf as their leader—John Wayne in another role—declares, "I've been smellin that for 40 years, never could get used to it" (cf. Dobie 1941). Film portrayals of branding animals as the property of particular men (and sometimes women) further reinforces notions of the bodies of animals as commodities to own, sell, buy, and use with impunity.

Among the scores of Gene Autry westerns, *Barbed Wire* (1952) and *Cow Town* (1950), with segments almost documentary in style, depict the real-life postwar carceral archipelago that developed in the mid-nineteenth century. They are unique in their almost seductive capturing of the essence of carceral spaces and logics made palatable and inviting by, among other things, beautifully portrayed herd scenes, the acting of the affable central character Autry himself, and the lovely tunes of this 'singing cowboy' who serenaded audiences. In *Barbed Wire*, Autry plays a cattle buyer in 1878 Kansas living at the railhead where buyers find their supply of herds gradually being depleted: "the pens are empty," declares a voiceover. In this story the Texas cattle trails have been blocked by homesteaders (and pro-homesteading laws) stringing barbed wire across their territories; these homesteaders turn out to be mostly imposters on the payroll of a rancher who plans to develop the railroad on his land. Autry travels to Texas to fix the problem, assemble a herd, and reopen the trails. He destroys a sizeable portion of the barbed wire fences, and with the trail now open the cattle drives continue north to Kansas. Conceptually the film is about barbed wire, but only a couple of images of wire fence actually appear in the film.

In contrast, the (oddly named) Autry film *Cow Town* focuses on barbed wire and the fence cutting wars, with competing ranchers illegally fencing public land. The film appears to be a wholesale advertisement for the wonders of barbed wire, though—an invention that we learn at the beginning of the film "keeps our homes and industries safe" as well as saves, controls, and prevents stealing of cattle on the open range. The message seems to be that without the fences, cattle suffer—they freeze in blizzards, die of starvation, or are "crippled or destroyed on the open range," meanwhile "turning neighbor against neighbor." Autry himself brings the barbed wire into town, with a voiceover declaring that "with barbed wire we can keep our herds where we want them, we can control and improve breeding, control bloodlines, get the prices we want." The film draws out tensions that arise between the ranchers and between ranchers and cowboys—the latter of whose jobs will be replaced by barbed wire, hence their fence cutting (which is also done by ranchers who want to keep access to the open range). It is the future unemployed cowboys who are seen

Fig. 5.2. Cow making an appearance in the sheriff's office. From the Gene Autry film *Cow Town* (1950).

to whip the hides of cattle at night to make it seem as if they were victims of barbed wire, "The tormented cattle becoming prey to infection and disease."

Of the films I viewed for this chapter, *Cow Town* features the most cattle by far, and some of whom we might even consider 'animal actors'. They stampede, graze in pastures, and roam through town, including a single cow making an appearance in the sheriff's office and others in shop windows (fig. 5.2). The film highlights the benefits of barbed wire; it is strewn through a town street (Autry instructs, "Go get that wire, boys") and manages to halt a stampede. The cows appear intelligent as they stop short of the wire in order to avoid injury. I return to unpack these images and what they might mean for bovine experiences in Hollywood filmmaking in a following section. First, though, I turn to another important message of these western films: that cowboys and cattle partnered together to heroically conquer and tame the American West via the cattle industry and the American colonial enterprise.

Masculinity and the Heroic Taming of the West

The 'breeding out' of brutish, uncouth, and uncivilized characteristics of cowboys—of animalistic and savage men being 'claimed by their environment' and subsequently civilized through their encounter with the American wilderness—has strong resonances with the much discussed and debated frontier thesis of early twentieth-century historian Frederick Jackson Turner (1893; Heffernan and Morin 2021). The themes of western films centered on the Turnerian portrayals of the frontier as a place where violence, lawlessness, and savagery met lawfulness and order; a place of barren landscapes and hard-bitten and adventurous men who confronted the wilderness and learned lessons that earned them heroic and romantic triumph and respect. However, scores of scholars, such as Russell (1993) and Aquila (1996), have argued that the cowboy as a hero has been thoroughly dislodged. Without rehashing the well-worn arguments here, such commentators have observed over many decades that the frontier that Turner described served effectively as a founding American myth but had little relation to reality—a reality that could be better described as a brutal colonial and imperial conquest of Indigenous peoples and land.

One important aspect of this founding myth of the American past, reinforced in Hollywood westerns, was that cowboys were typically depicted as being white people, whereas approximately one-third were actually Hispanic with Mexican origin (and some were likely newly freed Black men). This legend of the white cowboy owed considerably to Wyoming's Buffalo Bill Cody's Wild West Show, which began touring in the early 1880s. The Hispanic vaquero offers another aspect to the Spanish legacy of the U.S. carceral archipelago. Oftentimes these men were poor and unemployed, and so the cattle drive offered an employment opportunity (Sherow 2018; Cronon 1991; White 1991). The common portrayal of Mexican or Indigenous men as hustlers or thieves or as presenting dangers to the cattle drive north through Indian Territory, in memoirs as well as in films, reinforced the notion that the American colonial project was necessary and appropriate. Scofield (2019), in her study of the western rodeo, offers some additional insights into how performance of particular western characteristics and actions has helped sustain an idealized western identity. Despite reputation, many marginalized groups, including prisoners and women, have starred in rodeos and in so doing have widened the definition of the real American cowboy; yet, through performance they have also reinforced the persistent and exclusionary myth of an idealized westerner as a stoic, tough, independent individual.

As Hollywood served up the Turner myth to audiences, it depicted both cowboys and bovine animals working alongside one another, as creatures undergoing a civilizing process through their encounters with that wilderness and succumbing to, among other things, the 'order' that the carceral landscape offered. Though the animals are objectified as a commodity to be captured, stolen, bought, traded, and sold, and even as generic beef (à la *Red River*), they also served in western films as the mirror image of the cowboy—as enduring hardships on the trail alongside cowboys and accompanying them triumphantly into cow towns—and thus helping tame, conquer, civilize, and industrialize the wild, untamed West. Historically, the end of the cattle drive period in the 1880s coincided with Turner's thesis of the end of the frontier—settler colonial conquest had been completed across the continent, and the cattle drive had come to its own conclusion with the arrival of the locomotive. Together these etched a moment in history that glorified the ostensible hardships white settlers endured to usher in an industrial future.

The heroic cowboy in this calculation gendered not only hegemonically masculine, but also masculinist. The entire emerging industry of beef production was masculinist in terms of its profit motive and practices of carceral domination and control of animals, and this in addition to and aside from the gender identities, norms, and behaviors of the rugged men doing the controlling and dominating. Meat itself, and meat eating, resonates closely with machismo (Adams 1990; Rifkin 1991: 236–244; Sumpter 2015), a powerful symbolism in western cultures, with meat consumption representing strength, power, and virility (if also misogyny). As this thinking goes, "Meat is strength. Meat is power. Meat is life. It is the very king of foods. It gives us might, increases our potency, adds edge to our aggression, heats our passion, augments our sexuality, and turns us males into macho men" (MacClancy 1993: 145).

The low social status of the typical cowhand or cowboy—uneducated, oftentimes portrayed as unintelligent, and without means—conflicted often with the trail boss in particular, who appears in western films typically as stronger, smarter, more sophisticated, and with high moral standards. The film *Dodge City*, starring Errol Flynn as a Texas cattle agent (modeled after the real Wyatt Earp of Dodge City), offers a useful example. In the film Flynn appears cultured and moralistic, even if it means making deals resulting in lower profits. The film plays on the myth of a Wild West cow town circa 1872, rife with gunfights, hangings, mayhem, and drunkenness—"we're the disgrace of America," declares one disgruntled character. Flynn becomes sheriff to clean up the town and establish law and order, including by establishing 'fair practices' in the cattle industry. Such leaders, including trail bosses, were portrayed in western films as moralistic, honorable, and honed by a type of sophisticated masculinity, whereas the lower-status cowboy offered of image of a more animal masculine physicality. Yet, cattle-drive films portrayed both versions of manhood as laudable in their work and in their efforts in taming the West.

Importantly, as depicted in such films, cattle in this calculation were likewise gendered heroically masculine. This focus on masculinity offers an opportunity to explore the role of violence embedded in the colonial-cattle trails context, for the human animals involved as well as the nonhuman animals. Carceral spaces of captivity and exploitation are by definition spaces of violence, with bodily management, control, and domestication of animals taking many forms by use of many carceral structures, practices, and instruments. But cattle generally do not appear as subjects of violence in Hollywood westerns; quite the contrary. They mostly appear as background figures, as passive, willing participants of captivity, as part of ordinary cattle commerce and evidencing little response to carceral practices and instruments (e.g., the branding sequence in *Red River*);[2] or, their suffering was employed to teach lessons about the values and correctness of the carceral landscape (à la Gene Autry films). As Derby argues in another context (2011: 604), bovine animals served an important role in developing a culture of violence in the Latin American cattle frontiers before railroads and barbed wire began to close the open range. These conditions rewarded those humans with masculine values of courage and resilience; the cattle were the basis of production as well as indicators of social status. Thus, the animals served as a means to other (human) ends; they served as a foil for men needing to prove their masculine talents.

Many of the western films about cattle drives were coming-of-age stories about boys becoming men through their encounters with the rugged western environment and the emergent carceral landscape. In the film *The Cowboys*, the John Wayne protagonist declares to the boys he has recruited for the cattle drive, "You're dealing with the most ordinary, dumbest creatures on earth" [the cattle,] and horses aren't much better." These boys are recruited away from the feminized space of the one-room schoolhouse, and after the trail boss dies during the journey, they heroically finish the job by driving their 1,500 animals to their destination, overcoming environmental and physical challenges as well as cattle thieves. The Joel McCrea film *Cattle Drive* also centers on a boy becoming a man by participation in a cattle drive. This youngster—ornery and spoiled, whose inattentive father is preoccupied with plans to expand the railroad line—gets left behind at a railroad stop and joins a cattle drive to Santa Fe, New Mexico, becoming tough and ultimately rejecting his 'eastern', feminized ways.

Western films about the emergent cattle industry display heroic masculinity through character image and development but also, importantly, through sound and music. Nearly every cattle-drive western features triumphal music that accompanies and signifies important (albeit brief) moments—wide-angle and panoramic pastoral scenes of huge, majestic herds being assembled in preparation for the trail; men and animals crossing rivers; animals pasturing en masse along the trail; parties catching sight of the cow town railroad; and most significantly during concluding scenes within the cow town streets with their triumphant welcome by townsfolk (e.g., *Red River*, *Dodge City*). Perhaps the most obvious way that bovine animals became associated with the masculine taming of the West was through the climactic, triumphant music accompanying entry into the cow town after an arduous journey. The credits to the soundtrack to the film *Dodge City*, for example, features the upbeat "Columbia, the Gem of the Ocean" (1843), played by a band as the train pulls into town with its live animal cargo. And all of the musical selections in the soundtrack to *Red River* were from the Moscow Symphony Orchestra, composed by Dmitri Tiomkin. Southhall (2022) observes that it is ironic that a Russian composer (Tiomkin) will forever be associated with his scores for films set in the American West:

> He defined the sound of the cattle country as well as his illustrious contemporaries, but in a rather different way. Listen to a few bars of Red River and there'll be no doubt you're listening to music telling some story from the old west . . . [with its "muscular brass" and action music]. . . . [These affecting pieces] filled a dual role of representing great emotion while evoking the beautiful landscape as well. "Stampede" . . . [is] surprisingly dissonant, the orchestra seems almost in conflict with itself at times; quite brilliant. Of course, there is also a smattering of majestic, almost ceremonial music for some of the film's bigger moments, with two tracks in the album's centre—"Red River Ahead" and "Red River Crossing." . . . As the movie (and score) reach their climax, Tiomkin lays on fully orchestral versions of his main theme thick and fast, notably in "A Joyous Meeting" and "Approach to Abilene." Everything then ends with the triumphant, rousing finale "The New Brand," a great way to go out.

In this way the jubilant music becomes associated with the animals teeming through the streets, as if it were their own triumph to have arrived at the cow town, to have endured and prevailed through the hardships of the cattle drive.

Recuperating Bovine Experiences in American Westerns

Thus far I have argued that bovine animals appearing in mid-twentieth-century Hollywood cattle-drive films were depicted as largely and in effect complicit with the carceral infrastructures and landscapes within which they were embedded. With this in mind, it seems worth pondering what the lives and experiences of these animals might have been like as 'actors' in these films, and how their experiences might have compared to those of their nineteenth-century counterparts they were representing on screen. The historical context of the cattle carceral archipelago in film is important in that it foundationally rested on the theme of commodifying animals as food while at the same time depicting them as beings exempt from pain and suffering and perhaps even enjoying the pastoral, serene, and/or majestic landscapes through which they were captured or moved. Recuperating their lives as Hollywood actors involves seeing them anew as sentient beings with real experiences in these films, experiences that necessarily involved their own realities, preferences, and emotions. Their objectification in film is noteworthy in that they were represented as living commodities controlled and dominated by their human superiors, but also as partners to those humans in their work. Westerns thus created another absent presence for these animals, particularly as the plot lines of the films centered not on animal lives but (only) on human dramas such as those involving altruistic sheriffs and cattle outlaws.

As it turns out, depictions of cattle engaged in dramatic, dangerous, or seemingly painful events or procedures, such as branding, stampeding, crossing swiftly moving rivers, or running over cliffs, were representative of animal lives in real carceral spaces constructed and filmed in particular ways for moviegoing audiences. Archival and other sources reveal that film footage for many if not most bovine herd scenes was captured using animals from then-operating ranches and real-world cattle drives; that is, animal experiences were rented out for filmmaker profits and audience entertainment. There thus appears to be little difference between oftentimes gruesome real life and filmed life for these animals, affirming McLean's (2014) observations that animals acting in films was tantamount to 'life itself'. The overall effect, I would argue, led audiences to the plausible conclusion that animal lives within carceral spaces were ordinary and acceptable, thus neutralizing and further advancing their commodification and exploitation.

Examples precede the Hollywood heyday of the cattle-drive film. Tacking back a bit to the Silent Era, the film *North of 36* (1924) is a purported 'exact replica' of a cattle drive over the Chisholm Trail. This film features a drive of about four thousand longhorns, rented from a ranch near Houston, Texas, tracing the animals' being driven from Texas to the railroad terminus in Abilene, Kansas. "Strung out, they covered a distance of over four miles" (Gilks 1925). The animals and crew covered 20–30 miles per day for the first week, and then 12–15 per day in later weeks, with a daily routine (also) mirroring that of the cattle drives of fifty years' prior, with grazing until noon, 'marching' until twilight, and halting for grazing after dark. The film features animals fording a river a half-mile wide, and a stampede. And like actual drives of an earlier era, the owner of the cattle (a rancher named Bassett Blakely) planned to ship the cattle to market following the film's production.

Jack Lilley, a former stuntman and owner of an animal training and supply company called Movin' on Livestock, offers a number of insights into such uses of farmed animals in western films (Lilley 2022).[3] Lilley recalls that portrayals of big herds were oftentimes animals on their way to market—"There is a buyer waiting" at the end of filming. Like many others, his business is (still today, via his son Clay) renting animals for the movies. Just as in a historic cattle drive, when re-creating a filmed version Lilley "looked for a good lead steer"; cattle are "like chickens, they stayed together." When filming, he walked them slowly, making sure water was available: "just let them go awalkin', let 'em graze, let 'em water." His company filmed at ranches, with ranch owners providing access to the animals and helping create scenes.

But what about more dramatic scenes in films such as *Red River* and *Cow Town*? Many production notes, files, and articles on the history of the motion picture industry offer partial insights into how images of carceral practices and animalized animals were produced.[4] Very briefly, from 1934 to 1968, the Motion Picture Production Code (PCA), known popularly as the Hays Code (mentioned earlier), spelled out acceptable and unacceptable content for motion pictures, mostly related to sexual content, drug use, and other 'morally questionable' content, including cruelty to animals. All filmmakers were required to submit their films for approval before release. (As discussed, the AHA came into existence alongside and superseded it specifically for animal portrayals in film.) In the case of *Red River*, archival evidence illustrates contentious dialogue around the gruesome branding scene noted earlier. When the screenplay was submitted for approval, the PCA declared that showing brutality toward animals was unacceptable, including that the branding scene 'needed to be hidden' in order for the film to go forward (Hollywood, Censorship, and the Motion Picture Production Code 1946): "The brutal treatment of animals could not be approved under the provisions of the code." The director, Howard Hawkes, met with the PCA (discussing this as well as other objections to the film), and subsequently the parties agreed that no scenes would suggest cruelty to animals. Although cruelty to animals remained undefined, ultimately the branding sequence was filmed indirectly behind the actor's body, although the imprinted, burned flesh with smoke arising from it remained in the film.

Numerous trade articles on cattle-drive films discuss technical production issues related to filming cattle. Production notes about *Red River* report that the film was shot on location in Texas and in Arizona's Rain Valley, with nine thousand cows (numbers vary) milling on the banks of the Red River; and that walkie-talkies were used to facilitate communication among special-effects technicians, camera people, and actors who were working at a distance from one another (*Red River, Motion Picture Herald* 1948; Harlan 1956; *Red River, Home Movies* 1949). The stampede scene is *Red River* was the most expensive aspect to film, requiring elaborate equipment, as was the rental of approximately six thousand cows (Redelings 1949). The animals were often kept corralled or sequestered next to hillsides to keep them within camera range.

The filming of stampedes is an interesting subject of its own. The makers of the film *Stampede* (Redelings 1949: 580) took advantage of the news that the Mexican government "had ordered the destruction of a large amount of cattle. There were going to drive the animals—who suffered from hoof and mouth

disease—off a high cliff in a remote area of Mexico." The director made the de-
cision to film this "mercy stampede" for his movie. "He rented a fleet of jeeps,
rounded up his camera crew, and filmed one of the great mercy stampedes in
history." (The article does not elaborate on what exactly happened 'mercifully'
to these animals after being driving off the cliff.)

A number of observers have noted the difficulty of filming cattle. Eric
Fleming, cowboy star of the popular 1960s television show *Rawhide* (Bell 1961:
55–56), relates that the "unpredictability of cattle" was one of the biggest challenges facing that program. Most of the show's scenes were filmed on the fifty-
thousand-acre George Light Ranch in southwest Texas with about three thousand cows. But the finishing touches, the close-ups and looping and dubbing of
unusable scenes, were made with a herd of five hundred animals on California
ranches. "The cattle represent a real problem, because it is impossible to train
3,000 wild, range-bred animals." Fleming shares,

> Cattle are crazy. . . . They do exactly what they're not supposed to. Sometimes,
> when you're filming a big scene and you want them to stay calm, the slightest
> noise will set off the whole herd. Then, when you have a scene which calls for a
> stampede, you can try every trick in the book, make all kinds of noise and raise
> all kinds of Cain—and they just stand there and look at you. . . . We try to keep
> our wild rides to a minimum. It's just too expensive to spook the cattle. They
> run off too much weight. Once in a while, though, when we're filming a routine
> scene, something happens to start them running and we try to take advantage
> of it. The cameramen have learned to watch for it and they try to shoot as much
> film as possible. Then we use it in later episodes.

As with stuntmen like Jack Lilley from Movin' on Livestock, one difference between an actual cattle drive and one made for the movies or television was the
replacement of the human actors with stuntmen or experienced ranch hands.
With *Rawhide*, the stampede scenes were photographed as close to the animals
as possible, with experienced doubles doing the riding. "In the two and half
years we have been working on *Rawhide*," Fleming explains, "we've learned a lot
about handling cattle and what to expect from them. This way, if they do start
running, we can pitch right in and help the real ranch hands. In fact, they've
come to look to us for help. They know they can depend on us." "Besides,"
Fleming adds, "I enjoy working with cattle. A lot of times, I'll help the regular
wranglers bed down the herd after we finish shooting for the day. It helps me
understand my role better."

Archival sources oftentimes focus on the technical aspects of filming cattle.
Six airplanes were used in acquiring sky shots of a stampeding herd, a prairie
fire, and the burning of a complete settlement of homesteaders for the film *Sundown* (First National Films 1923). Rowan (1956: 176) discusses use of a crane in

shooting a big cattle roundup sequence in the 1956 film *Giant*, a film directed by George Stevens and starring James Dean, set on a cattle ranch. "With the Mitchell camera mounted on the boom we moved right out into the field, into the midst of the cattle, and made shots from every conceivable angle—all of which proved ideal material for the cutters who made it into one of the most thrilling sequences of the picture." Gilks (1925) notes that "camouflaging the camera from the cattle" was important in such sequences. And Herbert (1940: 300–301) discusses filming at Universal Studio's Going Places Travelogues Dude Ranch:

> Most important is it to have the cattle come down a ridge toward the camera. Worst of all is to have them on a flat or hill sloping away from the camera as the foreground as the first cattle will hide many behind them and a large herd will look unimpressive. But coming down hill and strung out a few hundred will look like a thousand. . . . If you have no alternative than to shoot them on a flat, then try to get your camera as high up as possible. In this case if no cliffs or natural elevation is available then it would be better to make the scene near the ranch house and put your camera up in a barn, on top of a water tower, windmill or silo. *Be sure to avoid fences in such a shot* [my italics].

While it is impossible to ultimately know the experienced realities, preferences, and emotions of the bovine animals appearing in these films, I suggest that whatever they were, they were simply life as the animals knew it. As McLean (2015) observes, it seems that no distinction can be made of bovine animals' 'performance' in film as anything other than their experiences of life. McLean argues that animals cannot 'act' like anyone but themselves, so in effect they are always playing themselves, not a fictional role. Experiences of branding or castration, or inducements to cross rivers or stampede, were the lived experiences of animals in life and in film.

Unlike beloved animal stars more explicitly coerced into their actor roles and who sometimes seemed to love the limelight that stardom brought (e.g., Collins 1993), or animals painfully coerced into actions they would not normally perform (Nance 2013), bovine actors' experiences of acting in the carceral spaces of films and the instruments and practices employed in them would have been much like any described within the carceral archipelago as it existed in the early to mid-twentieth century. While there would have been many differences in the experiences of animals on the actual cattle trails of the nineteenth century—prolonged thirst, snowstorms, death of loved ones, and so on—I find that there is something of a 'carceral continuum' of carceral structures and instruments across the nineteenth-century cattle-drive structures and instruments and those continuing to be employed in the mid-twentieth century—use of ranch pens, barbed wire, branding irons, castrating knives, and dehorning tools, to name a few. (And indeed, many are in use today.) These similarities are worth pointing out in that they carried attendant physical pain and suffering, as well as psychological or emotional trauma. In the end, it was the important role that the western films played in the rapidly expanding beef industry that should be kept in mind. These filmic representations kept alive a mythic portrayal of the American past, kept the carceral naturalized and neutralized, and allowed the carceral framing of animal lives to become enjoyable as entertainment.[5]

Conclusion

Instructive to my analysis in this chapter has been Burt's (2002: 137) observation that violence toward animals in film is not so much about concealing it as restricting it to its proper place. The message from films about cattle drives and cow towns is that the carceral archipelago was a 'proper place' for animal violence to occur; these were places where violence toward animals was acceptable and even encouraged. The ostensible heroism embedded in these films is, then, about the success of industrialized beef production; the success, if you will, of the carceral archipelago and its many human actors in exploiting and killing bovine animals for human consumption.

There is much evidence that animals, including bovine animals, were and continue to be subjected to a great deal of cruelty in the making of feature films—harm that is not, as noted, much different than their everyday lives on farms and ranches. Animal cruelty laws have, to date, ignored the vast majority of animals who are victims of human violence and mass killing in these ways, but that violence is considered acceptable, necessary, and normal—certainly not criminal.

There is some carceral logic to recognizing a much broader spectrum of acts of violence and cruelty toward animals as 'criminal' beyond those enacted on pets, such as those occurring daily in factory farms, slaughterhouses, and research labs. Relying on what is legally considered animal cruelty, and what to do about it, is obviously a problem, as many scholars note (e.g. Marceau 2019; Gruen and Marceau 2022). The preceding discussion offers an opportunity to circle back to the ostensible protections, deliberations, and practices of the AHA, especially with regard to animals not typically considered film actors. Coulter's (2022) 'harm spectrum' framework may be useful as a technique for evaluating the images on screen: it considers degrees of cruelty toward animals, from those that are not legally defined as criminal but which cause harm, such as withholding of sufficient water, food, shelter and medical care, to acts that are bona fide heinous. At the least, audiences must become attuned to animal cruelty when they see it, and not be seduced by the continued neutralization of it in westerns and other films.

Bovine Lives and an Ethical West

The Carceral West

The scholar Kathryn Gillespie describes a recent encounter with cows freely wandering the woodlands of central Washington State. These animals presented a perplexing image to her, and also present a contrasting one to the predominant image of cows mechanically grazing in small confined pastures or eating out of troughs in the agri-industrial operations with which many of us are familiar. Gillespie witnessed dozens and dozens of cows wandering the woods, drinking from the many lakes in the area, eating greenery, and resting.

> The surprising nature of [seeing] cows in the woods created a kind of fractured reality, a signal that something was askew—that cows are not the kinds of animals you imagine seeing in the woods of central Washington. Ideas about where cows do belong creep in, with images of pastures, fields, red barns, and the like. It was precisely these images that made me so delighted to see these cows in the woods, to see them living in a different kind of place, in different kinds of conditions. (Gillespie forthcoming)

As it turned out, however, and probably not that surprisingly, these cows were ear-tagged and had "large brands emblazoned on their sides," indicating they were part of a free-range beef operation. Today's version of free-roaming, foraging bovine animals live to some extent autonomously in such 'self-determined' communities of care and kinship—cows with their calves—seeming alert and decisive, choosing whether or not to interact with humans (and most likely they do not). Gillespie explains that these animals roam across ranges, foraging, until in the fall roundup the one- or two-year-old calves are captured for slaughter, the auction, or to be transferred to a feed lot for longer-term fattening, while the mother cows are returned to the farm for another impregnation. They endure the same violence as in other historical and contemporary beef operations—branding, castration, forced ejaculation and forced impregnation, familial separation, transport, and slaughter, but they do so with an "aesthetically pleasing veneer of cows grazing on the landscape." Their autonomous lives follow along this idyll until "humans on horseback come along suddenly rounding them up in a chaotic frenzy of panic and fear, rumbling down mountain roads on transport trailers to one destination after another—each more terrifying than the last."

Gillespie's encounter alerts us to the fact that things are not always what they seem. Beef production, however gentle and nice it is made to seem and be experienced, is by definition fraught with violence and death. The seemingly peaceful, self-directed lives of the animals in free-range, cow-calf 'regenerative' beef farming is offered to meat eaters as an alternative to the violence of other forms of beef production, yet the former turn out to be just as violent (and environmentally unsustainable) as the latter (after Stanescu 2019).

Documenting the origin story of free-roaming cattle on the continent—their migrations, capture, enclosure, and intensive commodification—offers tremendous potential to rethink what might have been for the lives and experiences of animals who became ensnared within the carceral archipelago of the early cattle beef industry, and to challenge the unprecedented levels of violence that remain inherent within it for their successors. Although this work is focused on the lived experiences of bovine animals in the past, in this afterword I reflect on the significant threats to contemporary animal lives as well. Appreciation for the lives and experiences of the ancestors of animals in today's agribusiness requires an analysis or rethinking of this history and historical geography. My intention has been to offer some basic understandings of bovine animal lives, adding new understandings about 'other others' whose lives and stories matter and yet have heretofore been left out of our histories and historical geographies. If nothing else, I align with what McLauchlan (2021) has labeled a process of attunement: if not understanding what it is like to be the other, at least becoming attuned to it.

The previous chapters have focused on a number of structural, infrastructural, and technological practices and apparatuses that produced untold social, emotional, and physical suffering among their bovine captives. Studying the centuries-long transport of cattle to the Americas via sailing or other ships and constituting such mobility as a forced migration is one conceptual intervention that I propose in this book. I have noted Hodgetts and Lorimer (2020) identifying the 'ordering practices' of sovereign, disciplinary, and biopower (or biopolitical) practices that governed animal mobility. Highlighting the power dynamics involved in forced migrations helps distinguish it from simple movement, recognizing that animal movements are always produced within (and are productive of) relations of power between various actors. These insights can be applied to the emergent cattle industry more generally and ultimately to the forced mobility of bovine animals across the entire carceral archipelago—the open range, the ranch, the cattle drive, the cow town, and the trains.

The foregoing chapters have amply illustrated that bovine animals' movements and experiences, outside of and within the carceral archipelago, included those of pain, suffering, pleasure, joy, grief, anger, care, and surprise, among others. Clearly, though, restrictions on movement—captivity and enclosure—along with accompanying carceral practices, elicited strong expressions of anxiety, distress, anger, protectiveness, suffering, and ultimately death. Cow-calf separation caused untold anxiety and desperation, and cold weather caused much suffering and death for animals frozen and trapped by barbed wire drift fences.

Certainly, use of instruments of torture such as wire fencing and branding irons has not abated—although perhaps today's cows are tattooed with identification numbers on their ears or lips or have computer chips inserted under their skin to indicate their status as property, and owners of the mass production of meat processing have become the twenty-first-century version of the cattle baron. In attempting to establish what may have been the lived animal experiences of carcerality, I have relied on a range of human narratorial sources and voices confirming the likely affective results of carceral practices on sentient beings, noting that they often required in humans a deep disassociation, disaffection, and objectification of animal life. Such life oftentimes was tantamount to an accounting of heads or pounds. As I have also documented, some cowboys, eyewitnesses, and other commentators were attuned to bovine animal sentience and expressed care and empathy toward them—even if this did not translate into 'anticarceral activism'.

One of my main interventions in this work has been to study the effects of material carceral artifacts on bovine bodies in order to help us understand the experience of their use and as juxtaposed to what human interpreters of the carceral landscape might have observed and recorded about them. Carceral structures and devices tell us much of the story of historical animal captivity, containment, and exploitation—pens, stockyards, stock crush devices, railroad cars, and so on; and the material instruments and tools as well deepen the story in so many ways—spiked blabs for the calves, castration and earmarking knives, dehorning tools—all of which destroyed the bodily integrity of animals while causing untold pain and disorientation. Most farmers and ranchers today are unwilling to use anesthesia or sedation when dehorning their cattle, although a small number employ a veterinarian or trained professional to perform the procedure, followed by longer-term pain medication (Dehorning and Disbudding of Cattle 2014). The practice of dehorning is so reprehensible that in 2018 a referendum was brought in Switzerland to outlaw the practice (Swiss Info 2018). Specht (2019: 3) argues that "technological advances and innovative management techniques made cheap beef possible, but they did little to determine who would benefit most from this new regime (meat packers and investors) or bear its heaviest costs (workers, small ranchers, and American Indians)." As my work hopefully illustrates, bovine animals obviously also bore a heavy, perhaps the heaviest, cost.

The American cattle trails and cattle towns remain an integral piece of American legend and mythology, and part of my project has also been to show how the carceral landscapes created for the emergent beef industry were and continue to be celebrated and honored in museums, at living history sites, and via western films as an important part of the American 'manifest destiny' and conquest of the West. Digging into these artifacts makes clear that what is actually being celebrated is the success of the carceral landscape itself. Though Hollywood films were fictional representations of cattle trails and cattle towns, the carceral landscapes depicted were real enough. The portrayal of western carceral landscapes and animals captive within them, during a period when the public validated a strong nostalgic hold on the nineteenth century, spurred intensive growth in the post–World War II beef industry. The extraordinary popularity of the genre helped perpetuate myths of the Old West that ensured heroic and romantic triumph for both humans and animals, albeit immediately followed by animal death. Thinking about the cattle trailing West as a rural carceral archipelago also offers clarity on how distant, relatively unregulated rural towns made them attractive nodal and developmental points in the production and commodification of animal bodies. In reality, many localities were wrung dry by ranching, not revitalized and developed through it.

Through study of available archival and material cultural sources and evidence, lives caught within an American carceral archipelago can be understood and appreciated anew. There are, in fact, many historical parallels to the current systems of mass production of meat, including the replacement of the historic cowboys and cowhands with the low-paid immigrant workers in rural meatpacking plants today. Centering the animals, and the violence enacted upon them, can offer insights into the experiences of currently living animals. To that end, I pick up where my story essentially left off, with the coming of the railroads into the cow towns. That is, I turn to the immediate aftermath of the carceral archipelago and then the problematical social and ecological foundations on which it rests. Subsequently, I offer some final thoughts on the environmental costs and violence embedded within contemporary bovine animal agriculture, and what we might consider as future ethical animal histories and historical geographies of the West.

Animal Historical Geographies and Ecologies

The heyday of the cattle trail and cow town prosperity was short-lived. By 1885–1886 the end of the cattle drives was evident. Farmers and ranchers were fencing their land, railroads had extended closer to the cattle in Texas and elsewhere, and the 1884 Kansas quarantine law prevented entrée for infected animals. Also in 1884, the U.S. Congress passed a bill creating the Bureau of Animal Husbandry within the Department of Agriculture; its purpose was to empower its commissioner to prevent interstate transportation of diseased stock (Dykstra 1968: 334). By 1886, overproduction and a subsequent drop in market prices, followed by devastating weather (a debilitating blizzard), temporarily reduced the numbers of ranches and herds. But as rail lines continued to proliferate extensively throughout the Great Plains and West, they increasingly reached their source commodity directly, and ranchers began relying on irrigated crops to feed their animals. The British influence on the emergent cattle industry was evidenced in numerous ways, including that the taste for fatted beef continued to transform the U.S. industry that had begun at the eve of the Civil War, by feeding animals surplus corn (Dykstra 1968; 78–111; Rifkin 1992: 70–100; Cronon 1991: 218–220; Pacyga 2015). Today we see the outcome in the most exaggerated form of the factory farm or CAFO (concentrated animal feeding operation). Cattle towns such as Dodge City and Abilene lost their significance in the cattle industry, but their influences as sites of historical knowledge of animal experiences and celebratory re-narrations of the cattle-raising past continues, however problematically.

The various loci of power over cattle meat production had developed quickly and intersectionally. This included control over the carceral infrastructures that developed within (and *as*) the cattle trails and cow towns, legal or extralegal control over grazing land, enclosure of animals by wire fencing, and control over and modification of their bodies—an intersection of sovereign, disciplinary, and biopower (after Hodgetts and Lorimer 2020). As captive animals were driven to the railroad sites in developing cow towns and once secured on the railroad cattle cars, another locus of power in meat processing unfolded, which included development of the vast infrastructure of railroad transportation, control over slaughterhouses in St. Louis, Cincinnati, Kansas City, and especially Chicago, and the distribution outlets of processed meat. McCoy (1874: 310–312), the Abilene, Kansas, cattle industry entrepreneur mentioned earlier, rather triumphantly described the stock pens constructed in Abilene as a developing technology in slaughterhouses in Kansas City (fig. A.1). As McCoy describes this structure and its use:

> When a herd of cattle is placed in the yards adjoining a packing establishment for the purpose of being packed, they are separated into squads of two or three and driven through a long narrow lane, and forced into a small box pen, the gate being securely fastened behind them. A dozen or more of those box pens are located side by side, all connected with the main lane, or driveway, so that the men in the yards always have empty pens to fill. So soon as a pen is filled, a man standing upon a narrow gangway, just above the cattle's heads, with a rifle loaded with fixed ammunition, shoots the bullocks in the head. The ball ranges down into or through the brain, producing instant death. Of course the bullock instantly drops, only to receive the falling body of his comrade. . . .
>
> So soon as all are shot down in any one pen, a rising door, which divides the pen from the inner portion of the establishment, is hoisted, and a man enters from within the house dragging a long chain with a noose formed at the end thereof. . . . This he drops over the bullock's head, around his neck, or horns, as may be convenient, then calls for power, which the man at the lever at once applies, and the bullock is drawn out on a narrow floor, including toward a gutter, or drain [then to be cut apart].

Restating McCoy, it was the case that these cramped, co-confined animals, prior to their own deaths, would have mercilessly and distressingly heard, smelled, and seen this brutality enacted on their companions.

The stock pens developed in the nineteenth-century cow towns served as models for early slaughterhouse designs. While Cincinnati provided the prototype of the 'disassembly line' of animals (hogs, in that case), Chicago set the standard in mechanization and mass production of animal killing and processing. The Chicago Union Stockyards opened on Christmas Day, 1865. Patterson describes the enormous complex of hotels, restaurants, saloons, and offices that were eventually built, and "an interlocking system of 2,300 connected livestock pens" that took up more than a square mile in southwestern Chicago (Patterson 2002: 57–64; Giedion 1948: 213–246; Pacyga 2015: 1–18; Rifkin 1992: 113–119). At the time, the meat companies Amour and Swift each employed more than five thousand workers within those yards. By 1886 more than one hundred miles of railroad tracks surrounded the yards, and each day trains with new refrigeration capability unloaded hundreds of cars full of western longhorn cattle, sheep, and pigs onto the planks and into the sprawling pens. The 450 acres of stockyards contained twelve platforms be-

Fig. A.1. Killing cattle—Plankinton & Armour, Kansas City, Missouri. From Joseph McCoy, *Historic Sketches of the Cattle Trade of the West and Southwest* (1874, p. 311).

hind which were long rows of chutes and holding pens, divided by those for cattle, sheep, and hogs. These divisions were laid out on a grid system with numbered alleys or streets running between them. As Rifkin (1992: 26) describes it,

> Everywhere the eye could see, there were cattle milling, moving, being separated and corralled into designated areas, to await their last walk up the chutes. . . . Hoisted onto chains and hooked onto rails, those noble creatures, venerated by much of western culture for the first few thousand years of recorded history, were hurried along from station to station, where they were hacked at, cut up, severed, divided, reduced, and reconstituted, ending up as disembodied cuts of meat at the end of the line.

Thus culminated the tragic beginning of the U.S. beef industry. The scarce few wild bovine animals left today are being destroyed rather than protected. In New Mexico's Gila National Forest, for example, the remaining feral cattle, 'unbranded and unauthorized' according to both the Forest Service and local ranchers, are being shot and killed from helicopters to keep them from eating the ranchers' pastures (Chung 2022).

The new cattle baron is the large corporate farmer or owner of a meat-packing company, controlling an industry that has continued to evolve and concentrate animal lives into the hands of a very few. In the United States it will come as no news that megafarms and giant feedlots are the norm, wherein tens of millions of animals are slaughtered annually. The enormous feedlots in Dodge City, Kansas, owned by two companies, National and Cargill, hold upward of 40,000 cattle and advertise the scenic overlook view to them as a worthwhile tourist attraction. The Harris Farm in California, one of America's largest feedlots, known to locals as "Cowschwitz" (after the Nazi concentration camp Auschwitz), has "120,000 wretched cattle pumped with hormones to boost growth," and produces a staggering 150 million pounds of beef every year (Graham 2020). Today there are essentially only four big meatpacking companies making the $66 billion annually on cow bodies: Tyson Foods, Cargill, and a pair of companies controlled by Brazilian corporate owners, National Beef Packing Company and JBS (Goodman 2021).

While we see some challenges to these monopolies, the motivations behind them are oftentimes the perceived guiding sanctity, almost, of protecting the small farmer or rancher—with 'building a better meatpacking industry' meaning breaking monopolies in ostensible favor of protections for cattle farmers, meatpacking workers, and consumers—the latter who individually eat an average of fifty-five pounds of beef each year (Appelbaum 2022). Flooding in the state of Nebraska in 2019 caused an outpouring of grief for farmers and ranchers losing their helpless livestock (Smith, Healy, and Williams 2019). We read frequent news reports that small farmers and ranchers are continually fighting against and being pushed out of their small-scale operations—which ostensibly harken back to a more authentic rural past and lifestyle (after Immerwahr 2023)—and are replaced by such huge conglomerate operations. But there is no evidence that small-scale farming is any less violent than contemporary industrial agriculture; both are inherently violent. Playing on the notion of protecting small operations in rural areas misdirects our empathy; in fact, there is evidence that contemporary small-scale agriculture, with its inherent violence, is a much closer replication of settler agricultural practices than contemporary industrial ones (Gillespie 2022: 4). Much of this type of rhetoric rests on the mythical democratic past of the little guy who wants to protect his animals and rural livelihood, when in any case the intention is to eventually sell the animals for slaughter. It is just a matter of scale, and obviously it says nothing about the intrinsic value of commodified sentient beings or their lived experiences.

Legal ownership of the land was secondary to simply gaining access to it, which to a great extent remains the case today, with public lands leased to ranching throughout the West for nominal fees. De facto privatization of public land is maintained through ranchers' leases for grazing rights, in addition to federal and state governments' heavy subsidies for animal agriculture generally. As noted, part and parcel of the American settler colonial project was this type of land acquisition—the process of turning the public domain into private property aided by an inefficient General Land Office ill-equipped or indifferent to handling the highly complex machinations of surveying, selling, and registering of public lands. Today, the farm lobby, combined with the Department of Agriculture, continues to allow seizure of public land for the financial benefit of a few, as the animals fed on public land are certainly not considered public property. (Although lease agreement fees vary considerably by state and region, the Agriculture Fairness Alliance 2020 offers some foundational understanding of this relationship.) As Gillespie (forthcoming) sums it up, "Animal agriculture was and continues to be a core institution though which settler colonialism was originally delivered and still maintained."

Transportation of live bovine animals is another arena within which useful comparisons across history and geography can be made. Rather than experiencing the 'foodless, waterless purgatory' of the railroad journey from the cow town (Rollins 1922: 262–264), today's live animals are moved by truck, and the experience of such as any improvement is debatable. This, despite the recognition of animals' stress and suffering acknowledged by the meat and dairy industry, with transport included in the Humane Methods of Slaughter Act. Today's version of the cowboy in Australia—the largest exporter of live animals in the world—performs the roundup by helicopter, where the animals are then herded onto giant trucks to cross the outback ("Where cowboys fly" 2022). From there, they are loaded onto boats and shipped to Indonesia for fattening and slaughter.

Such live export of farmed animals reaches the news cycle occasionally. One recent report described a 523-foot-long Kuwaiti-owned ship transporting 19,000 cows from Brazil to Iraq, and the atrocious buildup of feces and ammonia in the animals' cramped holding pens across several decks. The conditions created such a putrid odor for Cape Town, South Africa, residents when docked that the conditions on board for the animals made headlines (Chutel 2024). Another recent investigation focused on the shipping tragedy involving the deaths of 5,867 dairy cows from New Zealand: a typhoon struck, and the ship capsized in the East China Sea, drowning all the cows and all but one of the forty-two people aboard ship. Animal Australia reports that such occurrences are frequent around the world, and that the conditions of the live animal export trade (continued forced migration of animals) are exemplified by routine animal suffering and terror: "At 'best,' animals are confined in cramped and stressful conditions, living in their own excrement for days and weeks on end. At 'worst,' all those on board—people and animals—are at the mercy of climatic extremes—be it heat, storms or high seas" (Animals Australia 2021; Neuman 2020).

Toward an Ethical West: Future Animal Histories and Historical Geographies

Perhaps incongruously, I am still optimistic that history will be on the side of taking bovine animal lives seriously. Despite 'ag-gag' laws and other such industrial protections, much progress has been made in exposing the hidden geographies of animal cruelty in spaces such as slaughterhouses, and I find hope there. Sadists notwithstanding, I think that most humans, when they begin to understand animal sentience—including that of the most animalized of non-human animals—and the scale and extent of animal pain and suffering in these spaces, will find it indigestible and will become increasingly intolerant of it.

We see relatively quick recent cultural changes in the plant-based food industries, and I think we are living in a time of great cultural upheaval wherein humans are generally coming to a better understanding of (some) animal suffering and cruelty, and of our sharing of the earth and its resources with animals—although I also know this stretches only so far. Ninety percent of Americans (or more) eat meat, and meat eating is, at least for now, increasing in the world (Marino and Mountain 2015). Despite the current rising trends of veganism, 'flexitarianism', and 'reducetarianism' in some areas, global levels of animal-based protein consumption are on the rise—between 1993–2013 the global population increased by 29 percent, yet global demand for animals' products increased by 62 percent (Food and Agriculture Organization of the United Nations 2014). We also know that industrial-scale food production poses significant threats to environmental sustainability. The approximately one-third of all arable land devoted to growing feed for animals is obviously unsustainable, as is the phenomenal scale of the methane (greenhouse) gases produced by 1.5 billion cows and bulls exploited and killed worldwide each year. The Intergovernmental Panel on Climate Change (IPCC) has recently suggested that dietary shifts such as reducing meat consumption as well as shortening supply chains and lessening food waste could play a significant factor in climate change mitigation (IPCC 2018).

Many alternative 'regenerative agriculture' approaches today attempt to address the environmental concerns of industrialized beef production, but these are primarily focused on improving the health of the soil and more generally reducing global warming, not reducing beef consumption or violence toward animals. Such practices include engaging animals themselves as workers—as "land management tools" who stomp carbon-absorbing organic matter into the soil (Fountain 2021)—but who nonetheless eventually end up at the auction yard or slaughterhouse. The wide-ranging alternatives to the industrial-scale beef operations that animal studies scholars debate, such as plant-based faux meat and lab-grown meat (Struthers Montford 2022), are beyond the scope of this study but are worth consideration as they offer alternatives to live animal suffering and misery.

Gillespie (2022) observes that the future of farmed animals is undertheorized compared with that of other animals, with their lives so embedded and taken for granted within the very fabric of settler-colonial-capitalist agricultural systems that they are beings "never meant to live lives of flourishing." She, among many others (Donaldson and Kymlicka 2015; Pachirat 2018; Blattner, Donaldson, and Wilcox 2020) discusses farm animal sanctuaries as spaces within which animal agency, choice, and self-determination can be at least partially realized. Sanctuaries provide homes, rescue, and rehabilitation for abused and neglected animals; they are places where formerly farmed animals can discover, develop, and/or regain their autonomy, mobility, individuality, and self-expression, and can share their lives with those with whom these choose. Pachirat (2018: 347) cites Farm Sanctuary in New York and New Jersey, and the Vermont-based sanctuary VINE (Veganism Is the Next Evolution), founded by pattrice jones and Miriam Jones, as noteworthy examples of spaces that "function as active explorations, *through praxis rather than abstract theory*, of a range of possible liberatory futures for human-nonhuman animal relationships." If animals at such sites are able to live in comfort and security and self-determination, sanctuaries are nonetheless sites of captivity, and as Pachirat (2018: 349–350) observes, are problematically not perceived as threatening or challenging to the existing political or economic order. Instead, rescued animals potentially become, as he argues, "recirculated and recommodified as objects within a sanctuary economy," associated with eco-friendly, white benefactors who support them as life-style choices.

In my view, such possible immediate futures for farmed animals—sanctuary life, the total elimination of domesticated species (Francione 2018), or others—can only be truly envisioned through the lenses of the past. What might be the other implications of conceptualizing historical bovine animal stories and experiences of nineteenth-century carceral spaces and practices brought to center stage in this book? The broader implications of disturbing or disrupting normalized objectifications of abject animals such as cows into subjects who possess sentience, vulnerability, emotions, and psychologies—or, in a word, as Maneesha Deckha (2013b) would call it, 'beingness'—is to rearrange our ethics around their care and their work (Blattner, Donaldson, and Wilcox 2020).

Cattle Trails and Animal Lives challenges us to think about the broader implications of the carceral materials and practices, infrastructures, technologies, spaces, networks, economics, and laws surrounding the beef industry—which fundamentally was and is based on profound levels of violence and suffering. This intensive biopolitical formation and reformation of bovine bodies cause(d) not only pain, suffering, and injury, but also a loss of dignity to animals as procreative beings, the ethics of which must be rigorously questioned (after Gruen 2014). It almost goes without saying that animal science is wholly aware of these cognitive and emotional abilities. Agricultural scientists, for example, who focus on dairy cows report the trauma involved in cow-calf separation, so it is common practice to separate the calves from their mothers immediately after birth to sever the relationship, with both forced to live lives of alienation (Flower and Weary 2003). The cries of cows and their calves that I hear as I bicycle on a local rail trail in central Pennsylvania attest to the pain of this separation. The trail runs along a series of small dairy operations in which the mother cows are separated and confined in milking stalls by a matter of only feet from their calves, who are themselves chained to individual small plastic huts for veal production. The mournful and loud cries—sometimes almost screaming—of the mother cows with their calves so close, yet wholly inaccessible, punctuate with violence the otherwise serene surrounding landscape and soundscape.

Historical geographies of bovine animals heretofore have focused primarily on their impacts on land, agriculture, and human capitalist endeavors (e.g., Crosby 2003), but the present work asks us to consider their lives, experiences, and stories within the context of the carceral. In the preceding chapters I have documented historical bovine animals' cognitive and emotional expressions of, among others, maternal care and kinship, enjoyment, individual preferences, curiosity, fear, stress, frustration, and grief. Insights into these lived experiences of historical animals via the thriving fields of critical animal histories and animal historical geographies brings a new reality to contemporary animal life and their futures. My work foregrounds carceral sites, spaces, and practices where normalized meanings of animals were first exploited and commodified primarily for food. To consider and take seriously animal lives and experiences within this historical carceral network is also to imagine alternative futures for them based on our affective understanding of them as subjects as well as our entangled experiences with them—within the law and policy (Deckha 2013b), within our moral codes (Gruen 2014), and within our potentially and mutually 'abundant' futures (after Collard, Dempsey, and Sundberg 2015). Studying the past helps us understand how bovine animals have ended up in the violent carceral spaces of animal agriculture today, and helps us recognize that their lived experiences cannot simply be taken as 'givens' in their present circumstances, but were in fact transformations, produced and made into the circumscribed, taken-for-granted lives they, and we with them, inherit today. Understanding the carceral past, especially locatable, specific, significant pasts and periods, of groups as well as individual nonhuman animals, helps us imagine what might have been, and could be, a differently imagined future for them.

NOTES

1. Some of the foundational ideas presented in this introduction appeared first in my chapter "Bovine Lives and the Making of a Nineteenth-Century American Carceral Archipelago" (Morin 2022) and my article "Cattle Towns, Prison Towns: Historical Geographies of Rural Carceral Archipelagoes" (Morin 2019).

2. Kathryn Gillespie's *The Cow with Ear Tag #1389* (2018a: 8) offers an apt explanation about why referring to the animals under study here as "cattle" is problematical, as the term has etymological roots in the word *chattel*, meaning property. In her work Gillespie recommends the term "bovine animals" to either 'cattle' or 'livestock', to signal that they are more than mere property. As it will become clear, use of the term *cattle* and understanding its etymology prompts one to think seriously about what conceptual and material work the word *cattle* itself does—in terms, for example, of living property, claiming property, and movement of property. While *cow* is a colloquial term for a bovine animal, in animal agriculture 'cow' technically refers to a female animal that has given birth to at least one calf; a 'heifer' is a female who has not yet given birth; a 'calf' is a male or female animal under six months of age; a 'bull' is an intact adult male; and a 'steer' is a castrated male. While I cannot avoid use of the term *cattle* when referring to the many actors, practices, and processes that treated and named them as property (cattlemen, cattle barons, cattle towns, cattle prod, and so on), I opt for the terms 'bovine animals' or the more colloquial 'cow' whenever possible (and regardless of gender and breeding history of the animals under discussion, which in most cases will not be known).

3. Though not specifically relevant to my study, recent work in rural studies consider, for example, the interdisciplinary nature of rural studies and the differences in rural studies on a global scale, as well as articulate a deterritorialization or 'rematerialization' of the rural as breaking down conventional rural and urban dichotomies.

CHAPTER 1. FIRST ENCOUNTERS WITH THE CARCERAL

1. Kilgore (1983) offers a comprehensive list of works that discuss the early Texas missions, animals they brought or purchased, and the extensive numbers of wild cows that appear in a number of diaries and accounts.

CHAPTER 2. ENCLOSING THE RANGE

1. Portions of this chapter on land laws and enclosure of the open range first appeared in Morin (2022).

2. Rosenberg (2016: 7–13) studied the popular rural American 4-H culture, run by the U.S. Department of Agriculture. Among other findings, the 4-H program encourages young farmers to embrace modern farming techniques, and to cultivate efficient, capital-intensive farms under the expertise of the federal government. The system also carefully exercises biopolitical control on humans by cultivating and carefully managing gender-appropriate, sex-segregated, predominantly racially white, hetereonormative divisions of farm labor. As the American state produced heterosexuality in rural America, heterosexuality also produced the American state: it was an infrastructure "composed of prized calves, symmetrical ears of corn, hand-sewn dresses, cans of tomatoes, bags of seed, precise record books, and most important, the gendered bodies of rural youth" (14).

CHAPTER 4. COW TOWNS AND (LOST) ANIMAL LIVES

1. Immerwahr (2023), drawing on Conn (2023), describes this as also the story of the slaughterhouse industry being sited in rural areas. Refrigerated cars and trucking allowed stockyard owners to move wherever business conditions suited them and then staffed them with low-paid, nonunionized immigrants, who were often undocumented (Immerwahr 2023: 28). Immerwahr also notes that the industrialization of the rural landscape includes its militarization by the Pentagon seeking cheap land: the United States has more than four thousand military bases, which has had the impact of 'fusing' rural people with the armed forces, with those dying in military action disproportionally from small towns. The prison-industrial complex also dominates in rural areas (Morin 2019). In all of these cases, people have few other options but to work in corporate jobs such as in the rural mines, factories, military bases, and prisons.

2. Today, as White (1994: 258) observes, athletes at the University of Texas derive their inspiration from the longhorn mascot, an identification that is ironically "with neutered cattle."

3. Such breeding programs are associated with improved agriculture itself (after Ritvo 1987). This relationship is front and center at the National Ranching Heritage Center (which not incidentally dates the beginning of the mixing of Herefords and Angus with Texas longhorns beginning ca. 1870; Lust 2021). In addition to the 19-acre outdoor historical park, the museum presents something of a propaganda machine for the history of cattle ranching and contemporary breeding of meat. Using enormous images of

animals with body parts associated with different cuts of meat, the museum describes the breeding of animals using donor cows and enhanced donor eggs, various insemination techniques, testing of the right bulls for breeding, and DNA and genetic profiling of animals. Museum displays cover everything from the refrigerated truck replacing the refrigerated railroad car for animal transport, to signage declaring that humans need the essential proteins of meat.

CHAPTER 5. CATTLE-DRIVE WESTERNS

1. The American Humane Association of Hollywood publishes the lengthy *Guidelines for the Safe Use of Animals in Filmed Media*, first issued formally in 1988 and meant to cover all "sentient beasts." According to its website, the association's "'No Animals Were Harmed' program today oversees the safety of some 100,000 animal actors each year on 1,000 film and television productions around the world. It is the only industry-sanctioned group to monitor the safety and humane treatment of animals in filmed entertainment." The Guidelines chapter on horses and livestock (American Humane Association of Hollywood 2015: 75–112) covers everything from recommendations on 'simulating' harmful equipment such as spurs; healthful requirements for weather, rest, and water; requiring veterinarians on site; the fact that untrained animals may be used when filming of a herd providing that the herd is preexisting and on familiar terrain, 'with a safety plan in place to prevent animals from escaping or deviating from the intended path'; and that branding and death of animals must be simulated (among many other recommendations). Yet as McLean (2014: 19–20) writes, "No matter how strenuously the AHA website labors to assure me that 'no animals were harmed' in the making of this or that film, even they admit that they cannot monitor all of them."

2. Johnson (2022: 119) argues that male horses were also icons of nationalism, power, and beauty, and that male horses were treated differently than mares in this calculation, who were underrepresented and marginalized—and illustrating how humans transfer their own gender roles and aspirations onto animals.

3. Clay Lilley, current head of Movin' on Livestock, www.movinonlivestock.com, invited me to contact his father, Jack. The biography of Jack Lilley states that starting at age fifteen Lilley became a legendary stuntman, actor, and animal trainer and supplier; he worked as a livestock wrangler and actor in hundreds of films, including *The Man Who Shot Liberty Valence* (1962), *Blazing Saddles* (1974), *Little House on the Prairie* (1983), and *City Slickers* (1991) (see Blazing Saddle Falls: Jack Lilley Rides 2015). Lilley reports that he "learned how to fall off a horse from those old cowboys . . . but pulling horses down . . . don't know if you'd get away with it today." In some of these extraordinary stunts, both horse and rider fall to the ground and stand back up without becoming disengaged.

4. Animal trainers and members of the local Animal Trainers Union 399 did not return my calls or emails. Thus, much of the material for this section I derived through production notes, files, and articles on the motion picture industry history available through the Margaret Herrick Library Digital Collections from the Academy of Motion

Pictures, dating from 1927, including a database on the Production Codes Administration Records, and the Media History Digital Library.

5. I acknowledge the 'proxy' use of animal experiences in western films generally in this last section of the chapter, as opposed to animal experiences in the specifically cattle-drive films discussed in the first section. My analysis was restricted by available sources and archives, but I would also emphasize that there is a great deal of room for additional research on bovine and other livestock animals in westerns and other films.

REFERENCES

Acampora, R. (ed) (2010) *Metamorphoses of the Zoo: Animal Encounter after Noah.* New York: Lexington Books.

Adams, C. (1990) *The Sexual Politics of Meat: A Feminist Vegetarian Critical Theory.* New York: Continuum.

Agriculture Fairness Alliance (2020). https://agriculturefairnessalliance.org/.

Alio, G. (2018) *Speculative Taxidermy: Natural History, Animal Surfaces, and Art in the Anthropocene.* New York: Columbia University Press.

Alio, G. (2021) Keynote presentation, Animaterialities Symposium, Center for Material Culture Studies, University of Delaware, 24 April.

Alkan, H. (2022) Workshop organizer, Rooting together, growing together: Multispecies co-temporalities of migration. IMISCOE Annual Conference, 29 June–1 July, Oslo.

American Humane Association of Hollywood (2015) Guidelines for the Safe Use of Animals in Filmed Media, "No Animals Were Harmed" program. Studio City, Calif.

Anderson, V. (2004) *Creatures of Empire: How Domestic Animals Transformed Early America.* New York: Oxford University Press.

Animals Australia, Live Export (2021). https://animalsaustralia.org/our-work/live-export/.

Appelbaum, B. (2022) Building a better meatpacking industry. *New York Times,* 15 January.

Aquila, R. (ed) (1996) *Wanted Dead or Alive: The American West in Pop Culture.* Chicago: University of Illinois Press.

Argent, N. (2017) Rural geography I: Resource peripheries and the creation of new global commodity chains. *Progress in Human Geography* 41 (6):803–812.

Argent, N. (2019) Rural geography III: Marketing, mobilities, measurement and meta-narratives. *Progress in Human Geography* 43 (4):758–66.

Arnold, O., and Hale, J. P. (1940) *Hot Irons: Heraldry of the Range.* New York: Cooper Square Publishers.

Ballad of Buster Scruggs (2018) Coen, J., and Coen, E. (Directors and Producers). Annapurna Pictures, Mike Zoss Productions. Released on Netflix.

Barbed Wire (1952) George Archainbaud (Director). Gene Autry Productions, Los Angeles.

Bauder, H. (2016) *Migration, Borders, Freedom.* London: Routledge.

Bell, K. (2016) El Capitan arrives. *Dodge City Daily Globe.* 1 November. https://www.dodgeglobe.com/news/20161101/el-capitan-arrives.

Bell, K. (2021) Curator of Collections & Education, Boot Hill Museum, Dodge City, Kansas. Personal correspondence with author, 13 December.

Bell, R. (1961) Eric Fleming: Cowboy, realist and dreamer. *TV Radio Mirror* 55 (2 January).

Bennett, D. (1998) *Conquerors: The Roots of New World Horsemanship.* Solvang, Calif.: Amigo Publications.

Bennett, J. (2010) *Vibrant Matter: A Political Ecology of Things.* Durham, N.C.: Duke University Press.

Bennett, L. E., and Abbott, S. (2017) *The Perfect Fence: Untangling the Meanings of Barbed Wire.* College Station: Texas A&M University Press.

Blattner, C., Coulter, K., and Kymlicka, W. (2020) Animal labour and the quest for inter-species justice. In Blattner, C., Coutler, K., and Kymlicka, W. (eds) *Animal Labour: A New Frontier of Interspecies Justice?* London: Oxford University Press, 1–25.

Blattner, C. E., Donaldson, S., and Wilcox, R. (2020) Animal agency in community: A political multispecies ethnography of VINE Sanctuary. *Politics and Animals* 6:1–22.

Blazing Saddle Falls: Jack Lilley Rides (2015) *Legacy,* SCVTV, 29 December. https://scvtv.com/2017/03/22/blazing-saddle-falls-jack-lilley-rides/.

Braitman, L. (2014) *Animal Madness: How Anxious Dogs, Compulsive Parrots, and Elephants in Recovery Help Us Understand Ourselves.* New York: Simon & Schuster.

Brown, F. (2021) *The City Is More than Human: An Animal History of Seattle.* Seattle: University of Washington Press.

Brown, R. M. (1994) Violence. In Milner, C. A., O'Connor, C. A., and Sandweiss, M. A. (eds) *The Oxford History of the American West.* New York: Oxford University Press, 393–425.

Buller, H. (2015) Animal geographies II: Methods. *Progress in Human Geography* 39 (3):374–384.

Burt, J. (2002) *Animals in Film.* London: Reaktion Books Ltd.

Butzer, K. (1988) Cattle and sheep from Old to New Spain: Historical antecedents. *Annals of the Association of American Geographers* 78 (1):29–56.

Cacho, L. M. (2012) *Social Death: Racialized Rightlessness and the Criminalization of the Unprotected.* New York: New York University Press.

Castration of Cattle: Literature Review on the Welfare Implications of (2014). American

Veterinary Medical Association, 15 July. https://www.avma.org/resources-tools /literature-reviews/welfare-implications-castration-cattle.

Cattle Drive (1951). Kurt Neumann (Director). Universal International Pictures, Los Angeles.

Cattle History in North America (2023). https://allaboutbison.com/cattle-history -in-north-america/.

Cherokee Strip Live Stock Association (2023). Oklahoma City: Oklahoma Historical Society. https://www.okhistory.org/publications/enc/entry?entry=CH025.

Chung, C. (2022) Plan to reduce feral cattle in New Mexico draws objections. *New York Times*, 8 February.

Chutel, L. (2024) That 'unimaginable' smell in Cape Town? A Docked ship with 19,000 cows. *New York Times*, 20 February.

Cloke, P., Marsden, T., and Mooney, P. H. (eds) (2006) *Handbook of Rural Studies.* London: Sage.

Collard, R.-C.. and Dempsey, J. (2013) Life for sale? The Politics of lively commodities. *Environment and Planning A* 45 (11):2682–2699.

Collard, R.-C., Dempsey, J., and Sundberg, J. (2015) A manifesto for abundant futures. *Annals of the Association of American Geographers* 105 (2):322–330.

Colling, S. (2020) *Animal Resistance in the Global Capitalist Era.* East Lansing: Michigan State University Press.

Collins, A. (1993) *Lassie: A Dog's Life.* New York: Penguin Books.

"Columbia, the Gem of the Ocean" (1843) *Dodge City* soundtrack. Music by D. T. Shaw and arranged by T. A. Beckett.

Conn, S. (2023) *The Lies of the Land: Seeing Rural America for What It Is—and Isn't.* Chicago: University of Chicago Press.

Cooley, M. (2022) *The Perfection of Nature: Animals, Breeding, and Race in the Renaissance.* Chicago: University of Chicago Press.

Coulter, K. (2015) *Animals, Work, and the Promise of Interspecies Solidarity.* New York: Palgrave Macmillan.

Coulter, K. (2022) The organization of animal protection investigations and the animal harm spectrum: Canadian data, international lessons. *Social Sciences* 11 (1).

Cowboys, The (1972) Mark Rydell (Director). Sanford Productions III, Los Angeles.

Cow Town (1950) John English (Director). Gene Autry Productions, Los Angeles.

Cox, J., with introduction by J. Frank Dobie (1895; 1959) *Historical and Biographical Record of the Cattle Industry and the Cattlemen of Texas and Adjacent Territory.* New York: Antiquarian Society.

Cox, L. (2015) Finding animals in history: Veterinary artifacts and the use of material history. In Nance, S. (ed) *The Historical Animal.* Syracuse, N.Y.: Syracuse University Press, 99–117.

Creager, A., and Jordan, W. C. (eds) (2002) *The Animal/Human Boundary: Historical Perspectives.* Rochester, N.Y.: University of Rochester Press.

Cronon, W. (1991) *Nature's Metropolis: Chicago and the Great West.* New York: W. W. Norton.

Cronon, W. (2009) Foreword: Nature screened. In Mitman, G. *Reel Nature: America's Romance with Wildlife on Film*. Seattle: University of Washington Press, xi–xv.

Crosby, A. W. (1994) *Germs, Seeds and Animals: Studies in Ecological History*. Armonk, N.Y.: M. E. Sharpe.

Crosby, A. W. (2003) *The Columbian Exchange: Biological and Cultural Consequences of 1492*. 30th anniversary ed. Westport, Conn.: Praeger.

Crosby, A. W. (2004) *Ecological Imperialism: The Biological Expansion of Europe, 900–1900*. Cambridge: Cambridge University Press.

Culpepper Cattle Company (1972) Dick Richards (Director). Twentieth Century Fox, Los Angeles.

Dalke, K. (2010) Mustang: Paradox of imagery. *Humanimilia* 1:2.

Dalke, K., and Hunt, M. O. (2017) Mustangs and domestic horses: Examining what we think we know about differences. *Humanimalia* 8:2.

Dargis, M. (2010) Montana cowboys lead, coax and cajole their charges amid a chorus of bleats. *New York Times*, 5 January.

Davant, R., with Herskowitz, M. (2016) *Mystic Sails, Texas Trails: Captain Grimes, Shanghai Pierce, Range Wars, and Raising Texas*. Huntsville: Texas Review Press.

Dean, J. (2021) Public History. In Roscher, M., Krebber, A., and Mizelle, B. (eds) *Handbook of Historical Animal Studies*. Oldenbourg: De Gruyter, 227–242.

Deckha, M. (2010) The subhuman as a cultural agent of violence. *Journal for Critical Animal Studies* 8 (3):28–51.

Deckha, M. (2013a) Welfarist *and* imperial: The Contributions of anticruelty laws to civilizational discourse. *American Quarterly* 65 (3):515–548.

Deckha, M. (2013b) Initiating a non-anthropocentric jurisprudence: The rule of law and animal vulnerability under a property paradigm. *Alberta Law Review* 50 (4):783–814.

Dehorning Calves (2004) Agricultural Extension Service. Knoxville: University of Tennessee, PB 1684.

Dehorning and Disbudding of Cattle (2014), Literature Review on the Welfare Implications of. American Veterinary Medical Association. 15 July.

DeMello, M. (2014) Rabbits in captivity. In Gruen, L. (ed) *The Ethics of Captivity*. London: Oxford University Press, 77–89.

Derby L. (2011) Bringing the animals back in: Writing quadrapeds into the environmental history of Latin America and the Caribbean. *History Compass* 9/8:602–621.

Derry, M. E. (2003) *Bred for Perfection: Shorthorn Cattle, Collies and Arabian Horses since 1800*. Baltimore: Johns Hopkins University Press.

Dobie, J. F. (1941; 2010) *The Longhorns*. Austin: University of Texas Press.

Dodge City (1939) Michael Curtiz (Director). Warner Bros. Pictures, Los Angeles.

Domesticating Bison for Survival (2023). https://allaboutbison.com/domesticating -bison-for-survival/.

Donaldson, S., and Kymlicka, W. (2015) Farmed animal sanctuaries: The heart of the movement? *Politics and Animals* 1 (1):50–74.

Dykstra, R. D. (1968) *The Cattle Towns*. Lincoln: University of Nebraska Press.

Earth Policy Institute (2012) http://www.earthpolicy.org/data_highlights/2012 /highlights25.

"El Capitan" (2019) Historical Marker Database. https://www.hmdb.org/marker .asp?marker=65271.

Elder, G., Wolch, J., and Emel, J. (1998) Le pratique sauvage: Race, place, and the human-animal divide. In Wolch, J., and Emel, J. (eds) *Animal Geographies: Place, Politics, and Identity in Nature-Cultural Borderlands*. London: Verso, 72–90.

Falconer, P. (2020) *The Afterlife of the Hollywood Western*. London: Palgrave Macmillan.

Few, M., and Tortorici, Z. (eds) (2013) *Centering Animals in Latin American History*. Durham, N.C.: Duke University Press.

First National Films (1923) 250,000 Cattle. *Film News*, 15 October.

Flower, F., and Weary, D. (2003) The effects of early separation on the dairy cow and calf. *Animal Welfare* 12:339–348.

Food and Agriculture Organization of the United Nations (2014) The state of food insecurity in the world: Strengthening the enabling environment for food security and nutrition. Rome, FAO.

Foucault, M. (1977) *Discipline and Punish: The Birth of the Prison*. New York: Penguin Books.

Foucault, M. (2007) *Security, Territory, Population: Lectures at the Collège de France, 1977–1978*. Trans. Burchell, G. New York: Palgrave Macmillan.

Fountain, H. (2021) A different kind of land management: Let the cows stomp. *New York Times*, 17 February.

Francione, G. L. (2004) Animals—property or persons? In Sustein, C. R., and Nussbaum, M. A. (eds) *Animal Rights: Current Debates and New Directions*. Oxford: Oxford University Press, 108–142.

Francione, G. L. (2008) *Animals as Persons: Essays on the Abolition of Animal Exploitation*. New York: Columbia University Press.

Francione, G. L. (2018) Commentary presented at Conference on Animal Exploitation. Bucknell University, Lewisburg, Pa., 3 March.

Fudge, E. (2002) A left-handed blow: Writing the history of animals. In Rothfels, N. (ed) *Representing Animals*. Bloomington: Indiana University Press, 1–18.

Fudge, E. (2017) What was it like to be a cow: History and animal studies. In Kalof, E. (ed) *The Oxford Handbook of Animal Studies*. New York: Oxford University Press, 258–278.

Gardiner, A. (2021) History of Veterinary Medicine. In Roscher, M., Krebber, A., and Mizelle, B. (eds) *Handbook of Historical Animal Studies*. Oldenbourg: De Gruyter, 493–507.

Genzert, R., Anderson, A., and Anderson, L. (2014) *Animal Stars: Behind the Scenes with Your Favorite Animal Actors*. Notavo, Calif.: New World Library.

Gerald Peters Collection (1988) *The West Explored: The Gerald Peters Collection of Western American Art*. Santa Fe, N.Mex.: Gerald Peters Gallery.

Gibbs, L. (2020) Animal geographies 1: Hearing the cry and extending beyond. *Progress in Human Geography* 44 (4):769–777.

Giedion, S. (1948; 2013) *Mechanization Takes Command: A Contribution to Anonymous History*. Minneapolis: University of Minnesota Press.

Gilks, A. (1925) Photographing "North of 36." *American Cinematographer*, January, 5–6, 19.

Gillespie, K. (2015) Nonhuman animal resistance and the improprieties of live property. In I. Braverman (ed) *Animals, Biopolitics, Law*. London: Routledge, 117–132.

Gillespie, K. (2018a) *The Cow with Ear Tag #1389*. Chicago: University of Chicago Press.

Gillespie, K. (2018b) Intimacy, animal emotion and empathy: Multispecies intimacy as slow research practice. In Moss, P., and Donovan, C. (eds) *Writing Intimacy into Feminist Geography*. London: Routledge, 160–169.

Gillespie, K. (2022) An unthinkable politics for multispecies flourishing within and beyond colonial-capitalist ruins. *Annals of the American Association of Geographers* 112 (4):1108–1122.

Gillespie, K. (forthcoming) *The Sound of Feathers: Haunting and Bearing Witness in Multispecies Worlds*. Durham, N.C.: Duke University Press.

Glick, M. H. (2013) Animal instincts: Race, criminality, and the reversal of the 'human'. *American Quarterly* 65 (3):639–659.

Goetzmann, W. H., and Reese, B. D. (1983) *Texas Images & Visions*. Archer M. Huntington Art Gallery, University of Texas–Austin. Austin: University of Texas Press.

Goodman, P. (2021) Record beef prices but ranches aren't cashing in. *New York Times*, 27 December.

Gould, J. H. (1891) The ocean steamship as freight carrier. *Scribner's Magazine*, 5 November, 604–605.

Graham, C. (2020) Tale of two farms says it all. *The Mail Online*, 30 May.

Griffin, D. R. (1992) *Animal Minds*. Chicago: University of Chicago Press.

Gruen, L. (ed) (2014) *The Ethics of Captivity*. New York: Oxford University Press.

Gruen, L. (2015) *Entangled Empathies*. New York: Lantern Books.

Gruen, L. (2016) Carceral logic and an ethics of avowal. Lecture presented at the Race and Animals Summer Institute, Wesleyan University, Middletown, CT.

Gruen, L., and Marceau, J. (eds) (2022) *Carceral Logics: Human Incarceration and Animal Captivity*. Cambridge: Cambridge University Press.

Gustafsson, L., and Haapoja, T. (eds) (2015) *History According to Cattle*. Brooklyn, N.Y.: Into Kustannus and Punctum Books.

Halley, J. (2012) *The Parallel Lives of Women and Cows: Meat Markets*. New York: Palgrave Macmillan.

Hanson, H. (2020) Cows have unique moos. *Huffington Post*, 18 January.

Haraway, D. (1993) Teddy bear patriarchy: Taxidermy in the Garden of Eden, New York City, 1908–1936. In Kaplan, A., and Pease, D. E. (eds) *Cultures of United States Imperialism*. Durham, N.C.: Duke University Press, 237–291.

Haraway, D. (2008) *When Species Meet*. Minneapolis: University of Minnesota Press.

Harlan, R. (1956) Filming *The Last Hunt*. *American Cinematographer*. March, 172–176.

Havins, T. R. (1948) Texas Fever. *Southwestern Historical Quarterly* 52 (2):147–162.

Heffernan, M., and Morin, K. M. (2021) Between history and geography. In Domosh, M.,

Heffernan, M., and Withers, C. W. (eds) *The SAGE Handbook of Historical Geography*, London: Sage, 25–46.

Heintzman, K. (2021) Material culture studies. In Roscher, M., Krebber, A., and Mizelle, B. (eds) *Handbook of Historical Animal Studies*. Oldenbourg: De Gruyter, 357–373.

Hemsworth, P. H., Barnett, J. L., Beveridge, L., and Matthews, L. R. (1995) The welfare of extensively managed dairy cattle: A review. *Applied Animal Behaviour Science* 42:161–182.

Herbert, C. W. (1940) Making ranch picture that is real. *American Cinematographer*, July, 298–301.

Hetherington, K., and Munro, R. (eds) (1997) *Ideas of Difference: Social Spaces and the Labour of Division*. Oxford: Blackwell.

Hidalgo, J. S. (2018) *Unjust Borders: Individuals and the Ethics of Immigration*. London: Routledge.

Hodgetts T., and Lorimer, J. (2015) Methodologies for animals' geographies: Cultures, communication and genomics. *Cultural Geographies* 22 (2):285–295.

Hodgetts, T., and Lorimer, J. (2020) Animals' mobilities. *Progress in Human Geography* 44 (1):4–26.

Hoganson, K. (2012) Meat in the middle: Converging borderlands in the U.S. Midwest, 1865–1900. *Journal of American History* 98 (4):1025–1051.

Holloway, L., Morris, C., Gilna, B., and Gibbs, D. (2009) Biopower, genetics and livestock breeding: (Re)constituting animal populations and heterogeneous biosocial collectivities. *Transactions of the Institute of British Geographers* 34:394–407.

Hollywood, Censorship, and the Motion Picture Production Code, 1927–1968 (1946). Archives Unbound, Margaret Herrick Collection, p. 4.

Holt, R. D. (1930) The introduction of barbed wire into Texas and the fence cutting war. *West Texas Historical Association Year Book* 6:65–79.

Hook, M. (2021) Docent, Old Abilene Town, Abilene, Kansas. Personal interview and correspondences with author, May–November.

Howell, P. (2021) Historical animal geographies. In Roscher, M., Krebber, A., and Mizelle, B. (eds) *Handbook of Historical Animal Studies*. Oldenbourg: De Gruyter, 309–324.

Hribal, J. (2003) Animals are part of the working class: A challenge to labor history. *Labor History* 44 (4):435–453.

Hunter, J. M. (ed) with introduction by B. B. Price (1924; 1985) *The Trail Drivers of Texas*. Austin: University of Texas Press.

Immerwahr, D. (2023) The pitchfork of history: Beyond the myth of rural America. *New Yorker*, 23 October, 26–29.

IPCC (Intergovernmental Panel on Climate Change) (2018). https://www.ipcc.ch/sr15/download/#full.

Jackson, Z. I. (2013) Animal: New directions in the theorization of race and posthumanism. *Feminist Studies* 39 (3):669–685.

Jett, S. C. (2017) *Ancient Ocean Crossings: Reconsidering the Case for Contacts with the Pre-Columbian Americas*. Tuscaloosa: University of Alabama Press.

Johnson, J. (2022) Mareitude: Misogyny in the horse world. In Argent, G., and Vaught,

J. (eds) *The Relational Horse: How Frameworks of Communication, Care, Politics and Power Reveal and Conceal Equine Selves*. Leiden: Brill, 119–134.

Johnson, M. L. (1996) *New Westers: The West in Contemporary American Culture*. Lawrence: University Press of Kansas.

Jorgensen, D. (2015) Migrant muskoxen and the naturalization of national identity in Scandinavia. In Nance, S. (ed) *The Historical Animal*. Syracuse, N.Y.: Syracuse University Press, 184–199.

Kauanui, J. K. (2016) "A structure not an event": Settler colonialism and enduring Indigeneity. *Lateral* 5 (1).

Kilgore, D. (1983) The Spanish missions and the origins of the cattle industry in Texas. *Cattlemen Magazine*, January.

Kim, C. J. (2011) Moral extensionism or racist exploitation: The use of holocaust and slavery analogies in the animal liberation movement. *New Political Science* 33 (3):311–333.

Kim, C. J. (2015) *Dangerous Crossings: Race, Species, and Nature in a Multicultural Age*. Cambridge: Cambridge University Press.

King, B. J. (2013) *How Animals Grieve*. Chicago: University of Chicago Press.

Ko, S. (2016) Notes from the border of the human-animal divide: Thinking and talking about animal oppression when you're not quite human yourself. *Aphro-ism: Essays on Pop Culture, Feminism, and Black Veganism from Two Sisters*, 13 January. https://aphro-ism.com/.

Kowalewski, M. (ed) (1996) *Reading the West: New Essays on the Literature of the American West*. Cambridge: Cambridge University Press.

Lambert, D. (2018) Runaways and strays: Rethinking (non)human agency in Caribbean slave societies. In Wilcox, S., and Rutherford, S. (eds) *Historical Animal Geographies*. London: Routledge, 185–189.

Lilley, J. (2022) Interview with author, 14 March.

Limerick, P. N. (1987) *Legacy of Conquest: The Unbroken Past of the American West*. New York: W. W. Norton.

Lin, J. (2009) *Barbed Wire: The Fence that Changed the West*. Missoula, Mont.: Mountain Press Publishing.

Lippit, A. M. (2000) *Electric Animal: Toward a Rhetoric of Wildlife*. Minneapolis: University of Minnesota Press.

Longhorn, The (1951) Lewis D. Collins (Director). Frontier Pictures, Los Angeles.

Lorimer, H. (2006) Herding memories of humans and animals. *Environment and Planning D: Society and Space* 24 (4):497–518.

Loyd, J. M., Mitchelson, M., and Burridge, A. (eds) (2012) *Beyond Walls and Cages: Prisons, Borders, and Global Crisis*. Athens: University of Georgia Press.

Ludwig, W. (2018) *The Old Chisholm Trail: From Cow Path to Tourist Stop*. College Station: Texas A&M University Press.

Lust, L. A. (2021) Curator, National Ranching Heritage Museum, Lubbock, Texas. Personal communication with author, 29 May 2021.

M., Ben. (2019) "El Capitan statue." Clio: Your Guide to History, 8 September. https://theclio.com/entry/85305.

MacClancy, J. (1993) *Consuming Culture: Why You Eat What You Eat*. New York: Henry Holt.

Marceau, J. (2019) *Beyond Cages: Animal Law and Criminal Punishment*. Cambridge: Cambridge University Press.

Marino, L., and Mountain, M. (2015). Denial of death and the relationship between humans and other animals. *Anthrozoös* 28 (1):5–21.

Mayes, C. (2020) Governmentality of fencing in Australia: Tracing the white wires from paddocks to Aboriginal protection, pest exclusion and immigration restriction. *Journal of Intercultural Studies* 41 (1):42–59.

McCoy, J. G. (1874) *Historic Sketches of the Cattle Trade of the West and Southwest*. Kansas City: Ramsey, Millett & Hudson.

McHugh, S. (2004) *Dog*. London: Reaktion.

McLauchlan, L. (2021) Multispecies ethnography. In Roscher, M., Krebber, A., and Mizelle, B. (eds) *Handbook of Historical Animal Studies*. Oldenbourg: De Gruyter, 393–408.

McLean, A. (ed) (2014) *Cinematic Canines: Dogs and Their Work in the Fiction Film*. New Brunswick, N.J.: Rutgers University Press.

McTavish, E. J., Decker, J. E., Schnabel, R. D., Taylor, J. F., and Hillis, D. M. (2013) New world cattle show ancestry from multiple independent domestication events. *PNAS Journal*. www.pnas.org/cgi/doi/10.1073/pnas.1303367110.

Milner-Gulland, E. J., Fryxell, J. M., and Sinclair, A. R. (2011) *Animal Migration: A Synthesis*. Oxford: Oxford University Press.

Mitchell, K., Jones, R., and Fluri, J. L. (eds) (2020) *Handbook on Critical Geographies of Migration*. Cheltenham, U.K.: Edward Elgar.

Mize, R. (2021) Presentation, Animaterialities Symposium, Center for Material Culture Studies, University of Delaware, Newark, 24 April.

Monster Blizzard That Turned Kansas into a Frozen Wasteland, The (2019), 3 March. https://www.history.com/news/great-plains-blizzard-1886-kansas-big-die-up.

Moran, D. (2015) *Carceral Geography: Spaces and Practices of Incarceration*. London: Ashgate.

Moran, D., Gill, N., and Conlon, D. (eds) (2013) *Carceral Spaces: Mobility and Agency in Imprisonment and Migrant Detention*. London: Ashgate.

Moran, D., Turner, J., and Schliehe, A. (2018). Conceptualising the carceral in carceral geography. *Progress in Human Geography* 42 (5):666–686.

Morgan, K., and M. Cole (2011) The discursive representation of nonhuman animals in a culture of denial. In Carter, B., and Charles, N. (eds) *Humans and Other Animals: Critical Perspectives*. New York: Palgrave Macmillan, 112–132.

Morin, K. M. (2010) Unpopular archives. *Professional Geographer* 62 (4):534–543.

Morin, K. M. (2018) *Carceral Space, Prisoners and Animals*. London: Routledge.

Morin, K. M. (2019) Cattle towns, prison towns: Historical geographies of rural carceral archipelagoes. *Historical Geography* 27:141–165.

Morin, K. M. (2022) Bovine lives and the making of a nineteenth-century American carceral archipelago. In Gruen, L., and Marceau, J. (eds) *Carceral Logics: Human Incarceration and Animal Captivity*. Cambridge: Cambridge University Press, 261–275.

Morin, K., and Moran, D. (2015) *Historical Geographies of Prisons: Unlocking the Usable Carceral Past.* London: Routledge.

Mountz, A. (2010) *Seeking Asylum: Human Smuggling and Bureaucracy at the Border.* Minneapolis: University of Minnesota Press.

Nance, S. (2013) *Entertaining Elephants: Animal Agency and the Business of the American Circus.* Baltimore: Johns Hopkins University Press.

Nance, S. (ed) (2015) *The Historical Animal.* Syracuse, N.Y.: Syracuse University Press.

Neuman, S. (2020) 42 crew, nearly 6,000 cows missing after ship sinks in storm-tossed seas off Japan. National Public Radio, 3 September.

Netz, R. (2004) *Barbed Wire: An Ecology of Modernity.* Middletown, Conn.: Wesleyan University Press.

Ogle, M. (2013) *In Meat We Trust: An Unexpected History of Carnivore America.* New York: Houghton Mifflin Harcourt.

Ohrem, D. (2018) Western horizons, animal becomings: Race, species, and the troubled boundaries of the human in the era of American expansionism. In Wilcox, S., and Rutherford, S. (eds) *Historical Animal Geographies.* London: Routledge, 132–148.

O'Key, D. (2019) Animal borderlands: An introduction. *Parallax* 25 (4):351–357.

Pachirat, T. (2011) *Every Twelve Seconds: Industrialized Slaughter and the Politics of Sight.* New Haven, Conn.: Yale University Press.

Pachirat, T. (2018) Sanctuary. In Gruen, L. (ed) *Critical Terms for Animal Studies.* Chicago: University of Chicago Press, 337–355.

Pacyga, D. A. (2015) *Slaughterhouse: Chicago's Union Stock Yard and the World It Made.* Chicago: University of Chicago Press.

Patchett, M. (2008) Tracking tigers: Recovering the embodied practices of taxidermy. *Historical Geography* 36:17–39.

Patterson, C. (2002) *Eternal Treblinka: Our Treatment of Animals and the Holocaust.* New York: Lantern Books.

Pawley, E. (2016) The point of perfection: Cattle portraiture, bloodlines, and the meaning of breeding, 1760–1860. *Journal of the Early Republic* 36 (Spring):37–72.

PETA (2022) Animals in entertainment, film and television. https://www.peta.org/issues/animals-in-entertainment/animals-in-film-tv/ https://www.peta.org/issues/animals-in-entertainment/animals-used-entertainment-factsheets/.

Philo, C., and Wilbert, C. (eds) (2000) *Animal Spaces, Beastly Places: New Geographies of Human-Animal Relations.* London: Routledge.

Power of the Dog, The (2021) Jane Campion (Director). New Zealand Film Commission and BBC Film, Netflix distribution.

Probyn-Rapsey, F. (2018) Anthropocentrism. In Gruen, L. (ed) *Critical Terms for Animal Studies.* Chicago: University of Chicago Press, 47–63.

Razac, O. (2002) *Barbed Wire: A Political History.* New York: New Press.

Redelings, L. (1949) Film reviews: Outdoor productions cause camera problems. *Home Movies*, 580.

Red River (1948) Howard Hawkes (Director). Monterey Productions, Monterey, Calif.

Red River (1948) *Motion Picture Herald*, 17 July, 4241.

Red River (1949) *Home Movies* 16 (1 January):36.

Rifkin, J. (1992) *Beyond Beef: The Rise and Fall of the Cattle Culture*. New York: Dutton.

Ritvo, H. (1987) *The Animal Estate: The English and Other Creatures in the Victorian Age*. Cambridge, Mass.: Harvard University Press.

Ritvo, H. (2010) *Noble Cows and Hybrid Zebras: Essays on Animals and History*. Charlottesville: University of Virginia Press.

Rollins, P. A. (1922) *The Cowboy: His Characteristics, His Equipment, and His Part in the Development of the West*. New York: Charles Scribner's Sons.

Rosenberg, G. N. (2016) *The 4-H Harvest: Sexuality and the State in Rural America*. Philadelphia: University of Pennsylvania Press.

Rouse, J. E. (1977) *The Criollo: Spanish Cattle in the Americas*. Norman: University of Oklahoma Press.

Routley, L. (2017) The carceral: Beyond, around, through and within prison walls. *Political Geography* 57 (3):105–108.

Rowan, A. (1956) GIANT enhanced by bold, off beat photography. *American Cinematographer* 37 (March), 176.

Royle, C. (2018) Shaking the ground: Histories of earthworms from Darwin to niche construction. In Wilcox, S., and Rutherford, S. (eds) *Historical Animal Geographies*. London: Routledge, 37–50.

Russell, S. A. (1993) *Kill the Cowboy: A Battle of Mythology in the New West*. New York: Horseshoe Books.

Scofield, R. (2019) *Outriders: Rodeo at the Fringes of the American West*. Seattle: University of Washington Press.

Scott, J. (1998) *Seeing Like a State: How Certain Schemes to Improve the Human Condition Have Failed*. New Haven, Conn.: Yale University Press.

Shackelford, B. M. (2015) *The Wests of Texas: Cattle Ranching Entrepreneurs*. Denton: Texas State Historical Association.

Shea, T., and Saxena, S. (2016) *What Is Animal Migration?* New York: Rosen Publishing.

Sherow, J. E. (2018) *The Chisholm Trail: Joseph McCoy's Great Gamble*. Norman: Oklahoma University Press.

Shillingberg, W. B. (2009) *Dodge City: The Early Years, 1872–1886*. Norman, Okla.: Arthur H. Clark.

Skaggs, J. (1973) *The Cattle-Trailing Industry*. Norman: University of Oklahoma Press.

Sluyter, A. (1996) The ecological origins and consequences of cattle ranching in sixteenth-century New Spain. *Geographical Review* 86 (2):161–177.

Smith, M., Healy, J., and Williams, T. (2019) 'It's probably over for us': Record flooding pummels Midwest when farmers can least afford it. *New York Times*, 18 March.

Southhall, J. (n.d.) Review of *Red River*, The Big T Out West. http://www.movie-wave.net/titles/red_river.html.

Specht, J. (2016) The rise, fall, and rebirth of the Texas longhorn: An evolutionary history. *Environmental History* 21:343–363.

Specht, J. (2017) For the future in the distance: Cattle trailing, social conflict, and the development of Ellsworth, Kansas. *Kansas History: A Journal of the Central Plains* 40 (Summer):104–119.

Specht, J. (2019) *Red Meat Republic: A Hoof-to-Table History of How Beef Changed America*. Princeton, N.J.: Princeton University Press.

Spiegel, M. (1997) *The Dreaded Comparison: Human and Animal Slavery*. New York: Mirror Books.

Spivak, G. (1988) Can the subaltern speak? In Nelson, C., and Grossberg, L. (eds) *Marxism and the Interpretation of Culture*. Basingstoke, U.K.: Macmillan Education, 271–313.

Stanescu, V. (2019) Selling Eden: Environmentalism, local meat, and postcommodity fetish. *American Behavioral Scientist* 63 (8):1120–1136.

Starrs, P. F. (1998) *Let the Cowboy Ride: Cattle Ranching in the American West*. Baltimore: Johns Hopkins University Press.

Stillman, D. (2008) *Mustang: The Saga of the Wild Horse in the American West*. New York: Mariner Books.

Strom, C. (2010) *Making Catfish Bait Out of Government Boys: The Fight against Cattle Ticks and the Transformation of the Yeoman South*. Athens: University of Georgia Press.

Struthers Montford, K. (2020) Towards a theory of multi-species carcerality. In Struthers Montford, K., and Taylor, C. (eds) *Colonialism and Animality: Anti-colonial Perspectives in Critical Animal Studies*. London: Routledge, 277–296.

Struthers Montford, K. (2022) 'Cultured' food futures? Agricultural power, new meat ontologies, and law in the Anthropocene. *Animal Studies Journal* 11 (2):1–37.

Struthers Montford, K., and Taylor, C. (eds) (2020) *Colonialism and Animality: Anti-colonial Perspectives in Critical Animal Studies*. London: Routledge.

Sumpter, K. C. (2015) Masculinity and meat consumption: An analysis through the theoretical lens of hegemonic masculinity and alternative masculinity theories. *Sociology Compass* 9 (2):104–114.

Sweetgrass. (2009) Barbash, I. (Producer), Castaing-Taylor, L., and Barbash, I. (Directors). New York: Grasshopper Film. https://video.alexanderstreet.com/watch/Sweetgrass.

Swiss Info (2018) Are cows happier with their horns? 26 October.

Taylor, D. (2017) Historic vessel now in Baytown, 4 April. https://www.chron.com/neighborhood/article/Historic-vessel-now-in-Baytown-9604582.php.

Teller, H. M. (1884) Letter from the Secretary of the Interior to the General Land Office. National Cowboy Hall of Fame and Western Heritage Museum, Donald C. and Elizabeth M. Dickinson Research Center, Oklahoma City, Okla.

Tompkins, J. (1992) *West of Everything: The Inner Life of Westerns*. New York: Oxford University Press.

Tortorici, Z. (2015) Animal archive stories: Species anxieties in the Mexican National Archive. In Nance, S. (ed) *The Historical Animal*. Syracuse, N.Y.: Syracuse University Press, 75–98.

Tortorici, Z. (2021) Personal correspondence with author, 2 July.

Tolia-Kelly, D. P. (2011) The geographies of cultural geography III: Material geographies, vibrant matters and risking surface geographies. *Progress in Human Geography* 37 (1):153–160.

Treaty with the Cherokee (1835). Indian Affairs, Laws and Treaties, Vol. II. Government Printing Office, Washington, D.C. https://americanindian.si.edu/static /nationtonation/pdf/Treaty-of-New-Echota-1835.pdf.

Tuan Y-F (1984) *Dominance and Affection: The Making of Pets*. New Haven, Conn.: Yale University Press.

Turner, F. J. (1893) The significance of the frontier in American history. *Proceedings of the State Historical Society of Wisconsin* and *Annual Report of the American Historical Association*.

Urbanik, J. (2012) *Placing Animals: An Introduction to the Geography of Human-Animal Relations*. Lanham, Md.: Rowman & Littlefield.

US Department of Agriculture (1929; 1940) Farmers Bulletin No. 1600, Dehorning, Castrating, Branding and Marking Beef Cattle. Washington, D.C.: Government Printing Office.

US Patent Office (1892) Dehorning Implement (No. 480,246) Alva C. Brosius of Cochranville, Pennsylvania.

Wadiwel, D. J. (2015) *The War against Animals*. Boston: Brill Rodipi.

Wadiwel, D. J. (2016) Do fish resist? *Cultural Studies Review* 22:196–242.

Wadiwel, D. J. (2021) Featured speaker on violence. British Animal Studies Network (virtual) Animaterialities Symposium, 24 April.

Walby, K., and Piche, J. (2015) Carceral retasking and the work of historical societies at decommissioned lock-ups, jails, and prisons in Ontario. In Morin, K. M., and Moran, D. (eds) *Historical Geographies of Prisons: Unlocking the Usable Carceral Past*. London: Routledge, 88–105.

Walker, D. (1981) *Clio's Cowboys: Studies in the Historiography of the Cattle Trade*. Lincoln: University of Nebraska Press.

Washburn and Moen Manufacturing, Glidden patent pamphlet (n.d.). National Cowboy Hall of Fame and Western Heritage Museum, Donald C. & Elizabeth M. Dickinson Research Center, Oklahoma City, Oklahoma.

Welch, B. (2017) The Old Chisholm Trail, 25 April. https://www.americancowboy.com /people/old-chisholm-trail-150-anniversary.

Where cowboys fly and cattle sail: An epic food journey (2022). *New York Times*, 31 December. https://www.nytimes.com/2022/11/30/business/cattle-exports -australia-indonesia.html.

White, R. (1991) *"It's Your Misfortune and None of My Own": A History of the American West*. Norman: University of Oklahoma Press.

White, R. (1994) Animals and enterprise. In Milner, C. A., O'Connor, C. A., and Sandweiss, M. A. (eds) *The Oxford History of the American West*. New York: Oxford University Press, 237–259.

Wilcox, S., and Rutherford, S. (eds) (2018) *Historical Animal Geographies*. London: Routledge.

Wilkeson, F. (1885) Texas cattle: Peculiarities of the long-horned beasts. *San Francisco Chronicle*, 7 July, 6.

Wilson, R. M. (2015) Mobile bodies: Animal migration in North American history. *Geoforum* 65:465–472.

Wise, S. (2000) *Rattling the Cage: Toward Legal Rights for Animals*. New York: Basic Books.

Wishart, D. (ed) (2004) Cattle towns and Dodge City, Kansas. In *Great Plains Encyclopedia*. Lincoln: University of Nebraska Press, 162, 383–384.

Wolf, K. (2014) Promoting Lassie: The animal star and constructions of "ideal" American heroism. In McLean, A. L. (ed) *Cinematic Canines*. New Brunswick, N.J.: Rutgers University Press, 104–120.

Wolfe, C., and Elmer, J. (1995) Subject to sacrifice: Ideology, psychoanalysis, and the discourse of species in Jonathan Demme's *Silence of the Lambs*. *Boundary* 2 (22/3):141–170.

Wolfe, P. (1999) *Settler Colonialism and the Transformation of Anthropology: The Politics and Poetics of an Ethnographic Event*. London: Cassell.

Wolfe, P. (2006) Settler colonialism and the elimination of the Native. *Journal of Genocide Research* 8 (4):387–409.

Woods, M. (2009) Rural geography: Blurring boundaries and making connections. *Progress in Human Geography* 33 (6):849–858.

Woods, R. (2017) *The Herds Shot Round the World: Native Breeds and the British Empire, 1800–1900*. Chapel Hill: University of North Carolina Press.

Worcester, D. E. (1987) T*he Texas Longhorn, Relic of the Past, Asset for the Future*. College Station: Texas A&M University Press.

Wynter, S. (2003) Unsettling the coloniality of being/power/truth/freedom: Toward the human, after man, its overrepresentation—an argument. *CR: The New Centennial Review* 3 (3):257–337.

Yong, E. (2022) How animals see themselves. *New York Times*, 21 June.

Zivkovic, A. (2021) Presentation, Animaterialities Symposium, Center for Material Culture Studies, University of Delaware, Newark, 24 April.

INDEX

www.ingramcontent.com/pod-product-compliance
Lightning Source LLC
Chambersburg PA
CBHW032350280326
41935CB00008B/522